THE BACHELOR DUKE

THE BACHELOR DUKE

A Life of
William Spencer Cavendish
6th Duke of Devonshire
1790–1858

JAMES LEES-MILNE

JOHN MURRAY

© James Lees-Milne 1991

First published in 1991 by
John Murray (Publishers) Ltd
50 Albemarle Street
London w1x 4bd

The right of James Lees-Milne to be identified as the author of this work has
been asserted by him in accordance with the Copyright, Designs and Patents
Act, 1988.

British Library Cataloguing in Publication Data
Lees-Milne, James
The bachelor duke: a life of William Spencer Cavendish
6th Duke of Devonshire 1790–1858.
1. Great Britain. Devonshire, William Spencer Cavendish,
Duke of, 1790–1858
I. Title
941.07092

ISBN 0–7195–4920–5

Printed in Great Britain by
Butler and Tanner Ltd, Frome and London

Contents

Acknowledgements

My gratitude to the Duke and Duchess of Devonshire is but partly repaid by the publication of this biography. To them I am deeply indebted. The book's conception was theirs. Its data are almost wholly theirs for the 6th Duke's journals, correspondence and notebooks at Chatsworth have formed the basis of my text. Their kindness in putting all these things at my disposal, and their generosity, hospitality and encouragement throughout have been beyond my deserts. To Mr Michael Pearman, archivist and librarian, and Mr Peter Day, keeper of the collections at Chatsworth, I am likewise enormously indebted for their indefatigable help, advice and enthusiasm. As for Chatsworth itself, that treasure palace in the most beautiful of English settings, of which the subject of this biography wrote, 'I enjoy being here before all earthly things', 'I adore it', and 'I am drunk with Chatsworth', how can I, while echoing these sentiments, not offer it my unbounded love and thanks too?

To John Kenworthy-Browne, biographer-designate of Joseph Paxton and expert on neo-classical sculpture I owe more than I can express. His understanding of the Bachelor Duke's character and achievements is second to none.

To the following persons I tender thanks for a variety of kind services: Mrs (Kitty) Arkwright, Miss Betty Askwith (the Hon. Mrs Miller Jones), Michael Bloch, Patric Dickinson (*Richmond Herald*), Dr Leslie Harris, Eeyan Hartley (archivist, Castle Howard), Anthony Hobson, the Hon. Simon Howard, Bruce Hunter, Douglas Matthews (Secretary, the London Library), the Hon. Lady Mosley, Stuart Preston, Miss Diana Scarisbrick, George Speaight and Mrs Virginia Surtees; also to the following learned bodies: the British Library, the National Monuments Record, the National

vii

Register of Archives, Trinity College Library, Cambridge (relating to the 6th Duke's terms as an undergraduate), the University of Durham Library and the University of Keele Library.

Those friends, and there may be several, who have helped me in other ways and whose names escape my faltering memory, I beg to accept apologies and belated thanks.

It is a privilege to be published by the venerable firm of my old school friend Jock Murray and to find myself once again under the vigilant tutelage of Ariane Goodman. Finally I hope I need not condole with Alvilde for having basked with me in the radiance of the Bachelor Duke for three happy years.

J.L-M.
1990

To Andrew and Debo

The Houses of Cavendish,

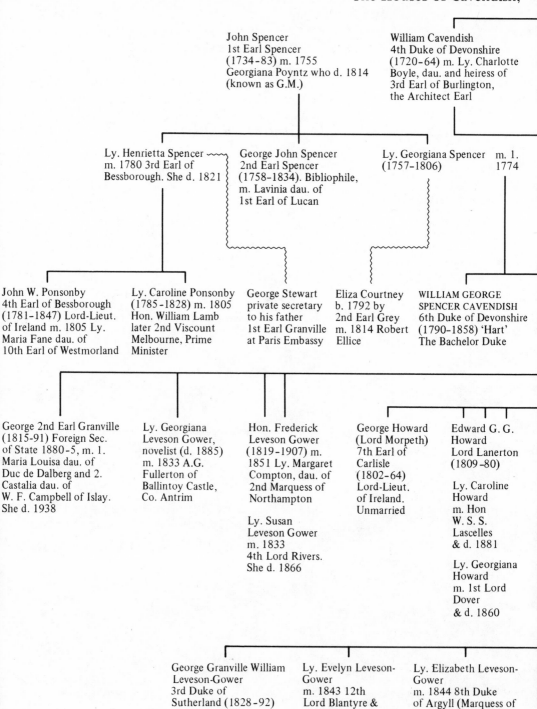

John Spencer
1st Earl Spencer
(1734–83) m. 1755
Georgiana Poyntz who d. 1814
(known as G.M.)

William Cavendish
4th Duke of Devonshire
(1720–64) m. Ly. Charlotte
Boyle, dau. and heiress of
3rd Earl of Burlington,
the Architect Earl

Ly. Henrietta Spencer
m. 1780 3rd Earl of
Bessborough. She d. 1821

George John Spencer
2nd Earl Spencer
(1758–1834). Bibliophile,
m. Lavinia dau. of
1st Earl of Lucan

Ly. Georgiana Spencer
(1757–1806)

m. 1.
1774

John W. Ponsonby
4th Earl of Bessborough
(1781–1847) Lord-Lieut.
of Ireland m. 1805 Ly.
Maria Fane dau. of
10th Earl of Westmorland

Ly. Caroline Ponsonby
(1785–1828) m. 1805
Hon. William Lamb
later 2nd Viscount
Melbourne, Prime
Minister

George Stewart
private secretary
to his father
1st Earl Granville
at Paris Embassy

Eliza Courtney
b. 1792 by
2nd Earl Grey
m. 1814 Robert
Ellice

WILLIAM GEORGE
SPENCER CAVENDISH
6th Duke of Devonshire
(1790–1858) 'Hart'
The Bachelor Duke

George 2nd Earl Granville
(1815-91) Foreign Sec.
of State 1880-5, m. 1.
Maria Louisa dau. of
Duc de Dalberg and 2.
Castalia dau. of
W. F. Campbell of Islay.
She d. 1938

Ly. Georgiana
Leveson Gower,
novelist (d. 1885)
m. 1833 A.G.
Fullerton of
Ballintoy Castle,
Co. Antrim

Hon. Frederick
Leveson Gower
(1819–1907) m.
1851 Ly. Margaret
Compton, dau. of
2nd Marquess of
Northampton

Ly. Susan
Leveson Gower
m. 1833
4th Lord Rivers.
She d. 1866

George Howard
(Lord Morpeth)
7th Earl of
Carlisle
(1802–64)
Lord-Lieut.
of Ireland.
Unmarried

Edward G. G.
Howard
Lord Lanerton
(1809–80)

Ly. Caroline
Howard
m. Hon
W. S. S.
Lascelles
& d. 1881

Ly. Georgiana
Howard
m. 1st Lord
Dover
& d. 1860

George Granville William
Leveson-Gower
3rd Duke of
Sutherland (1828-92)

Ly. Evelyn Leveson-
Gower
m. 1843 12th
Lord Blantyre &
d. 1869

Ly. Elizabeth Leveson-
Gower
m. 1844 8th Duke
of Argyll (Marquess of
Lorne). She d. 1878

The lines 〰〰〰〰 signify children born out of wedlock.

Howard and Leveson Gower

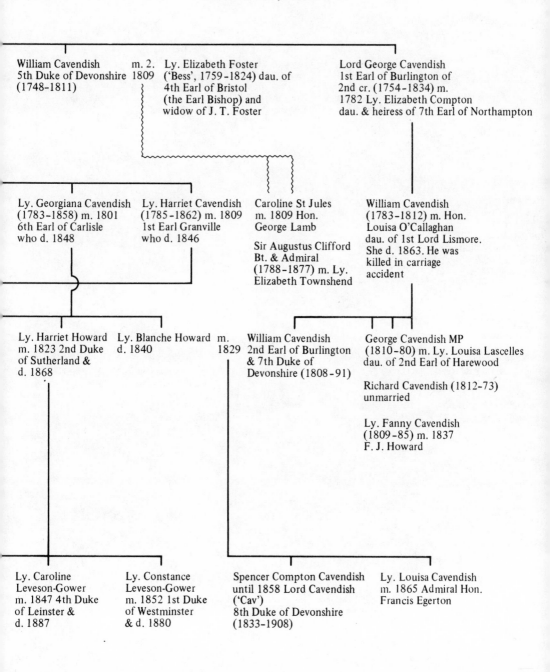

Lord Frederick Cavendish
Field Marshal
(1729–1803)
unmarried

Ly. Dorothy Cavendish
m. 1766 3rd Duke of
Portland & d. 1794.
Grandmother of diarists
Charles & Henry Greville

William Cavendish
5th Duke of Devonshire
(1748–1811)

m. 2.
1809

Ly. Elizabeth Foster
('Bess', 1759–1824) dau. of
4th Earl of Bristol
(the Earl Bishop) and
widow of J. T. Foster

Lord George Cavendish
1st Earl of Burlington of
2nd cr. (1754–1834) m.
1782 Ly. Elizabeth Compton
dau. & heiress of 7th Earl of Northampton

Ly. Georgiana Cavendish
(1783–1858) m. 1801
6th Earl of Carlisle
who d. 1848

Ly. Harriet Cavendish
(1785–1862) m. 1809
1st Earl Granville
who d. 1846

Caroline St Jules
m. 1809 Hon.
George Lamb

Sir Augustus Clifford
Bt. & Admiral
(1788–1877) m. Ly.
Elizabeth Townshend

William Cavendish
(1783–1812) m. Hon.
Louisa O'Callaghan
dau. of 1st Lord Lismore.
She d. 1863. He was
killed in carriage
accident

Ly. Harriet Howard
m. 1823 2nd Duke
of Sutherland &
d. 1868

Ly. Blanche Howard
d. 1840

m.
1829

William Cavendish
2nd Earl of Burlington
& 7th Duke of
Devonshire (1808–91)

George Cavendish MP
(1810–80) m. Ly. Louisa Lascelles
dau. of 2nd Earl of Harewood

Richard Cavendish (1812–73)
unmarried

Ly. Fanny Cavendish
(1809–85) m. 1837
F. J. Howard

Ly. Caroline
Leveson-Gower
m. 1847 4th Duke
of Leinster &
d. 1887

Ly. Constance
Leveson-Gower
m. 1852 1st Duke
of Westminster
& d. 1880

Spencer Compton Cavendish
until 1858 Lord Cavendish
('Cav')
8th Duke of Devonshire
(1833–1908)

Ly. Louisa Cavendish
m. 1865 Admiral Hon.
Francis Egerton

I

Childhood and Adolescence
1790–1811

———————•———————

'IT IS UNLIKELY now that any Life of the Bachelor Duke will be written apart from the account of him contained in this book,' wrote Violet Markham in an appendix to *Paxton and the Bachelor Duke* published in 1935. Certainly she produced a fine and sympathetic study of the 6th Duke of Devonshire in relation to her famous grandfather Sir Joseph Paxton. But remarkable as this relationship was between master and servant, enlightened patrician and plebeian of genius, friend and friend, there are many other aspects of the Duke, all recorded in a seemingly infinite number of papers, diaries and letters, which justify an exclusive biography of this versatile nobleman.

The subject of this biography bridged the Regency and the early Victorian periods. His life covered an era of European history which witnessed extraordinary changes, political, scientific, social and ethical, changes only surpassed in cataclysm by those of a century later. A survivor from the feudalism of the eighteenth century, he adapted himself by dint of an innate wisdom and circumspection to the tide of democracy which, patrician to the very fingertips, he had helped to bring about. Not a political figure of pre-eminence he nevertheless became by virtue of his inherited rank, riches and possessions, and his active patronage on a vast scale of the contemporary arts and sciences, the pattern of integration with a new and vigorous age.

In a sense the image of himself which he projected is even more significant than his achievements – and they were remarkable and various enough. The decades of his full maturity were those of constitutional reform – decades of indefinite promise in Great Britain. Over them brooded the romantic and benign figure of the 6th Duke of Devonshire. His character prefigured the qualities of understanding, compassion and a general liberal outlook on life which have much appeal for our own generation. No Georgian or even Victorian aristocrats strike us as more *modern* than this duke. For all their cultivation and elegance the Georgians were hedged by class conventions; and for all their hard work and sense of duty the Victorians distanced themselves from us by a humourless self-righteousness. Both enlist our historic sympathy, but not our absolute empathy. The Duke of Devonshire on the other hand is a man with whom we can readily identify our own ideals. He was neither narrow-minded nor stuffy. He was by no means exclusive or class-bound. His friendship with Paxton brought him in touch with scientists, engineers, inventors and leaders of industry, men risen for the most part from the peasantry, not even from the middle class. We feel that in spite of his exceptional privileges and distinctions he was someone whom we would dearly like to entertain to dinner, no matter how inadequate our dining-room table. And this, I fancy, sets him apart as a highly civilized being, a mirror as it were to the humanitarian age in which he conspicuously participated.

The future 6th Duke of Devonshire's entry to this vale of tears, and laughter, took place in a somewhat furtive manner for a baby of his exalted rank. His father and mother, William 5th Duke and the fascinating Duchess Georgiana, had been travelling in the unsettled Netherlands. Accompanying the 5th Duke were his four young children (two illegitimate) together with the Duke's mistress – his wife's greatest friend – Lady Elizabeth Foster, Georgiana's mother Countess Spencer, a governess, a family doctor Richard Croft, and a host of dependants and servants. On reaching Brussels the party were warned that the Austrians, profiting from the Continental instability, were about to reinvest the city, and that for their safety they should clear out. Owing to the Duchess's advanced pregnancy they decided on 1 May 1790 to make post-haste for Paris where they had friends. There they squeezed into the Hôtel de l'Université, but more accommodation was needed. Hastily the Duke managed to rent a house belonging to the Marquis de Boulainvilliers in the western suburb of Passy.

On 19th Georgiana wrote to the Prince of Wales, 'My dearest, dearest brother', that she was in a most terrible scrape from owing £3,000 to a certain creditor, one Baker, and begged His Royal Highness for a loan before her lying-in at Passy, 'upon repeated assurances that it is the safest place. Indeed, dearest Sir, if you should happen to be at all rich a very small *cadeau* would make me very comfortable' – her importunity was blatant – 'but if you are not rich, I entreat you not. God bless you my dearest Sir ... I do assure you that if you are a *poverino* as well as me, I can do very well without it.' This pathetic appeal was followed by assurances that her whole heart and life were devoted to him and 'I am sure my child will be bound to love you, as you have preserved it,' which was indeed to be the case. The ceaseless complaints about her gambling debts and her shameless sponging were expressed in such pitiable phrases as of an injured, innocent child, that those who loved her, and the Prince was certainly amongst the number, found them irresistible.

On the very day, 20 May, that the Duchess, her mother and Lady Elizabeth moved into the Passy house Georgiana's labour pains began. That evening the Duke and his daughters were installed. At one o'clock the following morning, 21 May, a son and heir was born with the clinical assistance of Dr Croft. Relief of the mother over this happy issue was immense. Georgiana's gambling debts were so large that she had not dared disclose to the Duke their full amount. By producing the longed-for son she in her feckless manner believed that all would be forgiven her and paid up by the doting father. Events did not turn out quite as she expected.

In the first place friends and society at home had been very suspicious of the Devonshires' motives for leaving England. Why, they asked, go abroad at a time when the French Revolution was reducing Europe to turmoil to produce a child instead of remaining at Chatsworth, the family seat, or at Devonshire House, the family palace in London? And why be accompanied by Bess Foster, who had lately borne the Duke a daughter and a son? The simple answers to these two questions were that the previous July, when Europe was still happily undisturbed, Georgiana who had not given birth for five years sought the waters of Spa to induce a pregnancy (had they not been efficacious with others?); and that for reasons best known to herself she loved the company of the Duke's mistress more than that of any living soul. Bess, forewarned of the interpretation by London gossips that if a son were to be born it would be hers by the Duke, made a point of going on the eve of the child's birth to the opera where she carefully displayed herself to the smart Parisians in the auditorium. Lord St Helens who sat with her in the box observed at the time that 'she looked as thin as a wrayle'. When in 1817 Dr (then Sir) Richard Croft shot himself after having been held responsible for Princess Charlotte's death in childbirth, ugly rumours of a Devonshire changeling again circulated. Bess was said to have confided to the Prince Regent that the child was hers. This rubbish was believed by many in spite of the fact that out of nine persons present in the birth-chamber seven gave oral and two (of whom the doctor himself was one) written testimony that the child was definitely Georgiana's.

Precisely a year to the day after his birth the Marquess of Hartington, the courtesy title of successive eldest sons of the Dukes of Devonshire, was christened William, after his father, and Spencer after his mother's maiden name, in St George's Church, Hanover Square, in which parish Devonshire House lay.

Any hopes that the Duchess's mounting debts would be wiped clean by a grateful and indulgent husband on account of Lord Hartington's appearance were dashed. Not only did the debts now stand at £60,000 but the Duke soon became privy to the fact that his wife was again pregnant, and not by him. Charles Grey, with whom Georgiana had long been besotted, was the 1st Earl Grey's handsome son, in his late twenties and seven years her junior. For the man who was to become 'the good Lord Grey' of the Reform Bill, Prime Minister, statesman of the highest probity and of whom Princess Lieven was to write, 'there is perhaps no man in England with morals stricter than his', young Charles treated his inamorata extremely cavalierly. To her heart-rending letters clandestinely addressed through mutual friends 'To Black' he paid not the slightest notice. As for the Duke of Devonshire, he behaved in the words of the egregious Bess like a brute and a beast. He banished Georgiana first to Bath where she was accompanied by her sister Harriet (Lady Bessborough), and then abroad. He cut off her money and refused to correspond with her. At Aix-en-Provence the sisters were joined out of loyalty by Bess.

The three ladies were in their separate ways disconsolate: Harriet Bessborough seeking relief from incipient tuberculosis, Georgiana nursing her shame and misery at being parted from her children in England, especially her baby son Hartington, and Bess lamenting her lover the Duke. Georgiana had got it into her simple head that she would undoubtedly die in her approaching childbirth. Certainly her health was declining and her looks were fading. Incurably sentimental and apt to be histrionic she wrote on 25 January 1792 a letter, addressed to Lord Hartington, 'to be given him in case of my death when he is 8 years old', conveying her blessing 'written in my blood'. She exhorted him to be obedient to his father and grandmother in all things, to be kind to his sisters and to love Lady Elizabeth Foster.

In fact she was not to die for another fourteen years of ever-increasing physical decay, manifested by terrible operations on the eyes (she lost the sight of one), swollen neck glands, wracking headaches, unnatural corpulence and a ghastly complexion. To such sad extremities was the former gay, enchanting and warm-hearted Duchess, painted by Gainsborough and Reynolds in all the splendour of youth and beauty, reduced. Presumably the little boy was not handed the pitiable letter on his eighth birthday. His mother's hopes for Hart's development of character were to be realized. He became a dutiful son to his father, with whom he had little in common, and an extremely affectionate and generous brother and cousin. He ministered to Lady Elizabeth towards the end of her life, and cared for her illegitimate daughter Caroline St Jules and son Augustus Clifford (his own half-sister and half-brother).

At Aix Georgiana gave birth on 20 February to Grey's illegitimate daughter who was given the name of Eliza Courtney. After being kicked around the Continent Eliza was brought to England and adopted by her grandparents Lord and Lady Grey at Falloden and Howick in Northumberland. She later married General Robert Ellice whose brother Edward was the husband of her father's sister Hannah Grey. Thus her aunt became her sister-in-law. According to Lord Broughton Eliza grew up 'a fine girl, sensible and talkative, and easy mannered'.

Eventually the Duke of Devonshire relented towards his wife. Graciously he allowed her back to Devonshire House. Whereas the servants went mad with joy and drank their dear mistress's health, welcome from the Duke and her two legitimate daughters Georgiana, known as Little G, and Harriet, known as Hary-O, was tepid. Regrettably that of the $3\frac{1}{2}$-year-old Hart, to whom she was now a stranger, was positively frosty. 'Hartington is very pretty but very cruel to me,' she complained sadly. 'He will not look at me or speak to me, tho' he kissed me a little at night.' She found that with his blue eyes, fine colour and infectious laugh he resembled the Duke. His face was alert and intelligent. He already had a way with him. At the age of 4 he reviewed the Derbyshire Militia at Bedford, standing in full regimentals in a field and solemnly doffing his hat as the troops saluted him, his fair locks blowing about in the wind. The officers were delighted with him.

In June 1794 Georgiana brought the children to Chatsworth. The girls were happy to be in Derbyshire where they belonged. Georgiana noted that Hart was the adoration of the country people, and not the least bit shy. Too much adulation may have swollen his head for his mother remarked, 'I am sorry to say that Chatsworth has made Hartington a little grand and he domineers too much' over the neighbours' children, even those older than himself. This was not wholly surprising since from the age of 18 months a retinue of servants attended his every need. He was however an affectionate little boy, though proud and at times ungovernable. One moment he was quiet and silent; the next argumentative and passionate. He would slope off on his own for hours, or would retire to the roof of Chatsworth, run along the leads and climb the pediment of the west front, sitting in front of Minerva, reading at her feet and pronouncing those adults sent to fetch him timid because they could not follow him. He nourished strange fancies. At the age of 7 he wrote to his father,

> I hear there is going to be a tax on watches and do not know what to do about mine. I have not got any Money and cannot pay it myself. I shall be very much obliged to you if you will pay it for me if not I must give my watch away.

For nursery tuition Hart inherited his sisters' governess Selina, the maiden daughter of Mrs Sarah Trimmer, highly esteemed authoress of *Sacred History selected from the Scriptures, with Annotations and Reflections adapted to the Comprehension of Young Persons* and thirteen other 'improving' books. Selina was a woman of forceful personality, prudish, puritanical, intensely proud of the Cavendish family, and intensely pious. Although she loved her she thoroughly disapproved of Georgiana and sneaked about her dreadful gambling and loose ways to Lady Spencer with whom she was in league. At one time Georgiana was so incensed by this disloyalty that she told her mother she would dismiss Selina. This she never did, and during her final illness relied upon Selina's selfless help and devotion. She even allowed the governess to correct her for spoiling the children. Selina adored the young Marquess and was loved by him in return although he often laughed at her narrow piety. Long after he was grown up and had succeeded to the dukedom she in her retirement at Brentwood would gently admonish him not to be taken in by toadies and to be kind to his half-brother Augustus. She left upon his childish mind an indelible impression of the evangelical doctrine of salvation by faith which, as we shall see, was deeply to influence his middle age.

When Hart was barely 8 Georgiana arranged for him to go to Harrow School. In July 1798 she took him there. 'As for my Hart,' she told her mother, 'he was a little hero, and seemed as if he had been there all his life.' He went through the customary curriculum of fagging, 'on his knees close to the fire in the little slip of a room, toasting some gingerbread upon his little scrubby knife.' His schoolfellow Lord Byron, two years his senior, told his sister Augusta Leigh that Hartington was on very good terms with him. 'He is of a soft milky disposition, and of a happy apathy of temper which defies the softer emotions, and is insensible of ill-treatment. So much for him.'

Apathetic and resilient he may have appeared, but he was sensitive and delicate within. All his life he was prone to catch colds and was a martyr to hay fever. In 1799 he fell ill of some undisclosed complaint. Georgiana took a house for him at Margate, sending him there with Bess to recuperate. For various reasons Little G was anxious about him. His mother allowed that she may have over-indulged him 'because of his ill health and peculiarity of disposition'. Miss Trimmer had most influence over him. She regretted that he was so reserved; he was not given to manly exercise and resented those who excelled at it; he would have his own way; he had lived too long among girls, his sisters and cousin Caroline Ponsonby. He needed, she opined, a good kind of young man who would be firm with him.

No tutor seems to have been immediately engaged, but instead of sending Hart back to Harrow Georgiana sent him to a kind of crammer's at Woodnesborough village between Ramsgate and Deal. The academy was kept by a Mr Smith in Holy Orders. There discipline was not strict nor teaching oppressive. If anything Smith was too conscious of his pupil's nobility, a fact which Hart recognized and deprecated at the time. Yet on his coming of age he supported Smith's retirement, extending an allowance after the old man's death to his daughters. Meanwhile Hart was permitted to go to London and Ramsgate at will. He made great friends with a fellow pupil two years his senior, Francis Tavistock, who in his turn became 7th Duke of Bedford. Georgiana was apprehensive lest Tavistock might lead her precious Hart into dissipation. While Hart was at pains to emulate his friend's man-of-the-world attitude he was under no illusions about his amours. 'Adieu dearest Tavistock,' he wrote in October 1806,

Will you make this rule for our correspondence? Never to make *excuses* unless the faults are very *atrocious*. So your idleness and my stupidity shall go free. Adieu once more, write as often as you can, but I do not require what I once did – and if we are ever together again I trust you will find it in other things.

To this slightly ambiguous letter Tavistock replied, exhorting him to take care of himself, 'as your constitution is by no means strong enough to bear much *night work* at present, and you may be seriously injuring your health without being aware of it.' There is irony in the older boy's admonition. Night work can be variously interpreted. Perhaps Georgiana's apprehensions about the rakish Tavistock's influence were not altogether unfounded.

In adolescence Hart was old for his age. On the whole he did not consort with other boys. He was happier with his parents' friends, particularly women. He kept up a correspondence with the famous blue-stocking Miss Mary Berry, intimate friend and legatee of Horace Walpole, even sending her a *Newspaper* of his own editing once a week. 'Nothing has happened worth telling you since my last ... except that on the 22nd [February 1803] Colonel Despard and his associates were executed at Newington, and had their heads cut off, but were excused the rest,' followed by some excruciating details.

The Devonshire House nursery was peopled by girls – sisters, a half-sister, cousins and the stray Corisande, a pretty daughter of the Duc de Gramont, whom for some reason or other Georgiana took a fancy to on her travels and brought back to England. Hart however was not attracted by the one girl in the coterie who was not a relation. At an early age he was smitten by his first cousin Caroline Ponsonby, the daughter of his Aunt Bessborough. Older than Hart, the engaging Caro with her piquant little face and high spirits was totally uninhibited. A vamp and a tease, she was no respecter of persons. She never treated the pedestalled young Marquess as the divinity the sisterhood and cousinhood revered. In that respect she was good for Hart who was by nature and position aloof. Besides, he adored her. When told of her engagement to William Lamb in 1805 he was appalled. The 15-year-old fell into hysterics and a doctor had to be sent for. He told Caroline that he had always looked upon her as his destined wife and no plan he ever formed of future happiness was dissociated from her. His pride was deeply wounded. He took long to recover from the shock; and until confidence was restored his relations with girls were guarded.

Caro's marriage however had not the slightest effect upon her feelings for him, or her manner of expressing them. 'With a cross heart and bad pen red ink and no time I write these few lines to you, my little kind cousin,' is a typical opening. Why had he quarrelled with her, his bread and butter? 'You are a bad good for nothing boy.' She bids him give Caroline St Jules three kisses for her. 'I never will give you another while you live.' Again, 'Your silence is absolutely provoking! write, write, write write.' Did he get the ring she sent him? He sends her a love potion, on receipt of which she writes, 'My most sensitive Elixir of Julep, my most precious cordial confection, my most dilutable sal polychrist & marsh mallows paste,' signing herself 'Your giddy cousin William Rufus Rex.' He was always to remain devoted, even when scandal broke over her head in the tragi-comedy affair with Byron and when her insupportable eccentricities, the break with her husband, and her final physical and mental collapse estranged family and friends. In the end he consented to be one of her guardians and had the pain of dealing with her finances and domestic tangles. Her misery and suicidal attempts tore at his heart-strings.

In March 1806 Lady Elizabeth took it upon herself to send for Hart from Woodnesborough on account of his mother's worsening condition. Still Georgiana managed to write to her son in between bouts of suffering, alleviated by ever-increasing doses of laudanum. Her notes got shorter and shorter. Desperately she warned Hart against falling into the errors which she now realized had ruined her short life. 'I was but one year older than you', she told him on the 9th of the month,

> when I launched into the vortex of dissipation – a Duchess and a beauty. I ev'ry hour however thank my protecting angel that all I have seen never weaken'd my principles of devotion to Almighty God ... But I was giddy and vain. You will have great temptations in the same way, but you have judgement and sense to protect you.

The following day the 18-year-old Tavistock went to see her. 'I made the room as dark as I could not to frighten the young man', she told Hart piteously. Apprised of his wife's desperate state the Duke now sat up with her night after night, taking turns with Lady Bessborough. On 1 April Hart wrote to his friend, 'Dearest Tavistock, I can hardly ... tell you that you must expect the worst. Pity me for what you yourself once suffered, but, bless you, dear friend.' How much did he really mind? Bess remarked that while her husband and sister were weeping by Georgiana's bedside Hart was watching her impassively.

9

Every future reference to his mother indicated affection mingled with pity for her foolishness and hopeless improvidence. He was probably embarrassed by her proprietary love of him. All boys flinch from maternal possessiveness. After all he was only 16 when she died. But when the time came he felt bereft.

> Never shall I forget [Bess wrote] Hart's look and figure first as I saw him in the Great Hall [of Devonshire House], as if to attend on his poor Mother there and then on the steps fixed – without his hat – his innocent, interesting countenance and looks bent to the last on the coffin as it was carried slowly down the steps, and on the Hearse as it was placed within. He did not appear to weep but his whole soul seemed absorbed by what was passing.

No doubt it was. The fact is that Hart and his two legitimate sisters gravely resented the intrusion and officious attentions of the interloper who in their eyes had usurped the place of their mother in the Duke's affections. They were also bewildered by and not a little contemptuous of their mother's acceptance of an untidy situation. Even so Hart, while then disliking Bess and declining to condole with her on the loss of her bosom friend, urged his less forgiving sisters not to calumniate her at such a moment of sorrow.

As soon as the funeral was over Hart, anxious to quit the gloom of Devonshire House, the reserve and taciturnity of his father and the bubbling effusiveness of Lady Elizabeth, retreated to Holwell, his grandmother Lady Spencer's house near St Albans. Not that Holwell with its black horsehair chairs in the hall, pervasive odour of sanctity and long family prayers conducted by Lady Spencer's bibulous chaplain, was exactly cheerful. But deeply devout though she was and disapproving (in her two daughters she had a good deal to disapprove of), Lady Spencer was a woman of the utmost common sense. Above all she lived for her family, children and grandchildren whom she ceaselessly chided without apparently arousing their resentment. She was a matriarchal figure beyond their criticism. Hart was devoted to her and until her death in 1814 listened respectfully to her sound advice if he did not always follow it. He kept up a steady correspondence, addressing her as 'My dear GM' (Lady Spencer spurned sentimental endearments) in journal form from day to day. His letters to her were necessarily guarded and cautious compared with those to his sisters.

In the autumn of 1806 young Lord Hartington under the guardianship of Dr Randolph, a quondam surgeon in the Navy engaged by the Duke on the grounds that he had travelled for a year with a friend without once quarrelling, toured his father's estates in Yorkshire, Lancashire and North Wales to get some idea of the extent of his future inheritance.

According to the Harrow school register Hart did not sever links with the school until 1806. His attendance all along had been spasmodic. Beyond participation in school speeches for 1805 and 1806 there are no records of his having distinguished himself academically. Clearly Harrow did not play an integral part in his education. Nor had Dr Smith's academy at Woodnesborough, to which he never returned. On the other hand Dr Randolph seems to have awakened the boy's desire to learn and instilled the elements of Latin and Greek if little scholastic knowledge besides. The doctor kept an academy at Bath where from time to time Hart was sent. Discipline under Randolph's roof was hardly more strict than under Smith's. But Hart respected and liked Dr Randolph. He kept up with him in later years and visited 'the dear old man' in his eighty-first year in 1835.

In October 1807 Hart was admitted to Trinity College, Cambridge, with the status of 'nobleman'. Here too in consequence of the privileges extended to noblemen Hart's attendance was irregular. Until Lent 1810 when he went down for good he was resident for six terms only out of nine. Nevertheless his status enabled him to take the MA degree without an examination. In return for the right to do a minimum amount of work the young Marquess had merely to pay higher university fees and to present a piece of plate worth at least £20 to the college.

In November 1807 Harriet told Little G that Hart was in raptures with Cambridge. She warned that it was a waste of time writing to him for he did not answer by return. Yet Little G must forgive him on account of his high spirits, his sweetness of disposition and his affection when one did see him. He captivated all who came in contact with him. His cousin Lady Sarah Spencer confirmed this impression. In May 1808 Hartington, supposed to be studying hard at Cambridge, was seen with another cousin, William Ponsonby, at a masquerade, dressed as two young ladies (Hart was six foot tall) in the latest fashion, 'with diamonds, spotted muslin and silver turbans and feathers'. Sarah was rather more critical than his adoring sisters. She thought it a little absurd for him to be practising French cotillions instead of hunting with her brother Althorp. Altogether he was too scatter-brained for the steady regularity of life at Althorp. He was getting into terrible scrapes and all the young ladies were throwing themselves at him.

When he wasn't in London or at Cambridge he was entertaining his young friends at Chatsworth *'en grand seigneur'*. His boon companion of the moment was Sir William Rumbold, a rackety baronet who accompanied him on flying visits to country houses. Sarah considered Rumbold 'a soft, silly person, but one can't tell properly after an hour's observation, be one ever so clever and learned'. All Hart's relations took a jaundiced view of Rumbold and considered him a toady – hence perhaps Selina's admonition – leading the Marquess into extravagant ways.

Hary-O was troubled by her young brother's disregard of their father's feelings. In remonstrating with him about his gadding about, riding, jumping, fishing and coursing at the expense of serious studies she exhorted him in January 1809 to inform the Duke that he was not keeping his present term at Cambridge. She begged him not to covenant with his tutors and undertake tours without consulting the Duke. 'I have had several conversations with my father about you,' she went on,

> and you are very much mistaken if you think his habits of indolence and carelessness have made him indifferent to his children. I am convinced that he loves us all but he is proud of you, and conscious about you and feels I am convinced, deeply, anything like neglect in your behaviour or dislike in your feeling towards him – Of the last I am certain he never can have had reason to suspect you ...
>
> I do not say that I have often lamented his coldness, and regretted the little communication between us, but I know that one expression of kindness or interest from him, has more influence over me than almost anything in the world.

This was generous of Harriet for it was fully recognized in the family that the Duke cared far more for his natural daughter Caroline St Jules than his three legitimate children put together. Indolence and seeming indifference were the most marked traits of this strange, buttoned-up man. Years later his son recorded how when woken out of sleep one night to be told by the servants that Chatsworth was on fire, the Duke turned over in bed merely observing that they had better put it out. On another occasion having lost a game of cards he muttered, 'That's unlucky, Chiswick was burned this morning,' which was the first intimation he had given anyone of the incident. And as an example of his extraordinary unconcern, when Mr Heaton, the crabbed old auditor, warned him, 'My Lord Duke, I am sorry to inform your Grace that Lord Hartington appears disposed to spend a great deal of money,' the reply was, 'So much the better, Mr Heaton, he will have a great deal to spend.'

Hart's calculated distance from his father was certainly enhanced by the omnipresence of Bess Foster. If he gravely resented it, Harriet who was obliged to live with her father detested it. In normal circumstances an unmarried daughter would act as her widower father's hostess. In this case the elder daughter Georgiana, Little G, had already left the fold on marrying George Morpeth, son and heir of the 5th Earl of Carlisle, in 1801. She was established under the sway of a tyrannical father-in-law at Castle Howard, Vanbrugh's immense pile in the North Riding of Yorkshire, where she gave birth almost annually to an enormous brood of Howards. Hary-O therefore was left to endure Bess's management of the household and entertainment of those of the Duke's friends who condescended to frequent his houses. On 14 October 1809 she wrote to her brother that

> Lady Eliz is unparalleled I do believe for want of principle and delicacy, and more perverted than deceitful, for I really believe she hardly herself knows the difference between right and wrong now.

Mercifully for Hary-O she did not long have to put up with this state of affairs. On the 7th of the month Little G had written to Hart about the 'most painful event' that was on the brink of happening. On 19th the Duke and Lady Elizabeth married. The fat was in the fire. The whole family of children, in-laws, nephews and nieces, were aghast. Only Hart kept his head and remained mum. Caro Lamb inferred that the wiles of the serpent had entwined themselves round her young cousin's heart. He indignantly rebutted the unjust imputation. 'When, I should like to know, have you seen me fawn upon that crocodile, as you have the cruelty to say I do in your wicket [*sic*] letter?' Belatedly the Duke thought fit to inform his son. Hart replied curtly: 'I had for some time had reports of the event, which has taken place and therefore was not surprised by your letter.' Hary-O's difficult situation was relieved by her marriage two months later to Lord Granville Leveson Gower, older than her by eighteen years and the father by her aunt Lady Bessborough of two illegitimate children. No wonder that strait-laced people in Regency times – and there were a few – looked upon the Devonshire House set askance.

The Duke of Devonshire's second marriage lasted less than two years. At least the poor man had the solace of being nursed during his decline and under a semblance of respectability by the only woman whom he had consistently loved. Moreover she had been his first wife's dearest friend, beloved too by Georgiana's sister Harriet Bessborough. Bess may have been a calculating woman, given to petty artifices. She certainly was tactless. Until 1809 a poor widow with two legitimate and impoverished sons, an illegitimate son Augustus Clifford and illegitimate daughter Caroline St Jules, she undoubtedly intrigued to get what money and advancement for them as well as herself that she could, while the going was good. Yet she was genuinely devoted to her duke and fond of her stepchildren in spite of the fusillade of hostility discharged against her by Hary-O and Little G. She was not a bad woman. On the contrary she was well-intentioned and generous besides being pretty and very attractive to men. She abounded in enthusiasm. Her vitality had, ever since the lethargic Duke first fell in love with her, been just what he needed to spur him into fitful activity.

On 21 May 1811 young Lord Hartington came of age. A magnificent ball was given at Devonshire House for which, according to Lady Charlotte Campbell, a thousand pairs of knives and forks and twenty-four carvers had been ordered. The hero of the day was much taken up with Lord Lucan's daughter, Lady Elizabeth Bingham, who was an outrageous flirt. 'She *faisait des yeux doux*, enough not only to have melted all the ice which he swallowed but his own hard heart into the bargain. "Much ado was there, God wot, She would love, but he would not,"' Lady Charlotte concluded. This does not suggest that the beau's intentions were very serious. The old Duke however, being more susceptible, was greatly charmed with her beauty, and showed it. So when the Marquess opened the ball with Lady Elizabeth Bingham all the guests mistakenly assumed that parental approval had been given for instant marriage.

Meanwhile at Hardwick Hall in Derbyshire the tenantry and neighbouring peasantry, as at the other Devonshire seats, were celebrating the coming of age to a less elegant but no less fervid tune. Young William Howitt, of Quaker origin and future author of *Visits to Remarkable Places*, walked over from Mansfield to witness the bucolic scene. Expecting a prosaic assembly he was confronted and not a little shocked by an unruly mob of rustic revellers. On approaching Hardwick he came upon a man in the park lying on his face under a tree, dead drunk. Then another, and another, and another. Further on they lay about like the slain on a battlefield. In a clearing before the house wild songs and cries accompanied a band playing folk music.

14

About the grass were scattered throngs. From the spigots of huge barrels cascades of ale were flowing. Men were catching the liquor in their hats. Sometimes two or three tried to drink out of the same hat. Others stooped to drink from the spigots. There was fighting, scuffling, and much clamour and confusion. At the garden gates strangers were forcing their way into the courts while hefty servants with staves thumped their skulls with all their might. The scene was like a picture by Bruegel.

Howitt, being slim and agile, slipped beneath the uplifted arms of a stout attendant and passed through to the house. In the rooms, which he was curious to see, scores of people were voraciously eating chunks of roast beef and plum pudding off heavy pewter dishes and drinking from leather jacks and tankards as though they had been fasting these twenty-one years, while footmen ran to and fro filling the foaming mugs. He made his way past the kitchens with their mighty fireplaces, tongs, pokers and spits, and a platoon of sweating cooks to the forecourt where under canvas awnings long tables were set for the grander sort of tenantry and yeomanry admitted by ticket. Around the forecourt the walls were swarming with yokels who had climbed up to get a view of the feasting of their betters. These spectators kept up a clamorous demand for the privileged guests to throw them succulent morsels. Sure enough hunks of beef and lumps of pudding were hurled. A score of hands caught at them and there were guffaws of laughter when the delicacies fell back into the court or flew over their heads. Suddenly at the height of the jollity there was a cry of horror. One of the stone finials on top of the high wall collapsed. It gave way with a man clinging to it. He was killed on the spot. The body was carted off and the riot resumed. A second man sprang at one bound over a low wall that stood on the edge of a precipice and fell a shattered corpse into a hollow. By then the greater number of guests were too intoxicated to mind very much. All around was Bacchanalian chaos, singing, yelling, reeling, dancing and tumbling. Bodies lay strewn around the court and in the hall. Mr Howitt left the scene determined to return on a less convivial occasion.

Little more than two months after his son came of age the Duke, worn out by the ravages of gout, expired on 29 July. His death must have been fairly sudden because only a day or two beforehand Hart was dancing at Carlton House with Princess Mary, a 38-year-old daughter of George III, to the tune of *Voulez-vous dancer, mademoiselle*. Dutifully he attended his father's deathbed, although Little G and

Hary-O were absent. Surprisingly the Duke, having reigned for forty-seven years and done the minimum for the benefit of the Chatsworth estate and its people, was mourned by his tenants. 'He appeared to me to possess,' wrote the Vicar of Edensor village, 'the kindest and gentlest heart, with the soundest & most extensive information, particularly on literary subjects; every soul in my parish appears to be struck with the deepest grief.' These words were not necessarily deferential for they were echoed by people who were under no social or political obligations to the Duke. He was undoubtedly very well read, deeply versed in Shakespeare, and he possessed a shrewd political sense. Fox and Sheridan who were his intimates preferred his literary advice to that of any man of letters they knew and would submit their writings to his judgement. When he dispensed his political seats the easy-going Duke, unlike most patrons, imposed no conditions on how the chosen candidates should vote; and he did not expect them to interfere with the way he voted. The only stipulation he made was that they must be in favour of any Bill for the suppression of cruelty to animals. Like nearly all Cavendishes he was absolutely without political ambition. On Pitt's death in 1806 Fox sent word that he could take any place in Lord Grenville's Ministry of All the Talents that he might choose. He answered that although there was nothing he would not do to mark his esteem for the ministry about to be formed, he would take none.

own right Baroness Clifford, the elder daughter of the architect Earl of Burlington. The heir to this union was Hart's father. The 5th Duke, passive and lethargic though he was, acquired through a process of steady purchases between 1773 and his death further property by way of investment in Buxton, Hartington and Chesterfield as well as land in the counties of Huntingdonshire, Nottinghamshire, Cumberland, the East Riding and Ireland. For these accretions to the Cavendish estate he paid in all £670,199.

The 6th Duke was therefore in receipt of an enormous income of which over £100,000 a year came from land. Moreover, since his father had no time between his son's coming of age and his own death to resettle the properties, the old entail was broken and Hart was absolute owner of all he inherited. This was of great advantage to him. On the other hand owing to the father's extravagance his inheritance was heavily encumbered. In addition his mother's gambling debts amounted to £109,135. What with the pensions and annuities he was obliged to dispense on top of interest rates at 5 per cent on borrowed monies and mortgages (in 1814 these came to £593,000), the young Duke was left with only 40 per cent of his net income to spend. For years he was to be dogged and harassed by money problems. He hated and was bored to tears by business, resenting as a personal affront any restraint on his own reckless spending. Not until Joseph Paxton took his finances in hand in 1844 was he really freed from anxiety.

The young Duke however acted wisely in one respect. Realizing that his estates had been shockingly mismanaged and neglected towards the end of his father's reign – the old family solicitor John Heaton, dubbed by Duchess Georgiana 'the corkscrew', though loyal had become imbecile – he put them all under the control of one auditor, James Abercromby. As yet the professional land agent had not made an appearance on the English demesne. He was to do so before the Devonshire estates became the property of the 6th Duke's heir. Abercromby, a dour Scot, extremely intelligent and shrewd, had been the 5th Duke's steward and in that capacity kept the accounts, acting as a sort of remittance man. Thus he had already acquired a thorough knowledge of the problems facing his new master. Also a barrister and MP, he was to be appointed Judge Advocate General in 1827 and Speaker of the House of Commons in 1835. Altogether he was a public figure of some eminence. Very enthusiastic about the Duke's affairs he visited the properties one by one, making improvements as he went along and encouraging his patron to plant two million trees on his various estates between 1816 and 1817.

There exists a memorandum headed *Household Establishments*, dated 25 December 1811 and directed to Mr Heaton for perusal and consideration. It was almost certainly compiled by Abercromby. It gives a list of 93 servants, indoor and outdoor, at Devonshire House, Chiswick, Chatsworth, Hardwick, Londesborough and Bolton, with the wages they had been receiving from the 5th Duke while he was in residence and the board wages allowed during his absence. It is interesting that whereas each residence had its own housekeeper, housemaids, porters, watchmen, even steward, and of course all outdoor staff, servants such as cooks, confectioners, butlers, under-butlers, grooms of the chamber, footmen and valets were itinerant, evidently preceding or accompanying the Duke from house to house.

When he had disposed of his mother's gambling debts which involved much disentangling and smoothing of ruffled feathers – Thomas Coutts, who had been undeniably generous to Georgiana but nevertheless felt that her husband had treated his requests for payment with aloofness, wrote absurdly to the son, 'I can boast of as noble a descent from ancestors as Your Grace or any man in Britain' – the young Duke next turned his attention to the well-being of those nearest and dearest to him. Far away and above others his full sisters Georgiana Morpeth (to become Countess of Carlisle in 1825) and Harriet Granville held throughout his life the highest place in his affections. During the whirligig of Devonshire House intrigues, love affairs, illegitimacies and the social round they had provided his childhood with the stability he needed, and failed to receive from his parents. On his mother's death Hart wrote to the elder sister, 'My own G., I cannot tell you how much I love you, and how I hope that you will be kind to me, now that it is one of the few things which can make me happy.'

Georgiana was a reserved and rather stern woman, thoroughly domestic, and wrapped up in her husband and thirteen children. She was also hypochondriacal to an extent verging at times on mental instability. Sydney Smith once addressed to her twenty pieces of *Advice on Low Spirits*, including 'Compare your lot with that of other people', and 'Don't expect too much of human life, a sorry business at the best.' Georgiana was extremely proud of her brother with whom her relations were always maternal and protective. Harriet, younger than her by two years, was highly intelligent, witty and sharp. Her devotion to Hart was no less intense, but devoid of emotional undertones. She was a more intellectual match for him than Georgiana, and their interests were wider. All three corresponded regularly at great length. Their understanding was so absolute that they scarcely needed to finish a sentence, knowing that the recipient would grasp the drift.

The very first thing the Duke did was to increase Harriet's settlement to £30,000, the same figure that Little G's had always been. Duchess Elizabeth's well-being was a trickier business and he was obliged to act firmly. She showed every intention of remaining at Devonshire House. He made it clear that she had to leave within a week of his father's death for Chiswick House where she might lodge for a year, after which time she must find a house for herself. Yet he was generous, increasing her jointure from £4,000 to £6,000 a year. To her credit Bess accepted the condition and acknowledged his kindness. Even so, before the year was up Lady Bessborough had to warn her that Chiswick was not her dower house. When his compassionate aunt pointed out to the stepson how ill Bess was looking he replied tartly, 'I see that she wears no rouge.'

Of Bess's two children by the 5th Duke, Caroline St Jules had been handsomely endowed by her father on her marriage to George Lamb, brother to William the future Prime Minister. Hart was obliged to break to her what her parentage really was. Until then she had supposed her father to be a Count St Jules living in Aix-en-Provence. She wrote a touching letter to Little G, overjoyed that she could claim her as a sister. In an age when stigma was still attached even by the tolerant to ducal bastardy Lady Georgiana Morpeth's pleasure was less fervent. Caro George, as the former Caroline St Jules was called to distinguish her from Caro William, her exact contemporary, remained discreet about her birth. 'A great dear', she was much loved by her family and pitied for her wretched married life with the boorish George who declined to cohabit with her.

Two years older than the Duke, Augustus Clifford found himself in an unenviable situation on the 5th Duke's death, that of an elder, natural, son inheriting neither title, name, possessions, nor money. To begin with he behaved ill-advisedly. But his congenital goodness and sound sense soon prevailed. Educated at Harrow, he entered the Navy at the age of 12. Egged on by his silly mother Bess, Augustus at first claimed that he should bear the Cavendish arms and be accorded the precedence of a Duke's younger son. On one occasion he stalked ahead of several peers into the messroom at Portsmouth, to be severely reprimanded by his Admiral. Hart however, who sympathized with his half-brother's awkward status, gently disposed of these pretensions. It is true that their father had meant to leave Augustus a lot of money by will, but on his death the much vaunted codicil could nowhere be found. Forthwith Hart settled on him £2,000 a year allowance, undertaking to give him more on his leaving the Navy or marrying, without however notifying him in advance. Within two years Augustus married Elizabeth Townshend and was duly endowed. In a letter to Little G, Hart justified his action on the grounds that it was his pleasure to make Augustus happy. Bess was effusive in her gratitude to 'dear, dear Hartington'. Clifford was to have a very distinguished career and remained one of Hart's closest companions. He rose rapidly in naval ranks, becoming an Admiral of the Blue and then the Red, but usually referred to affectionately by his half-brother as 'Captain'. Other honours such as that of Black Rod were to accumulate.

Within a matter of weeks after his father's death the Duke was appointed by the Prince Regent Lord-Lieutenant of Derbyshire, which office had in His Royal Highness's words been 'so long, so worthily, and so respectably held by [his] old and ever lamented friend', the 5th Duke. Hart wasted no time in taking his seat in the House of Lords. On 31 January 1812 he ventured in a few halting words to make his maiden speech in support of a Whig motion to examine the causes of discontent among the Irish Catholics. Lord Byron, who could not summon courage to address the House on that occasion and postponed his maiden speech till the end of February noted that the Duke of Devonshire spoke indifferently.

The years 1812 to 1815 are the least documented in the Duke of Devonshire's life. He was, as he told Lawrence the painter when he sat to him in September of 1811, planning to continue for three or four years in a state of wary consideration and to make himself fully acquainted with all that belonged to him, after which he would become more conspicuous. Those who knew his intentions and his mind predicted great excellence of conduct. Certainly he made a point of getting to know his estates. In September 1812 he crossed to Ireland with his Aunt Bessborough and her daughter Lady Caroline Lamb. It was not the Duke's first visit to Lismore. He had been there in the lifetime of his father, who practically ignored it. He did not record the initial impression made upon him by the massive structure which in years to come he was to transform from a jumble of cone-shaped, broken towers dating from King John's reign and pointed gables from King James I's, to what he believed exactly represented a castle of the ancient ages of chivalry and tournaments. We only know that for the rest of his life he was haunted by the magical setting of the dun-coloured fortress cushioned by trees sheer above the south bank of the bustling River Blackwater. There can be few castle sites in the British Isles more picturesque, certainly none that has changed less during our century. Although there were long intervals when the Duke did not go there he was constantly working out schemes for the castle's recreation and the fulfilment of his notions of medieval revivalism in architecture.

The 1812 visit to Lismore was as much for the benefit of his little cousin Caroline as for that of the sadly neglected castle of his Boyle ancestors. Caroline, trying to recover from her distressing love affair with Lord Byron which had caused much scandal in London, was in a state bordering on insanity. At all events when she saw the semi-ruined castle from a distance she prepared her mind, according to her mother in a letter to Lord Granville, for ghosts, knights in armour, echoing dungeons, a park of venerable oaks and every incitement to romantic horror. On arrival she was profoundly disappointed by a house without an acre of land on the edge of a dirty village. Hart, she complained, handed her into

> not a Gothic hall, but two small dapper parlours neatly furnished in the newest Inn fashion, much like a cit's villa at Highgate, that she cannot recover it and shall break her heart. She also persists in its being very damp. It certainly feels so, though I know not why: for though close to the water it is on a rock. Hart and Caroline had many disputes on the damp, when last night she suddenly opened the door very wide, saying, 'Pray walk in, sir. I have no doubt you are the lawful possessor, and my cousin only an interloper, usurping your usual habitation.' For a long time nothing came, when at last, with great solemnity and many pauses, in hopped a toad, Caroline following with two candles, to treat the master of the castle with proper respect, she said.

Hart was not at all pleased with Caroline's mockery, which he considered in poor taste. Yet it may have accelerated the initial phase of his extensive re-roofing and restoration of the castle between 1811 and 1822. First he commissioned William Atkinson, a Durham architect and the inventor of Atkinson's cement, to Gothicize the toad's very hall and the reception rooms on the north front overlooking the Blackwater with delicate groined ceilings supported on brackets in stucco, slender panelled doors and quasi-medieval chimney-pieces in black marble. He was very well satisfied with Atkinson's work and his own 'princely power of doing good', he told Georgiana, as well as 'the gratitude of hundreds daily saved from starvation and ruin.'

Little more than a month after his succession Lady Bessborough had remarked to her niece Harriet Granville that the young Duke was doing too much too hastily in the way of altering his numerous houses and did not seem to realize that he had all the time in the world ahead of him. As far as Chatsworth was concerned Lady Bessborough had little to worry about as yet. The Duke's work there in 1811 amounted to no more than repairs to the state room ceilings, some refurnishing and the projected building of a covered way from house to stables, which came to nothing. More grandiose ideas were merely fomenting. Meanwhile the young owner contented himself with complaining that the house he had inherited could not hold more than twenty guests at a time. He turned his energies to collecting coins and books. The first required little space; the second were a different matter.

The Duke spent in all £50,000, an enormous sum, on medals and coins immediately after his succession. This particular hobby was a flash in the pan. After the initial enthusiasm waned he did not add to the collection and in 1844 when very severely pressed for funds, sold it for a paltry £7,056. Medals were, he consoled himself, difficult to look at, and when you looked, seldom proved rewarding. Besides there was a new culvert at Chiswick that had to be paid for which justified the sale even at an appreciable loss.

Books, on the other hand, were to be a lasting passion. Not that he was deeply learned. He had a good working knowledge of the classics and early English literature, particularly sixteenth- and seventeenth-century playwrights. To the well-known scholar Payne Collier he owned, 'I am not worthy of my own collection, I am sorry to say; and I want you, as far as you can, to make me worthy of it by informing my ignorance.' His book mania may have been inherited. The 5th Duke had bought at the Lemoignon sale of 1791 rows of plain red, blue, yellow, green and brown morocco tomes with bold lettered labels. Unlike his son he read everything he acquired, preferring pages with wide margins on which to annotate. His preferences were shared in a wholly uninformed way by Duchess Georgiana. She had Bentley's edition of Bacon's essays printed on very large paper with six-inch margins all round. One of Hart's lasting memories was of his mother darting up and down library steps and eagerly poring over the open page at perilous heights. After all Georgiana's brother the 2nd Earl

Spencer was the greatest collector of incunabula and early printed books who has ever lived.

When the great bibliomaniac Thomas Dampier, Bishop of Ely, died in May 1812 the 6th Duke bought from his widow an entire library of rare books for £10,000. After the sale Mary Berry saw the collection stacked on the floor in a drawing-room of Devonshire House. It was shortly transferred to Chatsworth and arranged in the lower library on the west front. Notwithstanding being thus possessed of, in the eccentric bibliographer T. F. Dibdin's words 'the third longest bibliomanical spear in the metropolis', the Duke proceeded to buy forty-six extremely precious volumes at the 4th Duke of Roxburghe's sale that year. They included Caxtons and de Wordes. The Duke's agent Ridgway cunningly arranged for the French bookseller Nornaville to act for him secretly by making out that his client was Napoleon. The Duke continued to buy at other great sales in ensuing years, namely the Alchorne, Stanley and Townley sales. In 1815 at the Edwards sale he bought two books painted on vellum, one being the beautiful copy of Nonius Marcellus's *De proprietate sermonum* printed in 1476. When he brought all his books together from his various houses he found that the existing library at Chatsworth was not large enough. Without consulting an architect he adapted the 1st Duke's beautiful gallery which runs the length of eight windows on the east front. As early as 1815 he began pulling out William and Mary panelling to make way for shelves. These activities involved destruction of the carved fluted pilasters and at a later date the substitution of a projecting gallery, fine in itself but breaking the previous verticality of the room. In carrying out the alterations the Duke endangered the walls and certain flues which had to be put right in 1819 by the architect Jeffry Wyatt.

England's most eligible bachelor was like most normal young men a philanderer. He was always beguiled by someone, and by no one for very long. Lady Elizabeth Bingham, seeing no future in batting her eyelids at him, drifted off and married Mr Granville Harcourt MP. Harriet Granville, who had endeavoured in vain to promote the match, assessed her brother's problem not inaccurately. In a letter to their old governess Selina Trimmer who had broached the subject with some delicacy, she replied:

> I do not think it necessary to feel alarm about him as to his loves. He cares for none of them and is too babyish in his manner about and to them, to give any reason to them to hope or complain. He wishes them all married

most cordially and feels real relief as they go off his hands. He is a most amiable creature and only wants a little steadiness and right sort of ambition to make him all one can wish ...

Playing fast and loose with the feelings of peers' daughters was all very fine, but the young Duke was about to put his foot into more sensitive waters. By the summer of 1813 all London was linking his name with that of the Prince Regent's daughter and presumptive heir to the throne, the Princess Charlotte of Wales. This unhappy girl, shuttlecocked between her neglectful father and effusive, vulgar mother, Princess Caroline, who were separated and at loggerheads with one another, was treated as a bargaining counter in their domestic warfare as well as a political pawn between the Whig and Tory parties. At one moment the Regent incarcerated his child in Warwick House next door to Carlton House, in order to infuriate his wife. The unscrupulous MP Henry Brougham appointed himself adviser to the Princess of Wales simply in order to needle the Regent and advance his own interests in the Whig party. While the Duke of Devonshire was still hesitating over Lady Bingham in the summer of 1812 it was remarked that at the London balls he was often dancing with royalty.

The middle-aged Princess Mary gave no rise to gossip, and four years later was to marry her cousin the 2nd Duke of Gloucester. Princess Charlotte, aged 16, caused more chatter. In May Georgiana Morpeth warned her brother that the Princess had been lectured by her grandmother Queen Charlotte for talking to him too much and not behaving with due dignity and decorum. The Princess retorted saucily that she did not mind. At a ball given by the Regent for his daughter at Carlton House the Duke danced with her a great deal. He sent her presents of game from Chatsworth. The caricaturists pounced on the romance and the print shops depicted them on the ballroom floor together. When the Prince Regent's attention was first drawn to the affair he pronounced it 'complete stuff and nonsense'. That they could be more than friends was unthinkable. Urged on by Brougham however the Whigs in opposition encouraged the affair in hopes that the attractions of the Princess might attach the Duke to Carlton House to their benefit and to the discomfiture of the Regent, who now hated the Whigs and tolerated the Tories. Little did they realize the extent of Charlotte's dislike of her father or her capacity to mislead. She would go to almost any lengths to torment him. She did believe the Duke to be in love with her but displayed few signs of being in love with him, pronouncing him very plain. On the other hand she was determined by hook or by crook to be married to someone or other in order to have her own establishment and get away from her father's power, living as she did surrounded by his nominees and spies.

Miss Cornelia Knight, appointed by the Regent Lady Companion to the Princess, felt certain that the Duke was by no means insensible to the physical charms of his future Queen; and that, pursued by all the mothers and misses of London, while longing to be loved for himself, he fancied that this must be so if the heir to the throne paid court to him. 'A good young man, of a benevolent heart, moderate abilities, and romantic turn (which I understand was the case with him) might easily fall into such a snare,' Cornelia wrote. Snare is indeed what the young Duke was falling into.

By May the Prince Regent's suspicions were aroused. Rumour had it that he sent for the Duke telling him he must be pleased to recollect the difference between him and his daughter. And he accused her of flirting with the Duke and incidentally talking politics. A blazing row ensued. Charlotte defied her father and went on seeing her beau clandestinely. Lady Charlotte Campbell, who was Lady-in-Waiting to the Princess of Wales, thought that her mistress's daughter had a tender feeling for the Duke even when towards the end of the year she was likewise fooling the Hereditary Prince William of the Netherlands. She led this luckless foreigner so far down the garden path as to submit to a contract of marriage before she jilted him. Miss Knight's beady eye detected that the Duke's chances were for ever dashed. A print of his likeness which had been hanging with other portraits in a room at Warwick House was taken down and one of the Hereditary Prince substituted. Moreover the engagement between Charlotte and William was formally announced. The Duke's matrimonial chances, from the first slender, were thus truly dashed. But his relations with the Princess were not broken. Until her marriage to Prince Leopold of Saxe-Coburg-Saalfeld in 1817 they continued to correspond.

In a letter of 26 December 1812 to Georgiana Morpeth comes the first mention of one who until her death in 1849 was among the most intimate of the Duke's women friends. From Chatsworth he wrote that he was to dine with Mr and Mrs Robert Arkwright 'to meet old Melpomene Siddon'. Sarah Siddons, the legendary actress painted enthroned as *The Tragic Muse* by Reynolds, was the aunt of Frances Arkwright, herself the daughter of Stephen George Kemble, actor-manager. Mrs Arkwright's husband was a Derbyshire neighbour who had been given Sutton Scarsdale Hall, an exquisite early Georgian house near Hardwick, by his father Sir Richard Arkwright, inventor of the spinning jenny and immensely rich cottontot. Whereas Robert was a worthy, hard-headed man of business, though kind-hearted, Fanny like all Kembles was sensitive and artistic. Her portrait by Opie as a newly married woman in a high-waisted Regency dress shows a pretty and engaging little face over a slight figure which too soon turned plump. Music was her passion and she was well known in amateur circles for the sweet melodious voice in which she sang poems set to music by herself of contemporaries like her friend Tom Moore, even Byron and Shelley, hymns by Bishop Heber and popular ballads. Her intonation and the expression of her wonderful eyes 'had a strangely pathetic and exciting power. Her conversation was also singularly original and attractive', an admirer declared. Her sweet empathy was calculated to appeal to the romantic young Duke who must have known her before the dinner party given for Mrs Siddons. They became kindred spirits, deep in one another's confidence. Neighbours, friends and posterity have assumed that they were lovers. But from the Duke's casual references to her in his journals and the way in which Frances's letters to him consistently began 'My dear Duke', and ended 'Your Grace's truly obliged F. E. Arkwright' passion can, notwithstanding the era of correct forms of address, surely be discounted.

Fanny Arkwright's frequent display of hurt feelings, on the other hand, and her somewhat arch and whimsical manner suggest that she may have been covertly in love with the Duke. Never was she invited to Chatsworth alone nor did the Duke ever visit her clandestinely at Sutton although they spent hours together gossiping and discussing the arts while her husband, that 'impenetrable good man' in the Duke's words, was immersing himself in more mundane and practical matters like cow houses and sawmills on his estate. On his wife's death Arkwright wrote to the Duke that she was 'more sincerely attached to you than to any person except our own family'. The Duke for his part in asking himself with which woman he could live on a desert island without resources answered succinctly, 'Plenty, first Arkwright'. The Arkwrights were, by virtue of her, among the few country neighbours with whom the Duke could talk of other than local and rural events and whom he did from time to time invite to meet his sophisticated sisters and fashionable London friends.

And how did the rich, privileged and eligible Duke in his twenties strike beholders? He was tall, well-built if not exactly slim, and with a tendency to corpulence. But he was too vain not to take drastic slimming action in periodic abstinences. When 29 he agreed with his sister-in-law Lizzie Clifford that his figure was extremely good, only rather too round-shouldered. Fair-skinned under thick auburn hair, his oval face was arresting rather than strictly regular, and his nose was curiously downturned at the end. He was always conscious of the 'red tinge which sometimes in cold weather pervades that ornament of my own face', having a dread of a bottle nose.

He took enormous care of his person and would cross the Channel whenever he thought his teeth called for the particular attention of a Parisian instead of his London dentist. He was a dandy in that he made the best of himself, taking infinite pains with his dress. Yet although he was under no illusions about his appearance and even amused by the changes wrought by time, his jests did not conceal an inbred satisfaction. 'I am indeed beautiful to look at', he observed to his sister Georgiana in 1825, 'a lovely bloom on my face, my forehead white as snow shaded by my auburn locks and all the women in the street fall desperately in love with me the moment they see me. Some will, I fear, make away with themselves.' Precisely twenty years later he admitted ruefully, 'I walked out' into the bitter February weather of Derbyshire, 'like an old stiff blue butterfly'.

One disabling affliction he was never free from: deafness. He must have been born hard of hearing although no member of his family seems to have recognized it when he was a small boy. The first written reference comes from his cousin Sarah Spencer when he was 18. She said he was as deaf as ever, poor boy. And she noticed that when they were together at the play, *Henry VIII*, he was obliged to follow text in hand. His endeavours to conceal his deafness in conversation were exhausting. Throughout early manhood he suffered from excruciating throbbing in the head. He tried every remedy to stop it – sleeping on his right side, having his ears syringed. 'The noises in my ear are tremendous,' he told Harriet. 'That a coffee mill should always be grinding there is very well, I am used to it and don't mind, but sledge hammers going bang bang *pessantissimi martelli*, capriciously coming now and then without rhyme or reason is very tiresome, isn't it?' He constantly complained that in speech friends did not articulate properly. Toothless elderly women like Lady Sitwell of Renishaw dared not open their mouths wide enough. A fellow sufferer Miss Harriet Martineau introduced him to a trumpet, but it was of little use. In middle age he felt obliged to give up theatricals, which he loved, because in being unable to catch the cues he was afraid of putting out the others; and to his distress he had to give up shooting in old age because the noise of guns caused him pain.

In his youth and middle age however the disability did not prevent him from leading an active social life. At the age of 21 he gave *fêtes-champêtres* at Chiswick attended by royalty at which one or other of his two sisters did the honours, and dinners and balls at Devonshire House. These receptions were so magnificent and became so famous that people tumbled over themselves to get invitations. He entertained huge house parties at Chatsworth all the year round, and shooting parties at Hardwick and Bolton in the autumn months. He drove miles to stay with friends in great country houses, the Morleys at Saltram in Devon, and the Beauforts at Badminton for the Kingscote ball and races. 'Hart is so good-humoured and *facile à vivre* that he makes everything *couleur de rose*,' Lady Granville wrote with a plethora of affected French phrases, 'the sure way to have it so.' He was indeed welcome everywhere, the very spirit of fun and frolic. Nothing was too much trouble and he spurned special treatment on account of his rank. When he could not hire a room for the Derby races he begged one from Lord Scarsdale at Kedleston. 'I hope Lady Scarsdale knows me well enough to lodge me in the coalhole if it is necessary,' he wrote.

In August 1815 Lord Granville Leveson Gower was created Viscount Granville for no apparent reason beyond his noble birth and his having been sent to Russia as ambassador extraordinary in 1804. Harriet therefore became Viscountess. The following October she visited her brother at Chatsworth for several weeks bringing her great friend the Russian ambassadress, Countess Lieven. Dorothea Lieven was a woman of forceful personality and the greatest and most dangerous political intriguer in Europe. Born Benckendorff of a noble Livonian family, Dorothea had a very rich German mother who was a confidante of the Empress Maria of Russia. She married Christopher Lieven, ambassador to Berlin until 1812 when he was appointed to the Court of St James. She held extreme right-wing views although professing liberal sympathies. Feared and hated by those in high places who did not enjoy her friendship – Baron Stockmar found her manner disagreeable, stiff and haughty – she was welcomed by those who avoided her enmity. In a country house party she was an amusing and informative guest. By the time she knew the Duke of Devonshire she had become the token mistress (for they seldom met) of Prince Metternich with whom she kept up a regular correspondence. Clever

and artful she acted as a sort of female liaison officer spying for the
Russian court. She could wheedle cabinet secrets out of one minister
and blatantly pass them on to another. Being a strong supporter and
admirer of Lord Grey and hater of the Duke of Wellington she worked
for the Whigs against the Tories, behaviour not strictly correct in the
wife of a foreign ambassador. Aware of this trait, Wellington was
cunning enough not to have Count Lieven dismissed, believing that
the information his party gleaned from the wife's indiscretions out-
weighed her tiresomeness. It is doubtful if the Iron Duke considered
at the time the service he was rendering to posterity, for the subsequent
publication of her letters and journals has proved of inestimable value
to historians of British politics and foreign affairs in the first half of
the nineteenth century. With her lean figure, curly hair, pointed nose
(she was given the soubriquet of 'The Snipe') and contemptuous mouth
Dorothea had for some reason physical appeal for the Prince Regent
who usually preferred well-covered women. On the other hand William
IV, who was frightened of her tongue, loathed her. Lady Granville,
who was sharp herself, delighted in her conversation. Her brother
found her fun. He was to admit that one had to know her well to
appreciate her merits. Her first visit to Chatsworth was only moderately
successful. Her host complained of her crossness to guests and servants
and her officious way of shutting all windows unconscious of the
noxious exhalations arising from her person.

In return for Chatsworth hospitality Countess Lieven brought about
one of the most cherished friendships of the Duke's future life. Dining
in November 1816 with the Lievens in London he met the Grand
Duke Nicholas of Russia, then on an eight-month tour of Europe of
which four were to be spent in Britain. The Duke was instantly smitten
by the 20-year-old imperial youth who was generally acknowledged
the handsomest prince of the age. Destined to be the future Tsar of
All the Russias, Nicholas was the third son of Paul I who had been
murdered in 1801. Between him and the reigning Alexander I came
his brother Constantine, an ill-favoured creature with an ugly snub
nose and a character ungracious and unstable. On the assumption that
the Emperor begat no son the succession was still doubtful. Nicholas,
with his looks, charm and intelligence was literally the blue-eyed boy
of his countrymen. His every movement was followed by Russians and
Europeans alike with eager anticipation and admiration. The Court of
St James was not behindhand in offering this privileged youth every
facility for touring the country and meeting the King of England's

desirable subjects of whom the Duke of Devonshire was a foremost specimen. From the start the two young men got on splendidly. The acute Baron Stockmar, having sat opposite Nicholas at table at Claremont House where Princess Charlotte was then resident, observed him closely:

> He is a singularly handsome, attractive young fellow; taller than Leopold, and without being thin, straight as a pine ... perfectly regular features, a fine open forehead, well-arched eyebrows, a very good nose, a beautiful small mouth, a well-shaped chin. He has a soft young moustache and imperial. Wears the uniform of a mounted Rifleman – a simple green coat faced with red – the silver epaulettes of a Colonel, a shabby-looking star, a white belt, and a steel sword with a leathern porte-épée; he is lively without any shyness or stiffness, and yet very well-mannered. He talks a great deal, and speaks French with a very good accent; he accompanies his words with not unpleasing gesticulations. If all he said was not exactly clever, it was at least thoroughly pleasant, and he appears to have a decided talent for flirting. When he wishes in conversation to give particular emphasis to anything, he shrugs his shoulders, and throws his eyes up in rather an affected way. He shows great self-confidence in everything he does, but apparently without pretension.
>
> He did not take much notice of the Princess, who rather made up to him, than he to her. He ate for his age very moderately, and drank nothing but water.

The women present were all bowled over. 'I was told', Stockmar concluded, 'that when it was time for bed, a leathern sack was filled in the stable with hay for the Grand-Duke by his servants, on which he always sleeps. Our English friends thought this very affected.' Stockmar gives a brilliant vignette of a young man, aware of his public importance, determined to make a good impression, talking a lot with assumed self-confidence, gesticulating a little too much, and not unconscious of the favourable effect he is creating. Nicholas behaved with the utmost propriety, paying compliments to the ladies, yet resisting their blandishments. In fact ever since he had fallen in love at the age of 17 with Princess Charlotte, the eldest daughter of King Frederick William III of Prussia and his future wife, he had remained steadfastly faithful to their vows of eternal fidelity. In slightly over-doing the ascetic act of sleeping on straw there is a hint of emulating his Herculean forebear Peter the Great.

A few days after the dinner party at the Lievens the Duke wrote to the Count that during the forthcoming visit of the Grand Duke to the north of England he would be charmed to entertain him and his household at Chatsworth and to show him the natural beauties of Derbyshire as well as the manufactures of the county: *'mais j'ai peur, n'ayant qu'une partie de mon établissement à Chatsworth, très peu de domestiques, et étant tout à fait seul en* country gentleman *que je puisse paraitre manquer du respect pour S.A.I.'* He asked the ambassador's advice as to how he should set about an invitation. It is fairly clear that he had already broached the question with the Grand Duke who expressed approval and merely wanted confirmation. On 6 December the Grand Duke duly arrived at Derby where he was met by his host, who immediately took him to see the Infirmary and some cotton mills at Belper *en route* to Chatsworth. Unfortunately the Duke was rather lame, having fallen over a polished pedestal of black marble, but able to walk with a stick.

According to plan Nicholas was to have stayed only one night. He remained for several. He went out shooting and killed forty head of game in The Paddocks. He drove to Hardwick. There he insisted on climbing to the top of the old ruined house which was not at all safe. On his descent he took off his cap and, with an expression of much relief, made the venerable building a low bow. When in 1832 little Princess Victoria wished to mount to see the giant's chamber the Duke was obliged to say, 'Impossible, Ma'am.' Another day the two young men drove to Haddon Hall, the Duke of Rutland's romantic house a mere three miles from Chatsworth as the crow flies, and Ashford Hall, a lesser Devonshire house to the north of Bakewell. They weighed each other and their weight was exactly the same, 13 st. 7 lbs. The long winter evenings were spent by the two young men talking confidentially over the fireside far into the night, and sometimes playing the fool like schoolboys. They hammered away at the piano atrociously and sang ballads. Years later the Duke was to write:

> I did not know till afterwards how much he had liked [the visit]. In those days I declare myself to have been diffident, and especially so about my French in conversation – so that I was surprised when told that Nicolas was charmed with me myself abstracted from my sights and possessions – even then Chatsworth had its successes.

Never again were these delicious, uninhibited intimacies to be repeated and never again were subsequent meetings so carefree, so unfettered by the protocol which hedged nineteenth-century royalty, and in particular Russian princes. The golden days at Chatsworth were looked back upon by the Duke with a nostalgia that haunted him with bitter-sweet regrets for an affinity which, no sooner had it blossomed than it became a memory. Short though it was the Grand Duke Nicholas's visit was certainly the highlight of a romantic friendship between two congenial young spirits comparatively unmolested by hangers-on and free to follow their own devices.

When Harriet Granville came to Chatsworth in the middle of January 1817 the Duke was still in a state of euphoria. The Grand Duke and his small suite had departed, but her brother was buoyed up by plans for a reunion in London. She remarked that her brother seemed no longer at a loose end. 'The whole difference to me is Hart's no longer having habits of doing nothing,' she told Georgiana, 'and his library here facilitates everything.' The dinners were excellent, the rooms cheerfully lit, extravagance had given way to purposefulness, and the evenings were passed in reading, talking and much music.

On 21st the Duke left Chatsworth for London, recovered from his lameness. He remained at Devonshire House, with one short break, until 16 March. During that time he saw the Grand Duke almost every day. Nine times he dined with Nicholas in a house in Stratford Place provided for him by the British government. There he seasoned himself to Russian cookery, relishing the cold soups and salted cucumbers 'passionately'. Five times he dined with him at the Lievens, and several other times at the Regent's Carlton House, at the royal Yorks' and Cumberlands' and with the Duke of Montrose the Lord Chamberlain. He was even angry with the Duke of Gloucester and Prince Louis-Philippe (then living at Richmond) because they failed to invite him to their houses to meet his friend. Every day he and the Grand Duke rode at a great pace in Hyde Park. He was pestered by letters from ladies who wanted to know the Grand Duke, including the notorious courtesan Harriette Wilson. She fell in love with him and wrote to the Duke 'endless abominations', as he put it, about the handsome Russian visitor. The Duke had the opportunity of staging but one great dinner and one ball for the much sought-after prince although he accompanied him to several balls at Almack's and elsewhere. He attended Nicholas to the House of Lords and even at a cock-fight, which quickly sickened his friend. The two were in fact inseparable. Devonshire informed Mary Berry that he was 'quite taken in by' the Grand Duke. 'I liked him extremely and I think very highly of him; and, what is more, he supplies to me the place of Clifford,' his half-brother then on naval duty overseas. 'This is certainly an odd thing to have to say of a Czarovitch, but so it is, for he puts himself down to our English level, and still, I hope, without lowering himself.'

What was more, the Grand Duke proposed that when obliged to leave England in March he should take his friend with him to Berlin to fetch his bride and thence to St Petersburg for their wedding. The Duke accepted with alacrity. It was impossible, he confessed to his *Thought Book*, a record of his friendship and travels in 1817, to be more attached than he was to him. Even so he had the sense, during the mutual infatuation, to keep himself independent of the Grand Duke on the journey. They agreed to travel their separate ways and to link up whenever possible at stopping places, but not to make a point of that if either wished to linger for sight-seeing. There was something in the imperial character, a certain volatility, a certain hauteur which warned the Duke of Devonshire to keep a discreet distance, notwithstanding the warmth of the other's apparent affection. It was as if his natural wisdom cautioned him against giving vent to a tenderer affection which could not in all the circumstances be reciprocated.

The two young men set off separately, meeting at the Ship Inn, Dover, and embarking together on the *Royal Sovereign* yacht lent by the Regent. Nicholas would have it that the cliffs of Dover from a distance looked like St Petersburg. By now the Grand Duke was accompanied by a large retinue, and the Duke of Devonshire by a close friend Lewis Sneyd, future Warden of All Souls, and by Edwin Jones, a private physician. The Duke was a comparative novice at foreign travel, having made a first brief visit to Paris in 1815.

During the journey, in the course of which the two parties met up from time to time, Hart kept a close watch upon the development of his friend's character. Before leaving London he had confided in Madame Lieven his fear lest the Grand Duke's liberal intentions might turn to despotic leanings, for he made little secret of his contempt for British democracy. Besides he showed too absorbing an interest in military drills, army boots and cuirasses. The Duke wished he possessed the power and means to guide his friend along the straight and narrow path of British Whiggism. As it was, Nicholas's best hope of salvation lay in Princess Charlotte of Prussia (soon to take the Russian name of Alexandra Feodorovna), his betrothed, who was a pacific and eminently sensible woman. The couple had every disposition to be happy together. On 23 April they reached Berlin, the Grand Duke's goal.

When Nicholas left for Frankfurt-on-Oder to join military

manoeuvres, Princess Charlotte was bereft and the Duke somewhat at a loss. To console himself the Duke went to look at the legendary Queen Louise of Prussia's mausoleum at Charlottenburg – 'the most judicious thing of the sort I ever saw.' This Doric temple was built by Schinkel in the Queen's garden to contain her recumbent marble effigy, the arms folded and head inclined to one side exactly as she lay in death:

> more beautiful than any marble known to me. It was done by her protégé (Christian Rauch) a young artist whom she had sent to study in Italy – it is impossible not to feel emotion in the monument, it is so simple and she was so beautiful and so beloved. She is buried under it in a vault of which the King keeps the key in his pocket. Her rooms in the palace remain uninhabited as she left them.

The Duke was much moved to find King Frederick William III, her sorrowing widower, in the garden roaming the walks entirely alone and feeding the carp by ringing a bell to summon them. How pleasant it was that a pacific ruler could thus derive comfort and strength through solitude.

Without Nicholas a fortnight in Berlin was enough for the Duke. So he set out on a short jaunt to Denmark and Sweden, before ending up at St Petersburg. The truth was that over and above the scenery the post-Napoleonic courts of these countries aroused the Duke's curiosity. He admitted to a great partiality for governing royalties. In Denmark for contrast the party also stopped for meals in peasants' hovels, sharing one wooden spoon and eating together out of a large communal bowl of boiled milk and rye pudding. Their hosts were welcoming, immensely jolly and responsive to jokes whether they understood them or not. The children kissed the Duke's hands on his departure.

Stockholm at the beginning of June was a city of magical beauty which suggested to the Duke a Canaletto scene of Venice. Palaces, rocks, trees, bridges, huts, water and ships were so intermingled that the eye was dazzled in the sunshine. The whole city seemed in a bustling state of improvement. On arrival the Duke was delighted by the present of a large quantity of wine from the Prince Royal. He was Jean Baptiste Bernadotte, Prince of Monte Corvo, formerly a Gascon sergeant and one of Napoleon's marshals. In 1810 he had been chosen by the Swedes as Crown Prince, or Prince Royal, to the last King of the Holstein-Gottorp dynasty, the elderly and childless Carl XIII. His son Prince Oscar, aged 18, at once invited the Duke to dinner. So too did Count Eggerström, the King's Grand Chamberlain, and Mr Foy, the English Consul, 'a gentleman whose fare it will be quite impossible ever to forget', it was so disgusting.

The Duke, Sneyd and the doctor arrived at St Petersburg on 15 June. Exhausted by jolting across Finland in great heat they recovered in a lodging with a glorious view provided by the Tsarist government opposite the Winter Palace. Immediately the Duke ordered a droshky with graceful harness. Behind a bearded coachman wearing a huge hat and blue coat with red sash he travelled round the city. One horse drew the strange carriage like the wind while another called a *furieux*, fastened on the left, its head tied to that side, pranced and curvetted but without helping to draw and merely for ornament. No one in any circumstances walked in St Petersburg.

The city came fully up to the Duke's expectations. He found it a million times more beautiful than Paris and as clean as Chiswick in spite of being built like Venice on a bog. He was immensely impressed by the endless magnificent palaces with bronze railings rising from granite walls crowned by columns and urns; by the comfortable houses of rich merchants; by the towers like mosques and the Italian temples of which the new cathedral of Kazan was the most spectacular although about to be eclipsed by the domed Isau church; and everywhere by the lime trees in gardens peeping over walls at the River Neva so clear and deep.

At first the Duke, piqued that Nicholas was not present to welcome him, regretted that he had not stayed a few more days at Stockholm instead of hurrying away. In fact the Grand Duke had left that very morning to greet his bride at the frontier and introduce her to her new country. However he found time to write the Duke a most welcome letter signing himself 'Nicholas the Scotschman'. He expressed sincere regret at missing his friend and offered his brother Michael to do him the honours of the city in his stead. This the Grand Duke Michael, a droll and spirited youth, fulfilled with good grace. The Duke was delighted to learn how beloved was Nicholas not merely by the courtiers and princes but by the English merchants and the common people. Everyone went out of his way to be obliging to Nicholas's very special guest whose visit had long been awaited. Dorothea Lieven had written in advance to her brother Alexander Benckendorff begging him to be kind and attentive. 'You will find him very clever,' she wrote, 'and I am afraid of the judgement of fools on him.' Hart was now blissfully content. He told his sister Georgiana that he felt more at ease at St Petersburg than in London and yet was leading a life of hurry that would kill a horse. He was thoroughly spoilt. Every place was thrown open to him by the help of the British ambassador Lord Cathcart.

The greatest honour of all was not slow in coming: an invitation to dine with the Emperor Alexander I. He was struck by the overt benevolence of this tragic Tsar who, brought up on Rousseauesque principles, was on his succession in 1801 impelled by a genuine desire to introduce reforms and liberal government. His deeply ingrained love of peace was totally frustrated by the monstrous ambitions of Napoleon which obliged him to join the coalition of Powers against the French tyrant and then repel the invasion of his country. By now Alexander was under the sway of the mystic Madame Krüdener who directed his mind into a consuming pietism and turned his sympathies from French ways of thinking towards English ways, and even Protestantism.

The Duke was also received by the Empress Elisaveta Alexeievna, born a princess of Baden, from whom Alexander was now estranged. He was much impressed by this kind, gentle and lovely woman. 'What an engouement I could get up for her,' he told his sisters. In strong contrast was the Dowager Empress Maria Feodorovna, likewise a German princess and by birth a Württemberg. A handsome, fine figure of a woman with a Grecian profile like her son Nicholas's she had cultivated a grand and formal manner. Having been married to a criminal lunatic, Paul I, who had his sons publicly flogged in the market-place for the most trifling misdemeanours, she was not only fiercely protective of them in their childhood but also incorrigibly managing during their adulthood.

On 20th of the month Hart had the thrill of watching from his windows Nicholas accompany Princess Charlotte into the great square before the Winter Palace. For her he had high praise on this testing occasion – her lack of shyness, her self-confidence and her gracious demeanour.

A succession of festivities and fireworks followed the wedding of the royal pair. Towards the end of July it was time to leave Russia. 'I shall probably never see my friend again, but I leave him very happy with brilliant prospects and a heart to enjoy them,' the Duke wrote philosophically. Warm leave-takings followed in succession. Promising to be back within three years the Duke got into his new dark green calèche, built in St Petersburg, double crane-necked, strong, light, with a *dormeuse*, a bed, a cellar and a larder on board, and set off for Vienna.

Whether the Russian sojourn had completely come up to his expectations is open to doubt. The Grand Duke, preoccupied by his bride with whom he was very much in love, was not able to devote to his friend quite as much single-minded attention as would have been truly welcome. Moreover Dorothy Lieven told her brother that although the Duke of Devonshire was delighted with his reception by the imperial family he was not so satisfied with his treatment by the nobility. She feared that St Petersburg society amused themselves at his expense, wrongly in her opinion, for, 'notwithstanding his dull demeanour, he is full of cleverness and wit', and his reception would give people in London a bad impression of Russian courtesy. By dull demeanour Dorothea can hardly have implied lack of self-confidence on the Duke's part. Given his cleverness and wit, it is arguable that she meant a certain reserve rather than an inability to communicate. To shine, which is what he so consistently did amongst his sisters, half-brother and intimates, was not his forte in an alien society which he realized could not respond to his exclusive and very English sense of the ludicrous. Finding himself in such a society he became the remote observer of strange foibles rather than a contributor to its gaiety.

In Vienna he drove to see the Gloriette, that classical open folly above the palace of Schönbrunn. While he was there a boy drove up in a calèche and six horses, with one attendant, 'and notwithstanding the blueness of his eyes and his curling light hair, a breadth in his cheek, an expression in his upper lip made it easy to recognize the young Napoleon, the baby King [of Rome], the Prince of Parma ... there was no speaking to him or to his tutor, he seemed used to meet with curiosity, & willing and pleased to gratify it.' At least he returned the Duke's bow graciously.

From Vienna he made his way to Trieste, and thence to Venice, where the Duke's impressions were not highly original. St Mark's piazza reminded him of Moscow and the Palais Royal, Paris. The gilding of the four horses made them too smart for their surroundings. The theatres and Palladio's churches were most admired; St Petersburg had much the advantage of Venice, he thought, being the result of one conceived plan and not a haphazard accident of nature. The Duke called upon an acquaintance of the Travellers' Club in London, Byron's great friend, John Cam Hobhouse, whose cleverness made one forget his faults and 'democratic twist'. Hobhouse showed him Lord Byron's manuscript of the fourth canto of *Childe Harold*, which struck the Duke as superior to the previous cantos, although some of the stanzas were extremely melancholy. The Duke also visited the Armenian monastery on the island of S. Lazzaro and was puzzled over what Byron could have found to make a poem out of it, 'but poets are so fertile'.

He then went to Padua to hear Rossini's new opera, *The Barber of Seville*, to Verona and to Vicenza. He made a special study of Palladio's Villa Capra, the archetype of his own villa at Chiswick. It was, he found, Chiswick with a hump, the over-high attics swallowing up the dome. The superb situation on a vineyard-covered hill however was something Chiswick knew nothing at all about. Built of brick and not stone with plaster tumbling off the walls the house was uninhabited and decaying.

In Munich he dined with the King of Bavaria, yet another creation of Napoleon. Maximilian I was 61. 'No English country squire can live with greater comfort and hospitality,' the Duke wrote. 'He received us in his bedroom and ordering us to throw our hats upon his bed he entered into the most lively and droll conversation with a great deal of humour and sharpness.' Continuing his tour of European royalty, from Stuttgart Hart visited the King of Württemberg's stepmother, the widowed Queen Charlotte, who was the English Princess Royal and a daughter of George III. She lived in the enormous baroque palace of Ludwigsburg, by then happily established in recompense for the brutality with which the late monarch had treated her.

> Latterly he deprived her of all society and gave out that it was her taste to live quite alone. Accordingly she never appeared at court. He was very fond of the reigning Queen, she sat up with him the night before his death ... About ten minutes before that event one of the physicians worn out with watching threw himself into a large armchair in the royal bedroom. Unluckily it was a piece of musical mechanism, which upon his rising to give assistance struck up the merriest tune imaginable, and nothing could stop it so that His My was very much annoyed in his last moments and his soul went 'upon a jig to heaven'. We tried the experiment with the chair.

The Duke had barely arrived in Paris in November before he learned by the public telegraph of an event which as he expressed it years later, 'influenced, altered, must I add embittered the whole of my subsequent life.' The heir to the throne of the United Kingdom, Princess Charlotte, was dead. Having married the steady, prosey, pursy, but handsome

Prince Leopold of Saxe-Coburg in May 1816, thus escaping the alternative neglect and persecution of her father and the embarrassing fulsomeness of her errant mother, she had enjoyed but eighteen months of married bliss, only to die in premature childbirth. Perhaps because of the ambivalent reputation of her parents, perhaps because of her endearing tomboy manner, and certainly because of her youth – she was 21 – the event was received by her countrymen, high and low, with heartfelt mourning. People of every class met in the streets in tears, the churches were full at all hours, the shops shut for a fortnight ('an eloquent testimony from a shop-keeping community', wrote Dorothea Lieven) in a state of despair impossible to describe. That the Duke of Devonshire was deeply affected goes without saying. Whether he exaggerated his grief with hindsight is open to question. The elderly bachelor who in 1845 recorded his feelings in his *Thought Book* certainly hinted that his intimacy with the Princess was profounder than is borne out by what we know of her attitude to him in the years before her marriage, that is to say between 1811 and 1816 when he went abroad.

> The five years she had honoured me with her unreserved friendship and the most entire confidence – there was scarcely a day while I remained in England that she did not write to me in the most cordial and open manner. She consulted me on both her plans of marriage [to the Hereditary Prince of the Netherlands and Prince Leopold] and she continued to place her confidence in me afterwards. Who would not have been overwhelmed by such a loss? There was a charm in the intercourse, all the greater, from its being secret, and naturally I felt that in her station were it to continue for our lives it must be a source of endless and unceasing interest to me.
>
> Yet God knows how that might have been. Her charming ingenuous character would have thrown her into a thousand dangers. She was the most attractive clever and noble minded of women – full of warm and generous and spirited feelings, yet tractable as a child.

The Duke's first impulse was to get away from Paris and be with his cousin Henry Cavendish who had likewise been a devoted friend of the Princess. He left that very evening, sleeping at Beaumont-sur-Seine. At the inn he was vexed to meet some English friends, 'and there began the work of dissimulation, and of endeavouring to make my sorrow appear like that of other loyal subjects, and of suppressing the depth of grief, which as it could not be explained would have appeared like affectation.' He passed rapidly through London, retreating straight to Chatsworth to drown his unhappiness in a resumption of English rural life. During the first evenings he re-read Princess

Charlotte's letters, pored over her presents and cherished her memories that remained to him. Except with his sister Georgiana he never communicated with anyone on the subject of the Princess. Yet marriage with the Princess would have been out of the question, and his relations with her did not amount to a love affair as we understand the term. They amounted, if one of the French phrases to which all Cavendishes were so much prone may be employed, to little more than '*une amitié amoureuse*'.

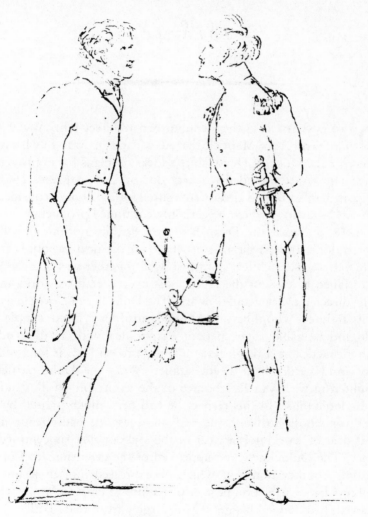

Drawing of the 6th Duke with Grand Duke Nicholas by Count St Antonio, 1817

3

Regency Duke
1818–1825

———————◆———————

ON 16 JANUARY 1818 the distinguished architect Jeffry Wyatt wrote to a friend from Matlock that he was on his way to Chatsworth to receive the Duke of Devonshire's ideas on plans for improvements which His Grace intended to carry out by slow degrees. The letter suggests that Wyatt had already submitted for the Duke's consideration plans and drawings which he certainly continued producing throughout 1818, and that the Duke had very definite notions of what he wanted done. Indeed the reason why over the next twenty years and more patron and architect got on so well together was because Wyatt never failed to consult the Duke over every detail of work, and the Duke directed every detail of work. The Duke became extremely fond of his architect whom he called 'a delightful man, good, simple like a child, indefatigable, eager, patient, easy to deal with, ready to adopt a wish if practicable, firm to resist a faulty project.' Their long relationship could hardly have been happier. What the Duke particularly delighted in was Wyatt's 'absence of the vanity of self-illustration in his undertakings'. In this respect he had been much praised by Lady Bath, for whose husband, the 2nd Marquess, he had already done a great deal of work at Longleat in the style of that sixteenth-century palace. The Duke knew and approved of the extensions to Longleat, the only country house of which he expressed himself jealous as a rival to Chatsworth. Longleat inspired him to employ Wyatt who, he believed, had derived his good taste largely from Lady Bath.

The 'improvements' to Chatsworth amounted chiefly to extensions on a prodigious scale to the north of the 1st Duke of Devonshire's building in order to provide additional and less archaic state rooms than the Hampton Court-like ones on the south front, as well as a gallery for sculpture and a greenhouse for plants, in other words a general aggrandizement. They were motivated by the 6th Duke's unashamed love of splendour, his sense of what befitted a great territorial magnate in a modern age of enhanced prosperity, and his evident passion for architecture. He wished to be able to entertain at Chatsworth on a scale which the house he had inherited could not accommodate, and to provide a worthy shrine for the works of art he was amassing. Chatsworth at the time of his succession was merely a large country house. He intended that it should become, like Longleat, a palace. Although his ideas changed as work progressed over the next two decades the general outline, decided upon in 1818 by the Duke and Wyatt, was adhered to.

The immediate priority was to contrive a new entrance to Chatsworth through an imposing screen of triumphal arches while concealing an unsightly jumble of office buildings. But the Duke was, as Wyatt had intimated, in no hurry. The new building did not begin in earnest until 1820, although Wyatt may have tidied up the great library where amateur hands had nearly caused serious mischief by interference with certain chimney flues. Writing to Georgiana Morpeth in March of 1818 her brother mentioned that the library was just finished, was beautiful, 'but the wind gets in'. The truth was that the Duke had other things on his mind. He was determined to travel to Italy, to study the architecture of antiquity and his own time (but not in-between) and above all to make purchases of sculpture, some ancient and most modern. A mania for marbles was now the vogue among the rich aristocracy of England. The 6th Duke of Bedford, father of Hart's boyhood friend Tavistock, had set the pace by employing Wyatt in 1815–16 to enlarge the sculpture gallery at Woburn and fill it with ancient and contemporary statues. The Duke of Devonshire felt impelled to do the same. Meanwhile tiresome estate problems had to be faced and dealt with.

In March he paid a rush visit to his property at Londesborough in the East Riding of Yorkshire with James Abercromby. The previous year the auditor had written to his master while in Germany with such enthusiasm and good advice about his affairs that the Duke had become more reliant upon him than ever. In approving of money being spent on Chatsworth as a worthy object Abercromby considered that certain outlying lands were disposable. The Londesborough estate was of long inheritance through the Duke's paternal grandmother. When young Lord Hartington went there with his tutor Dr Randolph in 1806 the parson told him ruefully that the 5th Duke had visited it once only in his life for a few days. The Duke and Abercromby reached a decision. The charming Caroline house was to be demolished and the wine packed up and sent to Chatsworth. The parson was dreadfully upset. '*Dictu miserabile*', he noted in an unpublished diary.

In January 1819 the Duke set out for Italy. With him, besides minor attendants unspecified, went a travelling companion and a private doctor. The two last assumed leading roles in the unvarying pattern of the Duke of Devonshire's retinues on this and all forthcoming journeys. The companion was James Brougham, a brother of Henry Brougham the Whig statesman, with whom it seems he shared a propensity for endless chat. To Georgiana the Duke wrote, 'Though not my lover do you think that James will make me grow thin with discussion as Henry does Mrs. Lamb [whose lover Henry Brougham then was]? I know very little of him, but he seems gentlemanlike,' an attribute very desirable in the Duke's requirements. As for Dr Eyre he must have answered the conditions which were laid down in a document entitled '*Arrangement with a Physician*':

The Duke of Devonshire offers to the Gentleman who accompanies him as his physician in travelling the sum of £50 per month.

He will be expected to undertake the superintendance of all travelling expenses and the examination of the courier's accounts, also transactions with the different foreign bankers when it may be necessary.

The second carriage will be always appropriated to his use, even when the Duke is not accompanied by any other person.

The Duke cannot undertake to introduce him or to promise his introduction to any of the courts which he may visit. Neither can he answer for it in private societies though it is likely that they will usually be open to all the party.

The Duke carries with him only the books with which he is himself occupied, therefore he requests that Dr. — will be provided with any that he may want for his own use.

At large towns where the Duke may stay some time and where he is in the habit of dining out there will be no table provided for Dr. — but his company will be very acceptable whenever the Duke dines at home.

These unequivocal directions intimate that socially the role of physician was a degree lower than that of companion, whose duties beyond being perenially agreeable were negligible.

The party crossed France. At Lyons the Duke met Duchess Elizabeth on her slow return from England to Rome where she had lived since 1814, and again at Marseilles and Nice, where the Duke and Duchess joined forces, he and his party on muleback, she in a *portantino*, a sort of black sedan carried by six men. Rome was reached before the end of March and the Duchess safely restored to her home. She instantly resumed supervision of her excavations in the Forum which were carried out by manacled convicts.

Rome was indeed the Duke of Devonshire's goal. It was already packed with English milords, numbering a few serious connoisseurs of the arts and antiquities, many more good-timers, and several profligate and drunken layabouts. On the whole they were loathed by the Romans for their insolence, outrageous behaviour and meanness, always wary of being cheated – not without reason. Their great riches were of course another factor to engender resentment among the poorest classes. Stendhal in *Pages d'Italie* of 1824 summarizes an account of their unpopularity in the following words: 'The late Duchess of Devonshire and the Duke of Devonshire are the only English, to my knowledge, for whom the Romans make exception in the profound hatred they bear towards their countrymen.' Both could speak Italian, were very open-handed and treated the citizens with the understanding and courtesy habitual to them.

The Duke spent three months in Rome with a short break in May of a jaunt to Naples, which he found a miracle of nature and antiquities combined, but falling short of the attractions of Rome. Having on this preliminary Roman visit rented the Palazetto Albani on the Quirinal Hill he acquainted himself with the popular ruins, of which the Baths of Caracalla and Diocletian and the Temple of Minerva Medici, where he picked up bits and pieces of marble in the garden, were his favourites. Most important of all he got introductions through the Duchess to several distinguished Romans as well as resident artists: among the latter the giant of living sculptors, Antonio Canova.

The Duke's admiration for the sculptor was instantaneous and overwhelming. A first visit to the studio convinced him that Canova was the greatest artist of modern times. Within four years he was to acquire Canova's statues of Endymion, Madame Mère seated, Petrarch's Laura, and Hebe (bought from Lord Cawdor), and busts of Madame Mère and Napoleon. Admiration turned to friendship and affection. 'The most talented, the most simple, and most noble-minded of mankind,' he called him. Canova reciprocated these warm feelings and expressed gratitude for the Duke's *'gentile generosità dell' animo'*. He took him to the casino Borghese to show him his recumbent *Venus* by torchlight, the house then being closed and shuttered. Gasparo Gabrielli, a painter turned dealer and a man of excellent taste and charm, acted in the interests of both the Duke and the sculptor. Gabrielli accompanied the rich English client to the studios of Canova's favourite pupils, John Gibson, Rudolph Schadow and Bertel Thorvaldsen. He executed all the Duke's subsequent commissions in Rome and protected him against being overcharged and cheated by dishonest traders in marbles. As early as April 1819 he presented the Duke with a long list of payments to a variety of persons besides sculptors, namely porters for carriage, custom officers for licences and duties, and others for packages and registering, the whole endorsed by the satisfied client, 'Gabrielli receipt for everything'. On his return to England the Duke received in September Gabrielli's announcement that he had already dispatched by sea twenty cases of works of art acquired in Rome, and that Schadow's *Filatrice* (today in the sculpture gallery at Chatsworth) would follow.

The Duke left Rome sooner than he had intended, by the end of June. The news from England was bad. The appalling conditions of the working classes were causing riots and bloodshed. Unemployment had followed conclusion of the Napoleonic wars. Power-weaving machinery was impoverishing the handloom weavers. The Tory government was dealing harshly with the disaffected Luddites. Habeas Corpus was suspended. Unfortunately the opposition's most active champion, Henry Brougham, was unreliable and his conduct unpredictable. The Duke felt his duty was to be at his post in case he were wanted. However on the eve of his departure he extracted a promise, willingly given, that Canova would create for him something to surpass all his previous works. There and then the Duke put down a handsome sum 'towards a statue in marble, of which neither the size nor the subject were decided'. Elated and excited the Duke quitted the city full of expectations of a masterpiece from the great sculptor's chisel. He was not to be disappointed.

The Duke's return to England coincided with the so-called Peterloo Massacre outside Manchester. Actually, of 50,000 people assembled to hear the radical demagogue Henry Hunt with banners proclaiming 'Equal Representation or Death', one man only was killed and forty were wounded. Nevertheless the government had the infamous Six Acts passed, making illegal all organized expressions of public opinion. Grey and Brougham were opposed to the Six Acts, but the Whigs as a whole, including the Duke of Devonshire, declined to co-operate with Grey and Brougham. They believed that although the magistrates had acted hastily in ordering the yeomanry to seize Hunt, yet vigorous measures were essential to suppress violence. The ugly situation did not prevent the Duke from going to Bolton Abbey in the middle of the month. Harriet Granville who was staying there told Georgiana that he was in a most perplexing uncertainty about his plans, quite apart from the national crisis. 'He cannot as yet find out what are those of the Grand Duke, upon which he must in great measure depend.'

Whispers had reached him that the Emperor Alexander was contemplating abdication and that the Grand Duke Constantine would renounce his claim to the Russian throne. Although the rumours worried him on behalf of his beloved Nicholas, there was nothing he could do about the situation other than hold himself ready to join his friend were the Emperor obliged suddenly to leave his country. And Nicholas apart, the Duke of Devonshire was very much preoccupied with his Roman purchases. He was unpacking the seated sculpture of Madame Mère which had reached London unscathed from Paris where he had bought it and was revelling in the purity and beauty of the marble. To crown his content he received a letter from the Duchess written from Rome on 1 September, announcing that she had seen the statue Canova had modelled for him:

> It lives, it breathes, it is all life, & youth, & beauty; yet it looks not, it wakes not. It is not Apollo, but it is a form so beautiful, of such nature, taste & loveliness, that I really think it is the most perfect of all his works. He is himself satisfied & contented ... He had worked at it as he says '*con amore*' & done it in the space of a fortnight. Much of the countenance and form might be taken from you – start not, it really is true ... it is beautiful, beautiful.

The sleeping *Endymion* and his dog had been born. The Duke was overcome with delight and excitement. Certain it is that the Duke never again was so absorbed in a branch of the arts as he was now by sculpture. He moved about his everyday occupations with an abstracted air like one possessed.

The death of George III in January 1820 caused a social and political hubbub which lasted throughout the year and put every other event into the shade. With the accession of the Regent as George IV his legal spouse saw no reason why she should not call a halt to her wanderings on the Continent, return to England and enjoy the privileges of Queen Consort. This was not at all to the liking of her husband. He promptly ordered that her name be deleted from the up-to-date Prayer Book. There were to be no prayers in the churches for Queen Caroline. Rejecting a handsome bribe of £50,000 to keep away and renounce the title of queen she crossed the Channel and advanced to London amidst the frenzied welcome of the populace, who were anxious to give expression to their detestation of the sovereign. The mob broke windows. The troops were called out. Urgent Cabinet meetings were held, no one in authority knowing what to do except postpone the coronation. Lord Liverpool's government attributed responsibility for the shocking state of affairs to Brougham who had promised them he would keep the Queen abroad. Finally a Bill of Pains and Penalties was promoted in the Lords by the Tories. From July till November the trial of Queen Caroline took place. It was not edifying.

The Duke came up to London and sat throughout the proceedings. The House of Lords was packed with peers eager to listen to the scandalous charges of ill conduct against Her Majesty during her late travels. 'These Lords are all old and fat and stinking,' Hart wrote to Georgiana from the House, 'and one is so fidgetty that he keeps the others in constant exercise by beating a tattoo.' He was strongly opposed to persecution of the Queen and blamed the King's ministers for the advice they had given their master. It looked bad for the King to be hounding the Queen. At the same time the Duke was not one to believe the Queen innocent; yet if it was impossible to prove guilt, he did not on that account favour her name being restored to the Prayer Book. He headed an address of protest from the gentry of Derbyshire to the King on whom it had no effect beyond irritation. It merely decided the King not to attend a rout followed by a concert and ball at Devonshire House.

The two figures who stood out most sharply in the drama were Brougham and Caroline. Brougham's temper hurt his cause. He was too passionate with the witnesses, and too insolent to the Lords. Yet the way he demolished the witnesses was masterly and his evidence for the Queen triumphant. Caroline in the role of injured wife, outraged by the gross imputations of one of her servants, the witness Théodore, was tragi-comedy at its height. 'Never did I see such a *coup de théâtre* as the Queen's throwing up her veil and sticking her arms akimbo, when she cried out Théodore! I think she wanted to awe him, and rage at his composure drove her out of the House. The Queen burst into laughter yesterday in Lord Wellesley's face.' Théodore, a rascal whom Brougham made contradict himself point-blank, was soon discredited. Gaetano, a gay, clever and quick Neapolitan sailor who had been in the ship which took the Queen to the Holy Land, claimed on examination that he saw her sitting on the lap of Luigi Bergami, her Milanese chamberlain, constant companion and almost certainly lover. As a witness he was never put out, and he never faltered. He seemed rather amused, if sorry to be obliged to testify against the poor lady. To the Duke's way of judging it was evident that anyone could have walked into the Queen's tent on deck at any time of night for she never undressed or had a proper bed made up. It could not thereby be inferred that she had committed adultery with anyone. Her casual, if squalid habits rather suggested the contrary.

At times the Duke was in despair that the Bill would pass, the House was so evenly divided. When things looked bad the mob would pelt him at Hyde Park Corner on his way back to Chiswick. When they looked bright he would be greeted with cries of 'Huzza for the aristocracy!' On 11 November the Prime Minister, Liverpool, deciding that were the divorce to go through the government would be besieged with petitions and revolution might even ensue, suddenly abandoned the Bill in spite of the fact that the second reading had received a majority vote of nine. 'Brooks's was such a scene of joy as I never saw,' he wrote. The crowds went wild with delight. This time the Duke was cheered all the way back to Chiswick, people shouting, 'God bless the noble House of Peers!' The country, in the emotion of the moment, as the Duke put it, was saved.

A distraction of 1821 was the Duke's purchase for £2,000 of John Philip Kemble's collection of old plays in print and manuscript. Kemble, uncle of Fanny Arkwright, through whom the deal may have been brought about, had recently retired from the stage and was in straitened circumstances. The collection was immensely important. It contained in all 7,500 plays, including one of the only two first editions of *Hamlet* to survive, and 111 volumes of playbills. It was estimated by Dr Waagen on his visit to Devonshire House in 1835 as the richest collection of its sort in the world. The 6th Duke greatly increased the collection. It was sold, together with 25 Caxtons, in 1914 to Henry E. Huntingdon.

'Sunday August 26th 1821, Chatsworth. I went to Church and

reflecting there on the little impression anything makes on my memory I resolved to keep a journal.' With these words the Duke of Devonshire began a day-to-day journal, or diary, which he conscientiously kept up, with only occasional omissions, until the last weeks of his life. It records his every moment, the places he went to and the people he met, being too often a mere catalogue of names. It is punctuated with every diarist's customary misgivings – 'O journal, journal, how stupid you are and how amusing you might be,' and 'Really my journal is a farce'. Yet his fits of disgust and threats to burn the whole thing were soon forgotten. On the other hand he erased several passages – 'I scratch out the worst bits' – so successfully that it has proved impossible to reconstruct them. That he wanted his journal to be read by posterity is most probable for he kept besides an astounding quantity of note-books full of his thoughts and ideas in a kind of desperate bid for immortality which is often peculiar to unfulfilled and childless persons. As a chronicle of a great patrician's life these papers are invaluable.

A visit to Paris in November enabled him to see much of Lady Hunloke whose name crops up repeatedly throughout the journals. Anne Hunloke was recently widowed, her husband, Sir Windsor, 5th baronet, having died of fever in Paris at the age of 42. The Hunlokes, an old Derbyshire family who had been friends of the 5th Duke of Devonshire, came from an early Georgian house, Wingerworth Hall, now demolished. With her grown-up children Lady Hunloke had gone to live permanently in Paris. Good-humoured, sprightly, flighty and totally unambitious to shine in society, she loved the Duke, and he her. The world considered that she was his mistress and some prudish countrymen refused to receive her in Rome the following year on that account. Mrs Lamb who was devoted to her affirmed that when among a few close friends she laughed and romped from morning till night. Lady Granville, always on the look-out to discredit her brother's intimates, pronounced her good, amiable, but childishly vulgar and at times silly. Try as she might Harriet could form no opinion about Hart's true feelings for the '*vedova*', she told Georgiana. 'Every supposition has an undeniable objection to it. Why do they meet – why do they part? Why live together, why live asunder – why marry why not marry?' And to crown her irony she added,

> 'I forgot to tell you that Mrs. Lamb told me … Hart's familiarity knows no bounds that he goes up before them all – pats her on the cheek, etc. it is certainly marvellous take what view of it you may.'

Lady Hunloke, being no toady, but proud, failed to make the advances expected by Lady Granville when she became ambassadress at Paris in 1824. Hart told his sister that he had the greatest respect for and interest in her. 'Every smile you bestow on her will add to the stock of happiness and gratitude in my heart.' And yet he considered her a figure of fun, though one that seldom failed to amuse. She was always putting her foot where it should not be, and was reliably disaster-prone.

During his three weeks' visit to Paris, when not listening to Madame Patti in *Otello*, gambling in the *salon* where he lost money, or ordering a quantity of rose trees for Derbyshire, the Duke rode and drove in the Bois with Lady Hunloke. On learning the distressful news of the death of his aunt Lady Bessborough in Florence, caused by catching cold through nursing a grandchild, he went home. At Boulogne he met Beau Brummel for the first time since that leader of Regency fashion had absconded abroad for debt. They shook hands twice. 'Poor man,' he commented, 'we tolerate greater swindlers in society.'

In December he was invited to stay with the King at Brighton. At first the Duke was surprised. He imagined he was in ill odour with his sovereign because he had not attempted to disguise his sympathies with the Queen at her trial and had been one of a number of rich peers endeavouring to supplement her income by a subscription. Furthermore the King had been vexed by the Duke's complaint in the Lords about the treatment of the Irish tenantry by English landlords, and the general persecution of the Catholic majority in that country. The Duke was by upbringing and conviction an unwavering Whig; and George had taken against the Whigs, his erstwhile supporters and boon companions, when in 1811 his father George III finally collapsed into insanity. The Regent feared lest the return of the Whigs, pledged to peace with Napoleon, would call off support of the war which was showing signs of being brought to a successful conclusion under Wellington. Whereupon all those Whig supporters who had enjoyed his favours, Grey, Granville and Holland, turned upon him with perfidy and ingratitude. The Duke of Devonshire's December visit to Brighton records some of the best and a few of the worst qualities of George IV: the transcendence of his good nature over slights and his fundamental generosity of spirit, not to mention his unfailing charm; and his evasion of issues by deliberate procrastination, and thereby the immense difficulty his servants and ministers had in bringing him to decisions, and keeping him to them when finally taken.

On 11th the Duke arrived at the Pavilion barely in time to dress for dinner. He was given two rooms upstairs, opposite the King's. A small party was staying, including the Marquess and Marchioness of Conyngham, the reigning favourite who now lived at court. The King received the Duke with his usual affectionate kindness and talked after dinner about Duchess Elizabeth and the late Lady Bessborough. The Duke was commanded to dance, although still wearing his black travelling gloves. He and five others supped with the King later.

The following morning soon after ten o'clock he was summoned to breakfast with His Majesty. This was what the Duke had hoped for. A second servant announced that he must go immediately in his dressing-gown. The King plunged into amusing gossip. After a pause the Duke took courage and asked outright if His Majesty was as pleased with Irish conditions as was reported. Oh yes; but he thought that everything done for the Irish must be gradual. He could not interfere himself, for constitutional reasons. 'Here I got extremely interested and was going to say something on my mind, but that beast Sir Edmund Naylor [Sir George Nayler] came in.' Before the subject could be resumed the King sent his guest with Lord Francis Conyngham to look at the Pavilion in detail. It was magnificent, and the Duke found the steam contrivances in the kitchen perfection, particularly one for keeping food warm on an iron table. For dinner the King had the Music Room fully lighted for the Duke's sake. It was like an oriental fairy tale. The band were playing Rossini. Hart was made to waltz with Lady Cowper.

At breakfast the following morning the King began again to burble about trivialities. What horse did the Duke ride? What did he think of the steam engine? He spoke of his yacht, its size, the merit of steam-propelled boats and the difficulty of navigating those with rigging. On his return from the state visit to Ireland he had been totally without fresh water. The Duke did not like to interrupt. At last the King touched upon the cruelties and disturbances in Ireland which were equal to the worst atrocities of savages. To remedy such horrors was not a question of Catholic versus Protestant, but of gradual improvement of education and amelioration of conditions. Here the Duke fancied the opportunity to press his point had at last arrived. But he could not get the King to stop talking. He just managed to convey that there were several matters he wished to discuss with him privately. At this point Francis Conyngham tactfully withdrew. Rather nervously the guest begged the King to follow up his highly successful visit to Ireland by granting some elementary concessions to the Catholics. Whereupon the King said he was not in the habit of talking politics, confided that his father's madness had been caused by worry over the Irish question, and by a deliberate process of parrying avoided committing himself. The Duke nevertheless thanked the King for his confidence while reminding him that he had been educated in certain political principles which it would be dishonourable to abjure. The King replied with great warmth. He considered him, the Duke, the spokesman of the most respectable profession of Whig principles. 'Good God, Hart,' he said, taking his arm, 'Sir, you shall hear me,' as though the Duke had not been listening respectfully to a non-stop monologue, and started all over again. The conversation lasted for three and a half hours. On its conclusion they embraced. That evening on going to bed the Duke kissed him. The following morning he was sent for to take leave. The King assured him a room would always be kept ready for him in the Pavilion.

On the penultimate day of the year Lady Bessborough's remains were buried in the vault of All Saint's Church, Derby, next to the coffin of her beloved sister Georgiana. All the funeral arrangements had been made and rooms for the bereaved prepared by Hart in the Judges' Lodgings. Caroline Lamb, who had been remarkably calm since her mother's death, became too agitated to attend the committal. Lady Bessborough's faithful maid Mrs Peterson and Selina Trimmer were among the mourners. The Duke took them all to stay afterwards at Hardwick. From Hardwick he went on riding expeditions to neighbouring country houses, Welbeck Abbey, Renishaw Hall and Wingfield Manor, accompanied by young William and George Cavendish, the grandsons of his uncle Lord George. William, who was eventually to succeed him as 7th Duke of Devonshire, and George were both to figure largely in their uncle's life. The Duke also took them woodcock shooting. He was a devoted and generous uncle, liking nothing better than to induct them into country pursuits as well as helping them financially. He was about to provide an apartment at Hardwick for his niece Georgiana Howard and her husband George Agar-Ellis until they could fine somewhere permanent to live. Whig politician, scholar and connoisseur Agar-Ellis helped bring about the admission of Catholic peers to the House of Lords and was largely responsible for the foundation of the National Gallery.

No sooner had the Duke returned to Chatsworth at the New Year of 1822 in order to supervise the restoration of Thorvaldsen's *Venus*, which had arrived from Rome broken across the wrist and ankles, than he was again summoned to Brighton.

In mid-March the Duke was obliged to get leave from the King 'to go to town' to speak in the House of Lords. In February, sailing perhaps a little close to the royal wind, he had spoken against the suppression of the Habeas Corpus Act in Ireland. Now he was about to advocate, almost from the steps of the Royal Pavilion, the abolition of tithes which were causing much hard feeling among the Catholic community. It was a cause for which the King had no sympathy at all. For a week in advance the Duke was horribly nervous about both the King's possible displeasure and his impending speech, which turned out to be highly successful. Lord Liverpool and Lord Lansdowne, Tory and Whig alike, praised it. The House was crammed, many members sitting on the steps of the throne. The Duke was particularly happy on Abercromby's account for that stern mentor had criticized him for not pressing the King with greater vigour over the tithes issue. When he got back to Brighton the King was very generous in his praise. 'There is no place where I feel less *gêné*, or more at my ease, from his unvaried kindness to me,' the Duke wrote.

In June he spent £1,000 purchasing furniture, chandeliers and antique busts at the thirty-two-day sale of magnificent Wanstead House in Essex. He visited the studios of artists Chantrey, Westmacott, Hayter and Jackson. He also went to see his old tutor Mr Smith of Woodnesborough. John the ricketty son slipped into his carriage an old ivory cup which he had bought in France. The Duke felt embarrassed. 'It is a bore to have that sort of present made one.'

In July he made a lightning visit to Paris accompanied by a new doctor, Richard Verity, who was to be associated with him for many years, and promised to be a sensible and agreeable companion. Verity was a character, alternately silent and absurd, 'the queerest man I ever saw, sometimes pleasant in society, but so absent and vain of his person & dress, gazing at himself in the glass that I sometimes think he is cracked.' In Naples twelve years later Verity astonished the natives by dressing alternately in fur and India rubber. Nevertheless the Duke trusted and had confidence in him.

On their way home a passing King's Messenger informed them that Lord Londonderry had cut his throat which gave rise to speculation as to whether Canning would go to India. 'Will the King offer me the Garter? That is what I long for that I may decline it.' – an opinion about honours commonly uttered by those who are *papabile* and one usually not borne out when the offer is made.

At the end of August the Duke went to Ireland to see the improvements carried out on his estate since his last visit eight years previously. The year 1822 marked completion of the re-roofing and structural restoration of Lismore Castle, begun in 1812. The house was at last comfortable; and fit for him to arrange the furniture, which was one of his favourite occupations. Nothing more was to be done at Lismore until Paxton was introduced to the Irish scene in 1840. The Duke attended ploughing matches and agricultural meetings; entertained dozens of neighbours to dinners and balls and made himself extremely popular. His attachment to the people and neighbourhood dated from this visit.

In early October 1822 he was back at Chatsworth to receive Jeffry Wyatt and Francis Chantrey who was in ecstasies over the progress of the architect's extensions. William Henry Hunt, a water-colourist, was busy painting detailed interiors of both Chatsworth and Hardwick which gave great satisfaction, and make a pretty record of the state of the rooms a hundred and seventy years ago. But Chatsworth did not detain him long. He was off within a month to Italy again, prompted by news from Gabrielli of Canova's death which not only distressed him greatly but also alarmed him, lest his precious *Endymion* might be requisitioned by one of the acquisitive admirers already thronging the great sculptor's studio. As recently as July Canova had written to him that no other hand but his would touch the sculpture, even if it remained unfinished at the time of his death. The Duke pictured the exquisite work as the seal on their mutual regard and understanding.

In Florence the Duke commissioned statues from Lorenzo Bartolini's studio and found time for three sittings for his own bust by Bonelli. Arriving in Rome on 12 December, he was conducted by Gabrielli to Canova's house. At last he was able to feast his eyes on *Endymion*. 'Deep and sincere grief mixed with the supreme happiness of possessing such a treasure.' The rest of the month was spent roaming from the studio of one pupil of Canova's to another. The Duke's choice of sculpture was largely governed by the master's approval of their work, either expressed to him by Canova verbally in 1819 or interpreted by Gabrielli who acted as his daily attendant and prompter. The Duke relished advice tendered by people like Gabrielli whose opinion and taste he respected, yet his decisions were very much his own and he would surprise experts who cautioned him against purchasing a piece of sculpture by promptly acquiring it. He made an invariable rule not to buy sculpture that was unfinished, or was nearly finished. He considered it a disgrace for a patron to possess a bad statue, however complete. And he would make an artist correct a model which had digressed from the drawing approved by him on commission. A bad painting could be turned to the wall. To dispose of a colossal and heavy group of marble was not so easy.

John Gibson the young English sculptor, whom in 1819 he had asked to carve a group of *Mars Restrained by Cupid*, was high on his list of protégés. The Duke bought a *Ganymede* from Adamo Tadolini, and ordered a statue of *Amor with a Butterfly* by Carlo Finelli, since 'poor Canova' wished him to employ this man. Tenerani and Trentanove were also patronized. At the studio of Thomas Campbell, another English sculptor, Mr Locke of Norbury so bored him with his praises that he could admire nothing. He met Thorvaldsen who showed him his grand works, but the Duke looked upon this eminent rival of his god 'as a modellist, not a sculptor'. He never thought his sculpture inspired. Moreover he was irritated by the Dane's procrastination. All the same he acquired some of his works including the standing Venus (*Venere Vincitrice*) commissioned in 1819, and of course he already possessed *La Filatrice* by Thorvaldsen's pupil, Rudolph Schadow.

During this concentrated tour of sculpture galleries the Duke returned several times to Canova's studio in order 'to adore Endymion', twice accompanied by his old friend Lady Abercorn who had deeply attached herself to the sculptor, and was so easily reduced to tears at the mention of his name that she was known as the *Acqua Infelice*. The 'dear good soul' took him into the sculptor's living quarters to show him Canova's pictures. He would have bought the great ancient hand in the street outside the studio had it not been public property. As though to compensate him for this disappointment Lady Abercorn let him have her bust of Canova's *Napoleon*. The Abate Canova, the sculptor's brother, an amiable cleric, allowed him to buy Antonio's favourite bits of ancient marble, of which the Duke had fifteen mounted. As a token of his feelings the Duke dispensed ten louis apiece to the sculptor's workmen. Indeed his generosity to causes connected with sculpture was remarkable. He gave John Gibson £100 towards the foundation of an Academy for English Sculptors and subscribed £50 towards Canova's monument in the Frari in Venice. He would have given more had it been erected in Rome.

The Duchess took him to the Vatican to see the Braccio Nuovo, just completed. It is part of the Museo Chiaramonti, a magnificent, luminous gallery with barrel roof and walls flanked by a continuous series of niches containing statues. The Duke endorsed the Duchess's high opinion of this cool and Greek-like apartment and wanted a sketch of it done, 'as we may take some hints from it', notably for Wyatt's new dining-room at Chatsworth. Built into an apse of the Braccio Nuovo are two antique columns of Egyptian alabaster which had been bought by the Duke and refused export.

In spite of the off-putting gush of Mr Locke he began sitting to Thomas Campbell for a bust which was to be the cause of much vexation. The sculptor took nine years to finish it owing, he protested, to the difficulty of procuring good Carrara marble. With Gabrielli's help the Duke ordered copies of Canova's two couchant lions on Pope Clement XIII's tomb in St Peter's, one by Francesco Benaglia, the other by Rinaldo Rinaldi. He had an audience with Pope Pius VIII. 'He received me very kindly poor old man, he is very feeble but has a fine countenance and animation still. He asked after the Duchess, talked of the arts, and I praised the braccio nuovo.' He left the Pope at midday to discuss Ireland with the Cardinal Secretary of State Consalvi, whom he conceded to be handsome and courteous but deemed 'no more than an old noodle'. With the Duchess he attended Canova's requiem mass in the church of SS Apostoli. The church was hot and damp and the service was not affecting. Then came the carnival into which he threw himself with gusto, and the fun of being pelted with sugar plums in the Corso.

If dear Canova's requiem was not affecting the Duchess's farewell party for him certainly was, particularly the long conversation he had with someone, whose name he coyly left a blank. In Florence he saw his bust by Bonelli, which was execrable, and bought an Italian greyhound bitch, called Spot, to which he became devoted and which accompanied him on many subsequent travels. At Suzzara, a familiar halt, the Duke wrote in his journal: 'Here I will make a solemn resolution,' whereat two and a half lines are erased. What was it that this discreet and outwardly correct man feared to leave for the prurient enjoyment of posterity? Casual sex? Drink? Sex seems unlikely for he surely would not have recorded such an irregularity in the first place. Drink on the other hand was a problem that accompanied him all his life and which he was not shy about. Only a week previously he had confessed that too much wine disordered his stomach. Five weeks later he was to be franker still about his propensity to drink more than he should. He got fuddled and made blunders. He repeatedly formed good resolutions which he failed to keep. Yes, too much wine did his health harm. Likewise, which was so tiresome, abstinence sometimes had the same baneful effect. 'Have been well punished for my temperance,' he wrote to Harriet in 1841.

> What I call temperance is ... 1 glass of sherry, and 2 or 3 sometimes, of claret. That, though plentiful, is an immense change from what you must recollect was my system of imbibing. Well, all I have got for it is much languor, inability to shake off influenza or cold quick – and (singular) a red nose.

Inebriates are often inclined to attribute symptoms of the bottle to the waggon.

A penchant for the bottle may have been contributory to his almost constant poor health. Until the end of his life, although seldom seriously ill he was perenially indisposed. He was victim to hay fever and slight asthma, afflictions of the spring and early summer. At other times of the year he was prone to colds, sore throats and influenza. He was certainly a confirmed hypochondriac. Practically every journal entry makes mention of a physical weakness or an anticipation of fell disease. Had he not been so rich and able to engage private doctors at beck and call he might not have concentrated so much on slight and imaginary complaints. As it was he suffered from real or feigned spasms, boils, chest constriction (which he interpreted as angina pectoris), hoarseness (cancer of the throat), shortness of breathing (rapid consumption). 'Such a day of porlitude', he would confide to his sisters, as they could never imagine. At the same time he was aware of and even amused by his dire pessimism and fears. When asked by his brother-in-law Granville how he was faring he replied, 'As ill as anybody who is well can feel'. Lady Granville, a great thrower of cold water on smoke without fire, attributed her brother's ill health to nerves. 'When he talks and gets eager, he forgets it and looks quite well.' And to his catalogue of remedies recommended or spurned, James's Powder, mercury, snuff and respirators, she turned a blind eye. 'He is the most wonderful person for keeping up our spirits,' she told Georgiana laconically. Selina Trimmer with her fussing and exhortations to the boy Hartington not to go out of doors in summer without wrapping up was possibly an early cause of his chronic valetudinarianism.

An occasion of great satisfaction to the Duke was the engagement of his niece Harriet Howard, the Morpeths' third daughter, to Lord Gower, son and heir of the Marquess (and future 2nd Duke) of Sutherland. The alliance was socially brilliant. Just as he had fêted the elder sister Georgiana on her marriage to Agar-Ellis, so he gave the bridal couple a great banquet at Devonshire House. The impression Harriet made of beauty and dignity allied to intelligence and humour established her overnight as an enduring favourite. Pleasure in the party was only a little dimmed by the prospect of another motion on the state of Ireland to be submitted by him in the House of Lords three weeks hence. Every moment he was worrying over it. 'I walk eternally in my garden dwelling on it. My health begins today to threaten.' Abercromby helped him prepare. He retired to Brighton in order to rehearse it and get away from distractions. He worked himself into such a state of nerves that he vomited all one night and was obliged to send for Verity. On the morning of the dreaded day he purged himself, which seems an unwise thing to have done. However in spite of a raging headache he delivered the speech on 19 June. There was something wrong at the bottom of the distracted state of Ireland, he said. The laws were not respected by the people. Nor were the people protected by the laws. The fault lay at the feet of a handful of Orangemen. The speech did good, he believed, although the majority of the Lords were against the motion.

During the disturbing period of anticipation and dread of his forth-coming speech Sir Thomas Lawrence, President of the Royal Academy and court painter, called on him with an overbold request for five drawings by Raphael in the Duke's possession. These were studies for the *Transfiguration* in the Vatican. The Duke declined. Then Lawrence reduced the request to three drawings while offering in exchange anything – a painting, a drawing of his own, even to get engraved a drawing he had once done of Duchess Georgiana. Lawrence's per-tinacity was made excusable only by his childlike desire always to have what he set his mind to. After mulling the matter over the Duke good-naturedly selected three out of his five Raphael drawings, reserving for himself the two best. In return he accepted three of Lawrence's drawings, of which one was of the King. The Duke acknowledged later that he had made a poor bargain; that he ought to have lent the Raphael drawings to the painter for his life only; and that had not the anxiety of his speech in the Lords been hanging over him he might not have been so weak. As it happened on Lawrence's death in 1830 the three Raphaels were sold by his executors for a large sum.

In July he went to the London docks and custom house to collect *Endymion* and Lady Abercorn's bust of Napoleon. *'Che gioia!'* They were taken first to Devonshire House and there unpacked. *Endymion* was intact although his spear was broken, which did not signify. The arrival of this treasure in London caused intense excitement. People called in droves to see and admire. *Endymion* became the rage. The statesman George Tierney claimed that all the Mayfair dandies aligned themselves on drawing-room sofas practising the *Endymion* attitude which was extremely uncomfortable and difficult to accomplish naturally and with grace.

On 16 September 1823 he set forth again for Rome with two britschkas. A britschka was a large and cumbersome carriage recently introduced from Hungary. It had a folding hood at the back and could be converted into a sleeping carriage. It was driven from the box or by postilions, usually to a team of four horses. In the first britschka drove the Duke and Spot, the Italian greyhound. Perched on the box were Santi, the Italian courier, 'a very handsome and picturesque person, with clever wicked eyes', and Meynell, the English valet. Santi was to accompany his master on several tours until accumulated misdemeanours led to his dismissal in 1838. Meynell, a character of charm who likewise led his master a dance, became an alcoholic and to the Duke's grief and relief, ultimately had to go likewise. In the second britschka sat Verity's partner, Dr Bellingham, a second cook and two footmen, William and Wassily. The crossing to France was extremely rough. 'I never was so sick, but it's salutary.'

In Rome the Duke made lightning visits to his sculptors Baruzzi, Albacini, Tenerani and Richard James Wyatt, to see how his various commissions were getting on. All but Pietro Tenerani were having difficulty in procuring good marble. From Gabrielli he ordered beautiful porphyry tables and through his agency commissioned a new statue, the *Discobolus*, from Mattei Kessels whom he called 'very clever and descrying'. During this short visit he found time to look at the basilica of St Paul's-Outside-the-Walls which had been burnt down in July. He contemplated the catastrophic ruins. 'What a scene, the crush of columns and the accumulation of soil explain how ancient Rome was destroyed by time & fire – this was in five hours! the lovely pavonazetto columns injured, some burnt *to earth*.'

His friends the Kinnairds and Normanbys and young George Howard were in Rome. Lord Kinnaird took him to call on the legendary Princess Pauline Borghese. He was fascinated by her traces of great beauty, her civility and graciousness. She instantly set to work with her notorious wiles upon the attractive English Duke who was ten years her junior. Since 1803 the little sister of the Emperor Napoleon had been married to Prince Camillo Borghese, a rich, handsome, but uncouth and unintellectual Roman nobleman. After eighteen months Pauline, bored by him and the parochialism of Rome, was pining for the excitements of Paris and the brother to whom she was consistently loyal and who adored her. On 19 February the Duke was invited to a party at the Palazzo Borghese where he was presented to Jerome Bonaparte, the ex-King of Westphalia, and his consort Catharina, with whom he waltzed. In no time Pauline had cast her spell over the susceptible Englishman. Outrageous flirtation led to little tiffs. Invited to call he was kept waiting. She 'was full of whims and childishness, but now and then very entertaining about her family,' he recorded. She would send for him whenever she felt like it. He would respond while remaining determined to be no woman's slave. Entries appear in his journal such as, '*Chez* Pauline, in bed; the lovely foot!' She made him call on the formidable Madame Mère who scolded him for having bought her statue, although he believed she had sold it greatly to her advantage. He was impressed by her stately bearing. Pauline was taken ill, whether genuinely or as a ruse he could not be sure. She put off a large party in order to entertain him alone to dinner. She showed him curious papers, a note of Napoleon's and two letters from the Empress Marie Louise. He persuaded her to sit for her bust to Campbell who was working on one of himself. She obliged him to accompany the sculptor to take casts of her hands and feet as well as her nose. Then she refused to sit.

The Princess sent him a pressed tussy-mussy (which survives) to which he attached a note, 'Bouquet given to me by Pcs Borghese March 15th 1824 and out of which I gave a double violet to poor Rose Bathurst ... the night before she was drowned in the Tiber.' The shocking event cast a blight upon Roman society. The horse of the pretty and much-liked young English girl slipped down a bank beyond the Ponte Molle into the rain-swollen waters under the eyes of the French ambassador, the Duc de Laval, who was powerless to save her. Devonshire's sorrow was not appreciated by the Princess. Her Corsican jealousy would alight upon any victim she chose to conjure up. Their intrigue soon reached the ears of Lady Granville who without delay wrote to Lady Georgiana Morpeth:

I am alarmed at Hart's new amusement, for beyond that I have no fears, but it is *assez de son genre* to squiddle with a princess, and he was sure to be taken with all those little clap-traps of embroidered cushions, satin slippers, dressing gowns of cachemire, morsels of Petrarch with which this one assails our nobility.

While being driven on 23 March along the Porta Pia road by Pauline, 'in high good humour', a message reached the Duke that his stepmother the Duchess was very ill. He rushed to her house where Dr Bellingham was bleeding her. He was assailed by ambivalent feelings. He would be sorry to lose Bess, yet 'selfish thoughts came on my mind of all the trouble and difficulty I should have being her only connection here, yet it is a comfort to her to have me. I trust she will recover.' She was not to do so. On 28th he was told that her condition was alarming. He consulted George Howard whose young opinion he valued as to whether he should warn the Duchess of her condition. George thought he should. She bore the information with astonishing fortitude. She had no special requests to make. She trusted Hart would take care of Clifford. She begged him to give her love to those she cared for most, named her dear servants and directed him to a red box in which would be found dispositions concerning her funeral.

At this stage the Duke allowed two of her intimate friends, Madame Récamier and the Duc de Laval, who were waiting outside the bedroom, to enter. She took leave of them. Madame Récamier was indignant that she had not been permitted to comfort the Duchess before she became insensible lest, she erroneously assumed, she might let fall confirmation that Hart was her son. The two friends were also shocked that no Catholic priest was called, because they believed the dying woman wanted to be received into the true Church at the end. On the contrary Bess had asked for an Anglican clergyman and Hart summoned the Revd George Frederick Nott who happened to be available. With this English clergyman, who had thundered against the heresies of Byron's *Cain*, she had a most interesting conversation. Her last action was to send for a box of Florentine workmanship inlaid with diamonds which Consalvi had left her. She died on 30 March which was the very day, Hart noted, on which '18 years ago my poor mother died – and between 3 and 4 of this morning I lost her whom my mother loved with enthusiastic affection'. She had recognized him and kissed his forehead when he first went into her room. Then she sank to sleep, her hand in his. He was deeply moved.

Illustrations

The author and publishers wish to thank the following for permission to reproduce illustrations: the Duke of Devonshire and the Trustees of the Chatsworth Settlement, Nos. 1, 2, 3, 7, 8, 9, 11, 12, 13, 14, 18, 20, 25 (photographs: Devonshire Collections) and Nos. 6, 15, 16, 17 (photographs: Courtauld Institute of Art); the Hon. Simon Howard and the Courtauld Institute of Art, No. 4; the Tate Gallery, London, No. 5; Royal Commission on Historical Monuments, No. 10; British Architectural Library/RIBA, No. 19; and *Illustrated London News*, Nos. 21, 22, 23, 24.

2

Youth and Responsibility
1811–1817

THE STATUS OF the 6th Duke of Devonshire on his succession in
1811 is to our eyes, although it was not, as we shall soon see, in
those of the Prince Regent, little short of royal. In a way it was superior
in that the responsibilities, although onerous enough to a man with a
conscience, were lighter; and unlike a constitutional sovereign the
Duke was his own master. He could behave as he pleased without the
threat of forfeiting position and possessions. The latter were immense.
They included Chatsworth and Hardwick Hall, both in Derbyshire,
Bolton Abbey in the West Riding, Londesborough Hall in the East
Riding, Lismore Castle in County Waterford, Ireland, Chiswick House
in Middlesex, and Devonshire House and Burlington House in Mayfair,
London. (The last of these he sold to his uncle Lord George Cavendish
for £70,000 in 1815.) With the country houses went lands of vast
acreage and with the London houses urban property of vast value.
Chatsworth and Hardwick were late Elizabethan houses built by the
Cavendish progenitrix, the famous Bess of Hardwick whose son was
created in 1618 1st Earl, and great-great grandson in 1694 1st Duke of
Devonshire. The last title was an award to the 4th Earl for the part he
played in bringing about William of Orange's invasion of England,
the crowning of that alien monarch and his Stuart wife Mary as King
and Queen of England and indirectly the foundation of the Hanoverian
dynasty in 1714. As for Bolton, Londesborough, Lismore, Chiswick
and Burlington House, Piccadilly, they accrued to the family through
the marriage in 1748 of the 4th Duke to Lady Charlotte Boyle, in her

The Duke took everything in hand. He wrote letters to Bess's brother Lord Bristol and various friends. He sorted her papers, putting them into trunks. He packed her plate and books. He paid off the weeping servants. He took her French footman into his own service. He had the body embalmed and soldered in a lead coffin, the face only left showing through a glass. Meanwhile Pauline was making ferocious demands. She complained that he was paying too much attention to his stepmother's affairs. She claimed to be very ill, and was bled and blistered. The guileless Duke asked if she too were going to die. She wrote him two disagreeable notes. He felt obliged to call on her in bed. She was in better humour.

Before leaving Rome he attended to some sculpture business. He supplemented the Duchess's payment for placing Consalvi's bust by Thorvaldsen in the Pantheon. He ordered a figure of Spot the grey-hound bitch with pups from Joseph Gott. And he commissioned a seated statue of Pauline from Campbell. He was not to get it till 1840. In fact Campbell behaved so casually that the Duke released him from the commission, only relenting when he received a distressed letter from the sculptor in 1838. Finally there came the announcement to Pauline of his departure from Rome. It was 'an affecting scene of farewell – a long and really melancholy farewell'. And that was the end of that flirtation. They did not meet again.

The Duke's journey to England was by slow stages. At Boulogne on 15 May he learned of Byron's death 'of one of the inflamations' which were so prevalent that spring. Whether or not the news moved him to remember his cousin Caro Lamb he went the day after his return to see her in Richmond. 'Poor Caroline, she were dreadfully agitated.' Things had gone very wrong with her. She was suffering from dropsy, her relations with her long-suffering William were at breaking point, and she was threatened with being put in an asylum. She begged Hart for protection for, as she explained, 'I loved you when an infant, adored you when a boy; for one or two years my heart wandered from you, but every early recollection, every early thought or wish is with you.'

One of the first things he was called upon to do on his return from Italy was to see George IV. The King, who had been favourably impressed by Jeffry Wyatt's drawings for Chatsworth, had engaged him to make improvements to the Royal Lodge, Windsor. He hardly needed the Duke of Devonshire's encouragement to appoint him architect for the vaster undertaking at Windsor Castle which amounted practically to a rebuilding. 'Hart, will you do me a favour?' the King asked in his rapid, breezy manner. 'What is it, Sir?' he replied. 'I wish you to be on the commission for improvements to Windsor Castle.' Respectfully the Duke declined because he was in opposition to His Majesty's ministers. 'Well, Hart, you have refused me that; will you do me another favour? Will you accept my picture, by Lawrence?' 'This', wrote the Duke years later in the *Handbook*, 'is one of a thousand things that did, do, and will attach me to him and to his memory, while I have breath in my body.' The portrait was the one intended first for Consalvi, and then for the Duchess.

Wyatt not unnaturally was overjoyed by the royal command. It was to give him the greatest opportunity and scope of his career. In no time he was worshipping the King, and was loved in return. He was allowed to change his name to Wyatville and in 1828 was knighted. The relationship did not prevent His Majesty from teasing him mercilessly to his face and mimicking him behind his back. As the Duke was to write, Wyatt spoke the oddest dialect.

> He would say, 'You enter thee 'ouse by thee sub 'awl ... The bastion is big enough for you to *iced* your tent there ...' Omitting the *h* so often he never conferred it upon words ... He was popular with all men, comrades or *ryal eyenesses*.

At Chatsworth this June Wyatt was busy planning an additional storey to the tower at the northernmost end of the new wing. This was the Duke's idea which came to him after seeing the great tower of the Bodleian Library at Oxford. It must be pointed out that Wyatt's neo-classical punctuation at Chatsworth in no way resembles the five superimposed orders in pseudo-Renaissance style at Oxford. The Duke was thrilled by the beauty of the architect's sketches for the Claude-like belvedere that swiftly arose, while vaguely worrying about the expense. Needless to say expense in the cause of the arts never weighed too heavily or too long with this prodigal patron. As it happened in October the sale of his Wetherby estate in the East Riding brought him £50,000 more than had been anticipated. It was a handy windfall.

Feeling 'very ill, such spasms as I thought must kill me,' the Duke went in August to Scarborough for sea air. On his return to Chatsworth he welcomed Sir Humphry Davy, inventor of the famous safety lamp. Davy was a great admirer of the Duke's deceased cousin Henry Cavendish, described as 'the weigher of the world' (to be accurate, calculator of the earth's density) who also discovered the constitution of water and atmospheric air. It was of him that the 5th Duke had

observed, 'He's not a gentleman. He works.' Cavendish died a millionaire and had his revenge in not leaving a penny of his fortune to the
head of the family. Sir Humphry Davy was full of information on all
subjects. His host was much impressed by his employment of a man
who made 'indian rubber the medium to keep one from all wettings',
in cloaks, boots and shoes.

In October the Duke spent two nights at Melbourne Hall on the
borders of Derbyshire and Leicestershire where poor Caro William,
finally separated from her husband, was in the custody of her brothers-
in-law, the odious George and Frederick-James Lamb. He was deeply
concerned about her wretched situation in that dank and gloomy den,
as he called Melbourne, where the soil was never dry and the male
Lambs like prison warders danced and whistled in her room with their
hats on. Having been appointed joint arbitrator with Lord Althorp
the Duke endeavoured to keep an eye on poor Caro, whose love for
him was unfeigned. To him alone she offered to surrender Byron's
letters and presents to her as though that action might appease her
persecutors and make her lot easier. Although Hart's powers to make
her life agreeable were limited by the omnipresence of the Lamb family
and by Caroline's periodic rages, which did not stand her in good
stead, he was at least able to answer her piteous appeals for help and
visit her from time to time at Brocket and, later in the year, at Richmond
under restraint. He and Althorp also succeeded in wresting from the
Lambs an adequate jointure for his unhappy little cousin.

In March 1825 the Duke paid the first of numerous visits to the
French Embassy in Paris where his brother-in-law Granville had been
appointed ambassador the previous autumn. Harriet, who had dreaded
Paris, the smart people and the late hours, begged her brother to come
over and help initiate her. In perfect raptures to be with his dearest
Tib again he brought over his diamonds for her to wear on state
occasions. Brother and sister held long discussions about her deport-
ment and *tenue*. They certainly bore fruit for, although Harriet was
plain and indifferent to fashion and made little attempt to vie with the
sophisticated French ladies in clothes, yet she held her own in acerbic
wit and repartee. Moreover Hart taught her to modify her scorn for
Parisian society's *de haut en bas* manner towards foreigners, and to
acknowledge their intellectual superiority to most of those who frequented the French capital. After witnessing a horrible spectacle, which
interested him, namely the close-up execution on the Place de Grève
of the murderer of two children, the Duke dashed back to Chiswick

and thence to Chatsworth where much progress in the building was apparent. The old offices to the north of the main block were now down and all the eyesores gone. He was enchanted with the improvements he found.

On 6 May he gave his first Chiswick party of the season. It was notable for the introductory performance in England of the famous Italian *castrato* Velluti. 'He sings divinely, but there are some unpleasant sounds,' wrote the Duke. In London there was much prejudice against his voice. He was heard by Mendelssohn with intense disgust. '*Non vir sed veluti*', not a man or nearly so, was said of him. Velluti sang from Meyerbeer and Rossini. By now in his late forties his middle notes had begun to fail; they could be harsh and grating although the upper register was still faultless.

In the House of Lords the Duke spoke with passion in favour of giving Irish Catholics full participation in the constitution; but the motion was defeated by forty-eight votes. Twice he stayed at the Royal Lodge, being given his usual pretty bedroom with a shower bath at the door. He drove to the Ascot races with the King, and the Dukes of Dorset and Wellington.

In July he travelled, with a Hungarian friend Count Karolyi, to Kedleston Hall near Derby. Lord and Lady Scarsdale were old friends but he did not like this exquisite Adam country house. He thought the decoration pretentious and the great rotonda frankly vulgar. He was helping to promote the marriage of his old bachelor friend John Beaumont to the Scarsdales' daughter Mary. His role was to persuade a reluctant father to entrust his daughter to an impoverished and elderly suitor. The wedding took place at Kedleston on 29 August. The Duke presented the couple with plate and lent them Hardwick Hall for the honeymoon. When Beaumont died nine years later he settled money on the widow who had never meant much to him.

The Duke's generosity to friends, relations and strangers alike was without stint. His note- and account books are packed with items, such as a present of £20 to the father of a poor man accidentally killed in the park; £20 to the architect Atkinson languishing in prison; to 'Lou Costello £50 for her book, knowing she was poor'; 'a late housekeeper at Chiswick in gt distress £5'; 'a poor Portuguese 5s'; 'a poor family recommended by Mrs. Siddons £5'; 'a convict at Cork £1'; a subscription for B. R. Haydon the artist (whose paintings he thought no good) 10 guineas. These alms doubtless meant little sacrifice for so rich a man, so constantly asked to put his hand in his pocket.

But the Duke did more than that. He would correspond at length with a railway company chairman to get the stationmaster at Portslade promoted guard of the Brighton–Portsmouth line. He would go out of his way to visit a poor starving woman in the Derbyshire dales whose plight had been brought to his notice. As for getting commissions and promotions in the Army for the expectant sons of acquaintances, this was a perennial duty, doubtless demanded of every duke but by no means unfailingly adopted.

To have 'the three dear boys' to stay at Chatsworth every August became a most longed-for ritual with the Duke. William and his two Cavendish brothers, George and Richard the grandsons of his heir presumptive Lord George, had lost their father William in a carriage accident in 1812. Their widowed mother Louisa brought them up. A daughter of the 1st Lord Lismore, Louisa was to the Duke like a red rag to a bull. Called the Viddy by Harriet Granville, the sad, lonely, self-pitying lady seemed to rejoice in her ill treatment by fate. She was jealous of her rights and her children's pleasures, resentful of the Duke's good fortune, prone to slights, and subject to unprovoked rages. Whenever she accompanied her children to Chatsworth there were unedifying scenes. The Duke was blissfully happy to take the boys shooting, riding and walking round the estate. 'Their mother is more repelling to one than ever,' he wrote. 'I mean that I cannot get over the dislike her manner & conduct have given me.' He felt obliged to tell her some home truths. She was odious to his other guests, and egged on her children to be rude to them. After a storm she calmed down, but the bitter taste remained. 'I despair of your ever understanding me,' she wrote after she left. He understood her only too well. She was consumed by envy.

Miss Emily Eden's visit overlapped the Viddy's. The future author of those entrancing novels, *The Semi-detached House* and *The Semi-attached Couple*, was the unmarried sister of George Lord Auckland, whom she was to accompany to India during his Viceroyalty. Clever, sharp, satirical and witty, she was a sort of patrician counterpart of the upper-middle-class Jane Austen. The Duke called her 'The Queen of Cleverness' and listed her amongst his best friends. From the following account of her visit to Chatsworth in August 1825 in a letter to Theresa Villiers, an account which would have distressed her host had he been aware of it, the claim was seemingly not reciprocated, at least at this early stage of the friendship.

I shall continue to think a visit to Chatsworth a very great trouble. You are probably right in thinking the Duke takes pleasure in making people do what they don't like, and that accounts for his asking me so often. We have now made a rule to accept one invitation out of two. We go there with the best dispositions, wishing to be amused, liking the people we meet there, loyal and well affected to the King of the Peak himself, supported by the knowledge that in the eyes of the neighbourhood we are covering ourselves with glory by frequenting the *great house*; but with all these helps we have never been so able to stay above two days there without finding change of air absolutely necessary – never could turn the corner of the third day – at the end of the second the great depths of *bore* were broken up and carried all before them; we were obliged to pretend that some christening, or grand funeral, or some pressing case of wedding (in this country it is sometimes expedient to hurry the performance of the marriage ceremony) required Robert's [her youngest brother was with her] immediate return home, and so we departed yawning. It is odd that it should be so dull. The G. Lambs are both pleasant, and so is Mr. Foster and Mrs. Cavendish and a great many of the habitués of Chatsworth; and though I have not yet attained the real Derbyshire feeling which would bring tears of admiration into my eyes whenever the Duke observed that it was a fine day, yet I think him pleasant, and like him very much, and can make him hear without any difficulty, and he is very hospitable and wishes us to bring all our friends and relations there, if that would do us any good. But we happen to be pleasanter at home. However private vices may contribute to public benefit, I do not see how private bore can contribute to public happiness, do you?

From this acidulous complaint one deduces that Miss Eden found the demands of the Duke's hospitality exacting, and his society dull. But then she was most definitely a blue-stocking, intolerant of social chit-chat and routine.

At the end of each year's entry in his journal the Duke habitually summed up the pluses and minuses of the past twelve months. Among the latter for the year 1825 he included, 'The worry of Harriette Wilson & the licentious personalities of the newspapers (foolish to mind).' Yet mind he did. In this year were first published the memoirs of the notorious courtesan. Sales were immense. The scurrilous anecdotes of the lady's experiences with gentlemen of London's high *ton* were in such demand that a barrier had to be erected at Mr Stockdale's bookshop to control the customers. Thirty editions of the work were sold in one year. Described by Walter Scott as 'far from beautiful ... but a smart saucy girl with good eyes and dark hair, and the manners of a wild schoolboy', Harriette dispensed her favours right and left. Certainly the 6th Duke of Devonshire may be numbered as an admirer, if he was not positively a client. Harriette's references to him are not flattering. They are certainly saucy. She narrated that His Grace, observing her to be alone in her box at the opera one evening, entered, 'believing that he did me honour'.

> 'Duke,' said I, 'you cut me in Piccadilly today.'
> 'Don't you know,' said Thickhead, 'don't you know, *belle Harriette*, that I am blind as well as deaf, and a little absent too.'
> 'My good young man,' said I, out of all patience, '*Allez donc à l'opital des invalides*: for really, if God has made you blind and deaf, you must be absolutely insufferable when you presume to be absent too. The least you can do, as a blind, deaf man, is surely to pay attention to those who address you.'
> 'I never heard anything half so severe as *la belle Harriette*,' drawled out the Duke.

After further disparaging quotations which do not at all accord with either the Duke's customary reserve and dignity or his well-bred manner towards women, Harriette turned to questioning his connoisseurship. Sham Vandykes and copies of Rubens could, she surmised, easily be foisted on the gullible Duke of Devonshire. In any case if it were not for the Duke's pictures, his fortune and his parties, 'he would be a blank in the creation ... Once indeed he was slandered with bastardy; but that passed off quietly, as it ought to do; for who would have made it their pastime to beget such a lump of unintelligible matter.' She inveighed against his affectation and stinginess. 'I remember him calling on me and pretending to make love to me.' She asked him for 100 guineas for favours which she implied had been granted. He sent her a very old, ugly, red handkerchief, and then a cheap ring, 'such a mere wire'. She returned the ring and gave the handkerchief to her footman. Clearly the Duke had either not come up to scratch or had rebutted the advances of this vulgar woman. No wonder he was affronted by the publication of her scabrous piffle. The wound however bit deep. When informed that his sister Harriet actually had a copy of the pernicious memoirs on her bookshelf he was extremely indignant. To think that one of her boys might have read it! Had he found it there he would have taken the liberty of removing and, what is more, destroying it.

Just before Christmas a report reached the Duke that the Emperor

Alexander was dead (*'Cela donne à penser* ... Poor Nicolas, what a state he must be in now.') This last event gave rise to all sorts of possibilities. How far would the consequences in Russia affect him? They remained to be experienced.

4

Reluctant Statesman
1826–1830

───────────◆───────────

THE NEW YEAR of 1826 opened at Chatsworth with the severest
weather known for decades. The Duke was entertaining a succession of large parties for shooting. In the snow he drove by sledge
to Derby on 12 January to address a county meeting on slavery in the
colonies. It was a subject he felt passionately about, and when he
walked on to the platform all his deepest Whig instincts were aroused.
He reminded his audience that the Tory arguments that abolition
would produce economic chaos in the colonies were specious; that
other methods more acceptable to God must be found; that, if not,
then rebellion would be the inevitable consequence; and that to be
afraid of raising the subject in Parliament was equivalent to the shed-
ding of blood in the West Indies. 'Let no one', he thundered, 'be
deterred by these awful warnings from the performance of that duty
we owe to humanity.' From a man in his secluded, entrenched social
position these were bold words uttered seven years before the slaves
were finally emancipated.

In February the Duke met Dorothea Lieven in London and talked
to her about Russia where all was confusion. The Emperor Alexander
had met his death at Taganrog from a fever caught from kneeling
before the tomb of Madame Krüdener. The reformist Tsar, idealist
and founder of the Holy Alliance of the Christian Powers against the
tyranny of Napoleon had, like other Tsars after him, felt compelled to
abandon Rousseauesque principles of liberty for all and adopt autocratic measures in order to preserve stability in his unruly country.

The volte-face was largely brought about by the influence of the arch-reactionary Prince Metternich, the revolt in Greece, and the Russo-Polish conspiracy against the house of Romanov. The Emperor's political disillusionment had been accentuated by personal tragedies. The deaths of his beloved sister Catherine Queen of Württemberg and of his natural daughter, and the terrible inundation of St Petersburg in 1824 finally broke the heart of this gentle monarch.

What was to happen now? The Emperor had left secret directions that his next brother, the ill-favoured and undependable Constantine, should not succeed him. Constantine was for a time undecided whether or not to claim the throne. Nicholas, the second brother, greatly reluctant to supersede Constantine, was after three days of unhappy deliberation, persuaded by their forceful mother, the Dowager Maria Feodorovna, to observe the late Emperor's injunctions. His assumption of the crown was accompanied by a mutiny in the army and the subversive activities of secret societies. Certain regiments stormed the Winter Palace in what is now known as the Decembrist Revolution. Nicholas, having failed to parley with the officers, opened fire on them. The worst interpretations were put upon the new Tsar's action by both the government and the opposition in Great Britain, a country in which revulsion towards Russian autocracy was endemic. The Duke of Devonshire was torn between love of his friend and Whiggish loyalty to democratic principles.

Madame Lieven convinced the Duke that Nicholas's conduct had been right. In her opinion he had shown an energy of character and determination which made him worthy of the throne he had been so unwilling to mount. She saw in him another Peter the Great. His ability was greater than Alexander's and his resolution rock-like. His domestic life was untarnished and his love for his family was exceeded only by love for his country.

The Emperor Nicholas's coronation was fixed for June 1826. The Duke of Devonshire hoped that he might be asked to represent the King of England; and 'the leader of the Whigs' as Dorothea Lieven called him was indeed in due course appointed Ambassador Extraordinary to Russia.

On 9 May, the very day that the Duke of Devonshire left London for Russia, a young man of 23 arrived at Chatsworth at 4.30 in the morning having travelled overnight from London by the Comet coach to Chesterfield. The new head gardener, little more than a boy, having scaled a gate, walked all round the grounds, examined the house, set the men to work at six o'clock, and fallen in love with the housekeeper's niece (whom he married within eight months), moved into his cottage, at a wage of 25s. a week, to remain in the same employment for the rest of the Duke's life while becoming a famous national figure and a knight. The Duke made no reference in his journal to the engagement of Joseph Paxton, whom he had got to know while strolling from the grounds of Chiswick House through a gate to the adjoining Horticultural Society gardens on land rented from him. He had been much impressed by the young man's knowledge of the creepers and new plants in his charge, and by his enthusiasm and brightness. The Duke's extraordinary sound judgement was to be more than justified by his impulsive action. Paxton turned out to be the best and most rewarding friend the Duke ever had, the sharer and largely the inspirer of his horticultural interests, and ultimately the manager of his vast estates and financial adviser.

The relationship between the Duke and Paxton must be one of the most satisfactory in the history of master and man and reflects enormous credit on both. The Duke from the first treated Paxton with the utmost confidence and consideration; Paxton treated the Duke with unvarying efficiency and loyalty. Moreover he never, even at the end when he became his master's right hand, overstepped the bounds of familiarity. The fact that the Duke saw fit to allow the young gardener to launch upon extremely important responsibilities at the very moment when he was sailing from England indicates foreknowledge of his new servant's trustworthiness and suitability.

On 25 May (which was 6 June by the Russian calendar) the steamer reached Kronstadt. The Duke was received by the British consul and three Russian Admirals of the Fleet while the men-of-war all hooted a welcome. On arriving in St Petersburg he was taken by carriage to a handsome and commodious palace belonging to Prince Demidov in the Nevsky Prospect opposite the Anichkov Palace, which had been chosen for him by his friend Count Stanislaus Potocki.

The Dowager Empress Elisaveta, Alexander's widow, had died only a few days earlier, and the Duke's relief on learning that the coronation date had been postponed on account of her death and that he was not late was countered by depression. His arrival seemed an anti-climax. To begin with on reaching land hay fever assailed him. Near starving he did not get dinner till ten o'clock and when it came it was filthy. On being driven next day in 'a horrible black charriot' to call on several ministers, everyone was out. And when he left his name on

Count Nesselrode, the Foreign Secretary on whom above all Russian ministers the new Emperor depended, there was no immediate response. Worse still Nicholas seemed in no hurry to send for him.

While crossing the North Sea the Duke gave vent in the *Thought Book* of 1817 (which he had brought with him) to misgivings as to how Nicholas would receive him in the altered circumstances.

> Nine years have passed since I wrote in this book and I now find myself again on my way to Russia ... Nicolas Paulovitsch my friend is on the throne, but I go prepared not to expect that, however well inclined, he will be able to receive me in the intimate and familiar manner in which we used to meet ... the times are difficult and critical for the Emperor, the thoughtless amiable boy is changed into a reflecting experienced man who has surprised the world by his firmness, courage, and presence of mind in the most difficult and trying events. How anxious I am to see him again, and how curious (in all reasonableness I hope) to know what his manner and that of the Empress will be towards me.

He did not have long to wait. From Tsarskoe Selo the Emperor sent him the kindest messages with the excuse that he was detained in the country on business consequent upon his sister-in-law's death. The Duke was mollified and a little chastened. Then Nesselrode called with more messages from the Emperor. 'I must not be *exigeant*', the Duke wrote, 'about seeing him, as formerly, he is so busy and he must go by rules to me as ambassador while as friend he might break through.'

On 14 June (Russian calendar), which was to have been coronation day, he first saw the Emperor. Joy of joys, he was commanded to come to the Anichkov Palace, Nicholas and his beloved wife 'Mouffy's' residence ('our little home'). He was ushered into the Emperor's private sitting-room. One glance proved 'that he was unaltered to me. Oh may God bless him!'

> To describe his affectionate kindness is more than I can attempt. He shewed me my picture hung up in his own room, he talked of old times, gravely, seriously, sensibly, and then in tearing spirits – he said it made him a year younger to see me. I stayed an hour with him, and neither could mistake each other's happiness.

The Emperor talked about England and the tumults there. They had them in Russia too and several deluded people in the Fortress were about to be tried for stirring up trouble. He talked of the Empress of whom he said, '*Nous sommes heureux comme au premier jour*', a rare condition among sovereigns. He wanted to know which ladies in

England remembered him – La Grêle (Lady Jersey), La Lune (Lady Palmerston), L'Arc en ciel (Lady Conyngham), referring to them by their old nicknames. He knew all about them and Mrs Arbuthnot's *tendresse* for the Duke of Wellington. 'He did not consider me as ambassador, but *un ami* Devonshire, good devil.' He thought the Duke '*rajeuni et embelli*', which was pleasant to hear. The Duke had to admit that Nicholas was larger and bald on the crown of his head.

The Ambassador Extraordinary gave a party for forty-eight guests. It lasted thirteen hours. He was hurt to receive an anonymous letter from one of the guests criticizing the food and lack of supper. He took his nephew Morpeth, who had accompanied him to Russia, in his state coach-and-six to present his suite to the Emperor and Empress at Yelagmine. This was a formal occasion and thereafter he saw little of the Emperor. Count Potocki, Grand Master of Ceremonies, had warned him that other diplomatists would take it ill if they surmised he was received by their Imperial Majesties too often. However the Empress was most amiable although she could not at a court reception say much. But while looking at him she fingered her row of magnificent pearls. At first the Duke did not make out her meaning, but presently beheld the yellow diamond he had given her in 1817, arranged as a clasp. This touched him and made him less depressed. The Emperor took him aside to present him to his son the Tsarevich. 'Perhaps I ought to let this satisfy me,' the Duke wrote in the precious *Thought Book*, 'but it is not enough . . .'

> Besides the Emperor told me in the first interview that I should come to Tsarskoe Selo, and he has several times repeated this to Prince Charles of Prussia, his brother-in-law, but it never happens. I do not complain, I am not surprised, but I grudge the opportunities lost of seeing those I love and admire . . . I begin to worry myself about Nicolas, whose conduct in neglecting me *I think strange and unkind.*

Poor Duke. He was clearly disappointed and felt lonely. The young men in his suite were well enough disposed and cheerful, but they were not what he wanted. Besides, the expense of the whole commission was exorbitant. Was it worth while? He felt flat. Furthermore he fancied he was eclipsed by Maréchal Marmont, the French plenipotentiary, in party-giving and general splendour. One consolation was Prince Charles of Prussia's attachment to him. They went sight-seeing together, and each enjoyed the other's company.

At last came the coronation. It meant a rapid and tedious journey in heat and dust in four calèches and a landau to Moscow. The Maison Batascheff put at his disposal was handsome outside, but tawdry and ill-furnished within. His bedroom was a dark closet and he could not sleep for flies. For a great military review, which meant rising at four o'clock, Count Benckendorff, Dorothea Lieven's brother, lent him a magnificent white horse to ride.

On 5 August, when he was least expecting it, an ADC called to summon the Duke to see the Emperor at 6.30 at the house of Countess Orloff where the meeting would be unobserved and resentment over preferential treatment avoided. They were alone together. Nicholas explained what the Duke should already have understood, that the funeral, the coronation and the convention of hundreds of foreign representatives allowed him precious little spare time for his English friend.

> He said enough about previously not having seen me, enough to satisfy me, enough to remove all the fancies I had formed. He was adorable, after a time the Empress came in & made tea for us, only us ... Happy evening, 2 hours there.

So all was well again, within limits which clearly prohibited much further intimacy. The Duke was of course present at the actual crowning in the Kremlin on 22nd. At the reception the Emperor whispered to him in English, 'Are you quite satisfied?' 'Yes, Sir.' 'But quite? Quite satisfied?' 'Yes, Sir, I am delighted with Moscow,' a reply surely indicating reservation of feelings; and at the ball afterwards he danced with the Empress and the Grand Duchess Hélène. 'Nicolas smiled at me, shook hands and spoke, but noticed me less than the other ambassadors.'

Then the Duke gave a ball for which he received dozens of unsolicited applications from would-be guests. A heavy rainfall failed to extinguish the spectacular illuminations. The ballroom was decorated in lavish simplicity with white roses and no green leaves. 'I rejected *clinquant*.' The party ended at seven in the morning. The Empress told him afterwards that his ball had been far the best of all those given, and it was indeed from all accounts an unqualified success. And so it should have been since it cost the Duke £60,000. At last the Duke of Devonshire had made his mark with the Russians. His houses, his equipages, his dinners and his balls and above all his habitual way of living made the greatest sensation, 'leaving my colleagues (I believe without self-flattery) far behind. As for Marmont he was quite outdone.' Moreover the Duke was far more popular than the French Marshal on account of his rank, his comparative youth, his spirit and his love of dancing.

On 13th he dined with the Emperor. There were present only the Empress and Prince Charles of Prussia. The four of them sat at a small round table with no servants waiting. The children came in afterwards.

When it was time to go, the farewells were prolonged. The Duke gave Nicholas three views of Chatsworth and one of Chiswick, receiving in return a pelisse of the finest white sable, besides the usual diamond-encrusted snuff-box bearing the imperial portrait. The Emperor added to his benefaction two jasper vases and five diamonds, to be collected at St Petersburg, and the Empress gave him a malachite table. 'I am quite satisfied, except that I should have liked the (credo) impossibility of St. André', in his eyes the most coveted honour in the world, even transcending that of the Garter. On 1 October he left St Petersburg by land, not feeling able to face the sea.

When he got home in November the King was as forthcoming as ever, talking on all subjects except the Garter, which 'I would not approach, but wanted inordinately'. The King knew it and delighted to tease by withholding the honour. However the following month he sent the Duke a letter which reached him at Chatsworth, proffering the late Lord Hastings's Garter. It was, he wrote,

> some consolation to have it in my power to give it to you my dr young friend, the son of my dr old friends the late Duke & Duchess. It is but justice to say that Lord Liverpool cordially enters into my feelings upon your nomination.

Not every Tory was pleased and Mrs Arbuthnot criticized the King's action to the Duke of Wellington who excused it. But then Mrs Arbuthnot never had a good word for a Whig whereas the Iron Duke was magnanimous. Madame Lieven said the Emperor would be delighted. '*Questo non so*', wrote the recipient, still piqued at not having been offered the St André.

In his journal entry of 9 December the Duke wrote, 'Chatsworth, *che goia!*', fervently rejoicing over the great progress made there during his absence by the new gardener Paxton. He looked forward to an uninterrupted spell at Chatsworth on his own. But events did not permit him to remain in that beloved paradise for long. Politics claimed him in London through most of the year 1827. He once wrote that he could not care for and did not turn his attention willingly to politics except in extreme cases. And now a series of crises at Westminster was to occur which called upon his participation. He had long been a dutiful attendant at the House of Lords. Although a nervous speaker who went through agonies beforehand, he was a faithful and fairly active champion of liberal causes. Moreover in pre-Reform Bill days the expenses which his standing as an influential landowner with a political conscience brought him were immense. A mere twelve months previously he had received from old Lord Fitzwilliam, a cousin and neighbour, the modest proposal that he might subscribe £30,000 towards an election in Yorkshire. To this particular plea he paid no heed. On the other hand he offered to Lord John Russell his Irish borough of Bandon which was accepted; and to Henry Brougham his Yorkshire seat of Knaresborough because he believed the brilliant but unpopular statesman would be a greater danger to the country were he to remain outside the House of Commons than within it. Speaker James Abercromby, who was largely indebted to him for his parliamentary advancement, acknowledged him to be the most painstaking and discerning of political patrons.

Within the past five years a Tory government under Lord Liverpool had paved the way towards extensive financial and legislative reforms. The criminal code had been modified; Chancery reformed; and a police force founded by Sir Robert Peel. Huskisson and Canning had relaxed the Navigation Laws; the interests of Britain and her colonies had been declared one. Owing to Huskisson's abolition of tariffs and duties the country was enjoying a zenith of prosperity. The first steam railway line from Stockton to Darlington was opened in 1825, and a modern era seemed to dawn. On 17 February 1827 Abercromby called on the Duke at Devonshire House to announce that Lord Liverpool had suffered an attack of apoplexy. A new first minister must be appointed immediately. The obvious candidate was George Canning, Foreign Secretary in Liverpool's administration, who on account of favouring the Queen during her trial had been in ill odour with King George.

Canning, a Liberal by upbringing who became a Tory through horror over the excesses of the French Revolution, occupied an ambivalent position in party politics. Like a tight-rope walker he tried desperately to maintain a precarious footing between radicalism and reaction. In foreign affairs he had worked steadfastly to prevent a recurrence of French domination of Europe. In home affairs he refused to concede that constitutional reforms were a necessity. The Duke and the moderate Whigs realized that to win him over to their faction would in the current dilemma be a knock-out blow for the Tories. The Duke of Devonshire, who was known to be a close friend of the King, offered to act as intermediary between the monarch and Canning. Lord Lansdowne, leader of the moderate Whigs in the Upper House, expressed himself pleased with this gesture of goodwill. Thus the Duke was precipitated into delicate transactions at a time when the Irish Catholic question, on which he held very strong views, was at the forefront of political controversy.

He did his utmost to convert the monarch to an indulgent policy over Ireland. It was not easy. The King was bitterly opposed to the Catholics and his objections were strengthened by the House of Commons' rejection of the bill to grant constitutional rights to Irish Catholics. On 20 March the Duke in the Lords voiced his disappointment over the decision reached by the Commons. His task as mediator was made more awkward still by Canning's equivocation, for in spite of his declared pro-Catholic views the Foreign Secretary suggested to George IV that he should form a Protestant-inclined administration of which he, Canning, would not be a member. 'I tremble for Canning's honour and character, not to mention courage,' the Duke observed.

During these worrying weeks, shuttlecocked between the Royal Lodge where he was expected to be his normal entertaining self and Canning's house where he endeavoured to fortify the Foreign Secretary's wavering resolution, he nevertheless managed to visit with George Agar-Ellis some sculptors' studios and artists' galleries which held far more interest for him than the crisis on hand. So he looked at statues by Gibson and the Roman Angelo Bienaimé, at Haydon's colossal canvas of Alexander the Great (which he considered very inferior to Eastlake's picture of Isidas, commissioned by him) and Landseer's latest animal portraits. With Landseer he established a warm friendship. Soon the faithful Spot was sitting for her likeness to the popular canine painter.

On 4 April the Granvilles, to whom the Duke had lent an apartment in Devonshire House on their temporary withdrawal from the Paris Embassy, confided that Canning had kissed hands the day before on receiving the King's orders to form a government. 'Unfettered, unshackled! I dined with her and Lord Granville alone & then went to Ld Hertford's concert, very happy & elated.' Granville was to be made Foreign Secretary *ad interim* until Canning could resume that office. But the crisis was by no means over. The Duke of Wellington and other ministers resigned. On hearing the news King George's phlegmatic comment was '*Nec aspera terrent*' – Difficulties do not daunt – the motto of the Order of Guelph. No one seemed to know who was out and who in. Everything depended on Lord Lansdowne hovering in the wings. The Duke was in and out of Lansdowne House and Carlton House. The King was very anxious that the Duke, as chief promoter of the coalition of the moderate Whigs with the Canningites and a sort of guarantee for the Whigs' votes, should become Lord Chamberlain. The Duke abhorred the idea but considered that, provided Lansdowne joined the administration, he ought to accept for his country's good. In the meantime he hedged while Canning and Lansdowne stalked warily round each other. Canning added his persuasion to the King's that the Duke should accept the office of Lord Chamberlain. The Duke called at Lansdowne House to ask whether his acceptance would help Lord Lansdowne and his party, for he had no inclination for the office. Lord Lansdowne replied that it would not help and that the Duke had other means of showing his support of Canning's government. When the Duke acquainted Canning with this snub the new Prime Minister begged him notwithstanding to accept the Lord Chamberlainship. His refusal would sour and discourage the King, already upset by the conduct of Wellington and his friends. Devonshire protested that Lansdowne's argument was sound and that acceptance would separate him, the Duke, from his party connections and turn him into a mere courtier. Canning failed to understand Lansdowne's reasoning and hinted that he might include a place for the Duke in the Cabinet if he consented.

It became clear that Canning's coalition with Lansdowne, which was extremely important if the new ministry was to last, hinged largely on the Duke's falling in with the King's wishes. The Duke spent the next few days driving round London seeking his friends' advice, particularly Abercromby's, and getting nowhere. Brooks's club were unanimous against Lansdowne's view; Lord Holland was in favour. Canning paid the Duke a visit, reiterating his unqualified confidence and renewing his persuasions. Finally the Duke consented to serve if the Cabinet (there was no further mention of his being included in it) were to be equally divided into pro-Protestant and pro-Catholic members; in which case he would agree to there being a pro-Protestant Lord-Lieutenant of Ireland. All that now remained was for Lord Lansdowne to change his mind.

On 22 April the Duke left for Bowood, Lord Lansdowne's seat in

Wiltshire, sleeping at Marlborough on the way. Lord Lansdowne was not agreeable to a change of mind. He begged to be left alone to think things over. 'But that animal Thomas Moore has called & got at him. Now that provokes me more than anything,' the Duke wrote. While waiting for Lord Lansdowne to think things over he read yesterday's *Courier* at the window, '& an extract from an Irish paper stating that Moore the poet received £2,000 a year for being writer to *The Times*; and at that instant the little urchin waddled by.' In fact Moore, who had a cottage nearby, had just strolled over to Bowood, passed the Duke in the hall and was shown straight into Lord Lansdowne's room. 'You find me', said the Earl to the poet, 'in the greatest worry and perplexity possible'. He explained how in order to avoid the conflicting issues he had left London for the country. He wished to support Canning's government without joining it. Now here was the Duke of Devonshire at his bedside that very morning, sent to re-open negotiations. How could he honourably support, were he to be in the Cabinet, the appointment of an anti-Catholic Lord-Lieutenant after all his pro-Catholic motions in the Lords? Moore's advice was that in such an event he could resign immediately without his character being impugned, advice which as the Duke later acknowledged was not so animal-like. Moore withdrew and joined the Duke and Lady Lansdowne in the library. 'Did you ever expect,' said the Duke, 'to see such changes as have happened? One can hardly believe it.' Moore said he hoped His Grace would not let His Lordship decide against joining Canning too hastily. 'I think he will hardly get me out of the house', was the reply, 'without a favourable answer'. Lady Lansdowne tactfully 'got the little man out to luncheon'. By four o'clock Lansdowne consented with certain stipulations which his guest noted down on paper. The Duke left Bowood and reached London at 2.30 in the morning.

On 8 May Dorothea Lieven wrote to her brother: 'The Duke of Devonshire has had an important share in these negotiations, and it is he who has brought the two parties together,' an opinion confirmed by Charles Greville in his memoirs.

The following day the Duke communicated Lansdowne's conditions to Canning who thereupon appointed William Lamb Irish Secretary. He waited upon the King who for four hours renewed his entreaties that he should accept the Lord Chamberlain's wand. But since Lansdowne had not yet retracted his objection the Duke stood firm. Finally Lansdowne himself took the Duke to Carlton House where the

Duke accepted the wand on the understanding that the two of them would act together. 'Oh to be sure, to be sure,' said the King in transports of delight. On 30th the Duke was made a privy councillor. The King was kind but in a great fuss at not being able to lay hands on either the key of office or the recipient's Garter ribbon.

The Lord Chamberlain has to be distinguished from the Lord Great Chamberlain, whose office has been hereditary since the Norman Conquest, and whose function is the charge of the Palace of Westminster, especially the House of Lords. The Lord Chamberlain on the other hand was always a member of the political party in power, by which he was appointed, a peer and a privy councillor. Soon after the accession of the young Queen Victoria however Lord Melbourne, during what is known as the Bedchamber Question, transferred the right of appointment of the Lord Chamberlain and other officers of the royal household to the sovereign absolutely.

The Lord Chamberlain carries a white wand of office and wears a golden or jewelled key. He is responsible for state ceremonies at court, coronations and royal marriages, christenings and funerals. At drawing-rooms and levees he stands next to the sovereign. The Bedchamber, Privy Chamber and Presence Chamber, the Wardrobe, housekeeper's room, guardroom and chapels royal are in his province. He is chief officer of the royal household. Other domestic duties fell to the Duke of Devonshire's share, barely distinguishable from those expected of a superior housekeeper or a police detective. For instance, he had to look for an upholsterer to recover the throne and he had to clean up an illicit gin-shop kept in Windsor Castle by a certain Mrs Miller who imported the alcohol wholesale from the town and retailed it by the glass to the royal housemaids. One of the more important duties attached to the office of Lord Chamberlain was the censorship of all plays and the overall control of London theatres. The Duke's salary for the first year of office was £1,045 4s. 11d.

In June he stayed at the Royal Lodge for the Ascot races which tired him very much. They must have tired his fellow-guest George Canning even more for he was stricken with mortal illness.

The death of Lady Abercorn in May grieved the Duke. After listening to the reading of her will at Coutts Bank he bought to console himself a bird from Sumatra, black with a yellow head, which talked like the birds in Arabian tales. It said, 'Drawing-room', 'How d'ye do, my Lord', spoke ship language, which was rather broad, and laughed, 'Hear, hear, hear!' On 7 August the Duke learned the dreadful news that Canning's condition was fatal. The following day Canning died at Chiswick, which the Duke had lent him, in the very room where Fox had died, also in office, twenty-one years previously. The Prime Minister's death caused the utmost concern among the Devonshire House faction. 'There never was a man so lamented, so honoured, so done immediate justice to,' wrote the Duke. He might have substituted the adjective 'belated' for 'immediate' since neither the monarch nor the Whigs had a good word to say for him until the last months of his life. Now even George IV was shocked. He decided to maintain the present government. At a Privy Council he talked of his sorrow if he had to part with his government and, amongst others, 'his young friend' the Duke of Devonshire. But he would not have Lansdowne as premier. Instead he sent for the nebulous Lord Goderich to whom he expressed his strong hostility to Catholic Emancipation. Goderich to his credit would not give way to the King on this issue. Supported by Lansdowne he reiterated the terms on which the Whig members had taken office with the Tories; and the King caved in. Not however without submitting to the persuasive advice of the Duke of Devonshire who was obliged to spend hours at the Royal Lodge. There he had to listen to the King's interminable stories about his salad days with Lady Melbourne and Bess Foster and to visit the monarch's newly acquired giraffe which had been landed somewhere on the embankment with two Egyptian keepers. 'Sister,' the Duke wrote afterwards to Harriet, 'it is the most wearying of things to contend with that man.'

Canning's funeral occasioned a bitter renewal of grief and the Duke retired to Chiswick

> in quiet and sadness. I make solemn and for the first time real true resolutions to get well [in other words to drink less]. I long to pray but cannot. I ought to be wretched but I have such an elastic disposition & such spirits of frivolity that I cannot feel strongly enough. I have dark forebodings, I wish to pray to God to save me.

He was candid and ingenuous in analysing his own weaknesses which were inextricably woven with a perfectly laudable love of life and the good things thereof, material and artistic, with which he was endowed. Shaking off gloomy thoughts he rushed to the sculptor Francis Chantrey's studio and ordered a bust of Canning.

It was a foregone conclusion that Goderich would not have the strength to stand up long to George IV. The King refused his earnest request, in which he was strongly supported by Devonshire, to accept the uncompromising Whig Lord Holland, Canning's great friend and erstwhile ally, in the Cabinet. Within five months the Prime Minister resigned, to be succeeded by Wellington with his ultra-Tories. Devonshire attributed Goderich's failure entirely to unaccountable indecision and sheer imbecility. After tumbling into all sorts of blunders he did nothing but burst into tears.

Under the date 29 November appears the following entry in the Duke's journal: 'At 5 I paid a visit which may have great influence on my whole life.' That it certainly did for a decade there is no question. On 8 December comes the entry, 'Called on Eliz Moss and returned at night to no. 50 Gloucester Place,' against which is a marginal note of a later date in his hand, 'Mrs. Warwick who lived with me for 10 years.' And on 9th, 'I managed so that my servants except Meynell ignored my absence.'

Of Eliza or Elizabeth Warwick, never again to be referred to as Moss, nothing is known beyond what the Duke vouchsafed in his journal and his personal account book. How and through whom she slipped into his life is a mystery, just as the manner of her leaving it is glossed over. And as for her subsequent career it too is as blank as was her existence before November 1827. We do not know what she looked like for no identifiable portrait, although two were certainly made, survives. She had a mother and sister Bess who were occasional causes of embarrassment and annoyance. As to whether she was married we have no clue, and the Mrs may have been a courtesy title like a cook's. It is possible that she had a husband living called Moss, and that her lover made her change her surname to the seemlier Warwick, her mother being referred to in the journal by the latter. That the Duke was sincerely attached to her at the beginning is evident from many ecstatic declarations, such as, 'Every day I like her better. She is perfection for me.' He confided in Georgiana and Harriet a few months after the affair began. Both sisters took it well, but they probably never met her. She was not allowed to see his friends with the exception of a few chosen males, such as Clifford and George Cavendish. Although given a house in London and another in Brighton, showered with presents, jewellery and every luxury, and eventually handsomely endowed by her lover, Mrs Warwick cannot have led a wholly satisfactory life. She resented her isolation on social grounds and was, not surprisingly, to make scenes.

On the fall of Goderich's ministry in January 1828 a letter from George IV reached the Duke at Chatsworth commanding his immediate attendance at Windsor. The King entreated him to remain 'in his family' and about his person. On the Duke's arrival he beseeched him not to resign the Lord Chamberlainship. He said it would break his heart and drive him out of his senses. He had already told Wellington that he cared only for Devonshire and no one else. Accordingly Wellington added his plea to the King's. In vain. The Duke explained that having taken office as the means of uniting Lord Lansdowne and the moderate Whigs with Canning it would be impossible for him to retain office under Canning's enemies and accept an arrangement which would exclude Lansdowne and his brother-in-law Carlisle, the Lord Privy Seal, from the government. In other words he behaved with firmness and honour. Yet he told Georgiana that when he considered the King's kindness about his going he felt less than the dust, and his wits were diminished through deserting his master. A further act of goodness by the King heaped coals of fire upon him. In a letter to Harriet the Duke wrote:

> last night as I was going to bed [he did not disclose that this was in Gloucester Place] there arrived [one presumes through the complicity of Meynell] a large parcel from the King, which contained what do you think – why *les ordres de Russie* at last with a letter authorising me to wear them, as kind as possible, not mentioning late events. The Emperor's letter is beautiful and I am very much pleased.

Furthermore Lord Hertford, who had been delegated to take the Garter to the Emperor Nicholas, was not given the Order of St Anne, which was gratifying. As the Duke wrote to Dorothea, now Princess Lieven, the Russian order was 'the greatest favour ever conferred'. Probably this moment marks the apex of the Duke's happiness in life. His great diplomatic achievement was rewarded by the most coveted honour (even more coveted than the Garter) bestowed by his best friend while his only experience of a sustained love affair was crowned by the as yet unalloyed bliss bestowed by Eliza Warwick. Even the death of poor Caro Lamb on 28 January did not cast more than a fleeting shadow, so wretched to her had her existence become.

During the last week of April Robert and Fanny Arkwright were staying with him at Devonshire House. 'Poor Elizabeth wrote me a nervous & unreasonable letter. I answered firmly but dryly.' Mrs Arkwright was probably not the cause of the unreasonable letter. More likely it was Henrietta Sontag, a young German singer who made her début that month at the King's Theatre in London as Rosina in *The*

Barber of Seville, and as Desdemona in *Otello*, both by Rossini. She quickly
became the idol of society. Sir Walter Scott gave her a souvenir album
containing the signatures of 2 dukes, 87 earls, 23 lords, 168 knights,
113 gentlemen, 59 authors, 43 musicians, 38 painters and (surprisingly)
26 ladies which signatures, particularly the female ones, must add up
to a record. Sweet, doll-like and bewitching, Sontag's coquetry with
an air of innocence seduced both sexes. The Duke went so far as to
disregard class distinctions and invite her to a ball. He was even said
to have lost his head by proposing marriage. In which case he must
have been unaware that she was already the wife of a Count Rossi, as
Harriet Granville delighted to inform him. However the very night of
the ball the Duke on slipping away to Gloucester Place found Eliza
seriously ill with pains. She had repented of her letter, and was fretting.
He sent for Verity and the next day she had a miscarriage. That evening
he gave a dinner party and listened to Fanny Arkwright's delicious
singing. On 21st he celebrated his thirty-eighth birthday and felt,
'never so happy as now if I would only behave well.' And did he? It
is open to question. After a visit to the Royal Lodge for the Ascot
races he went to Brighton for relief from hay fever and there made an
acquaintance on the chain pier – which he pronounced magnificent –
'with a sharp clever woman' unknown.

May was the most social month in the year, and the Duke of
Devonshire's presence at assemblies and routs set the seal on London
entertainments. Invitations to his parties at Devonshire House and
Chiswick – at the former he gave a concert for Sontag and at the latter
two breakfasts for 60 and 150 people respectively – were more sought
after than those of any host or hostess, apart from the King. On 17
May Sir Walter Scott recorded his impression of breakfast at Chiswick,
'where I had never been before'.

> A numerous and gay party, assembled to walk, and enjoy the beauties of
> that Palladian demesne, make the place and highly ornamented gardens
> belonging to it resemble a picture of Watteau. There is some affectation in
> the picture, but in the ensemble the original looked very well. The Duke
> of Devonshire received every one with the best possible manners. The
> scene was dignified by the presence of an immense elephant, who, under
> charge of a groom, wandered up and down, giving an air of Asiatic
> pageantry to the entertainment ...

The Duke was the most attentive host, making no distinctions among
his guests, and seeking out artists and writers who found themselves

for the first time among royalty and the *beau monde*. Tom Moore recorded how on his first attendance at Devonshire House,

> the Duke on coming to the door to meet the Duke of Wellington, near whom I stood, turned aside first to shake hands with me (although the great Captain's hand was waiting, ready stretched out), and said, 'I am glad to see you here at last.'

The poet considered him 'one of the civilest persons in the whole peerage'. Nevertheless he declined to stay a week at Chatsworth for reasons which he explained to Samuel Rogers:

> I have no servant to take with me, and my hat is shabby, and the seams of my best coat are beginning to look white – and in short if a man cannot step upon equal ground with these people, he had much better keep out of their way. I can meet them on pretty fair terms at a dinner or a ball; but a whole week in the same house with them detects the poverty of a man's ammunition deplorably; to which, if we add that *I* should detect the poverty of *theirs*, I think the obvious conclusion is to have nothing to do with each other.

Moore even discussed the matter with Fanny Arkwright who admitted that the Duke had not liked him at first, having felt the barrier between them, not social as Moore absurdly supposed, but from the Duke's tallness and deafness combined. 'Besides [he added] Moore is not the sort of man to stand on tip-toes to a duke.'

There arose the problem of where Eliza was to live. From the start the Duke never intended to set up house with her. Yet he wanted her to be close at hand. She stayed a night or two at Chatsworth while the Duke considered whether the Rookery would be suitable. The proposition was strongly disapproved of by Abercromby, 'sour as possible'. Nevertheless the Rookery was put at her disposal. But Eliza found the country very lonely when her lover was away, and even when he was at home. She was a confirmed townee and far happier tripping along the pavements.

In London she soon moved out of Gloucester Place to the far side of the Marylebone Road which was not then chic but was considered respectable. The Duke bought for her 22 Dorset Square where she resided until the affair ended. He commented that the interior was beautiful for she furnished it in 'perfect good taste'. Likewise he bought her a succession of houses in Brighton which she tolerated as a compromise between adored town and detested country, finally settling in 23 Brunswick Square, not far from the Pavilion which she was never to enter. In December 1828 they were at Brighton together house-hunting, the Duke staying by himself discreetly at the Ship Hotel. During the visit he had her drawn by the French miniaturist Simon Jacques Rochart which gave rise to an access of unreasonable jealousy on her part. Eliza became angry on discovering that her lover had also had his niece Susan Granville drawn by the artist. Then there was another scene, this time in Rochart's studio, for which there was an understandable reason. Eliza flew at Dolly Lyndhurst, a real rival, which embarrassed the Duke very much.

Sarah Garay, wife of Lord Chancellor Lyndhurst, was a great beauty of Jewish extraction, with large black eyes. She was flighty and coquett-ish and threw herself at the Duke's head. He was amused by her up to a point beyond which he hesitated to go. She had undoubtedly made mischief by gossiping about the liaison with Eliza. He and his mistress were, she said, the talk of Boodles Club and of 'all the people who ought not to have seen' them out together. Lady Holland in her brazen way became involved and questioned him mercilessly about Eliza. What with one thing and another, and in spite of sal volatile, he could get no sleep at the Ship until relieved by violent vomiting. 'Elizth's kindness and quiet attentions were adorable.' But he had the candour to add, 'This illness will add strength to the resolution I have made for 1829 to be more temperate.'

The New Year of 1829 was spent at Windsor Castle which, now finished by Wyatville, was revealed in full splendour. The architect's masterpiece was the long gallery off which all the rooms opened. The Duke found it strikingly beautiful. It was gorgeously furnished and filled with pictures, busts and bronzes. Perhaps there was a trifle too much gilding. Yet that heightened the fairy-like glamour. The lighting was beyond everything, coming from immense ormolu chandeliers, enough to darken daylight. The heat was accordingly suffocating, and would have been intolerable had not Harriet Granville who was staying insisted, in spite of Princess Lieven's protestations, on opening a window. The bedrooms were prettily upholstered in chintz wallhang-ings, beds and armchairs alike. With its splendour the castle was not cosy like the Royal Lodge. And the visit was made dull and flat by the King's indisposition. For although kind and in good humour he was suffering from spasmodic attacks of gout. He was thin, weak and made languid by continual perspiration. His complexion was pallid, and he had shadows under the eyes. Nevertheless he gallantly kissed all the women on their arrival while the band played as usual in the inner rooms, too loudly. The Duke, when not obliged to play *écarté*, went for walks with Harriet or inspected the castle with Wyatville.

After several affecting interviews at Brentford with his old governess Selina Trimmer who was dying the Duke took Eliza to Chatsworth. On the surface the love affair, in spite of the Brighton tiffs, still appeared perfection. Eliza made no fuss and no nonsense. All was gentleness and good sense. 'How happy I am, how much happier than ever,' he wrote. 'Walked over the woods with Paxton. They are thriving with a vengeance ... Went in droschki to Hassop & Stoke & paid long visits to the ladies thereof. It is so comfortable to find Eliz at home after my outgoings.' No doubt it was; and there was never a question of Elizabeth being received by the ladies of Hassop and Stoke. When Lord and Lady Newburgh came over to luncheon poor Eliz was kept at the Rookery that day. It was 'comfortable' too showing Eliz over the house when they had gone and perambulating her round the four-mile walk from Granville Corner on the south front. 'She was very happy but it knocked her up quite.' It was fun having her help unpack and place in the orangery the beautiful Berlin vase and the sculptor Kessels' *Discobolus*. It was cosy having her to an early breakfast with him before he drove off to Stanton '& sat with Miss Thornhill'. Then suddenly there comes the abrupt journal entry: 'My head is full of fancy, I can think of nothing else, and but for poor Elizabeth I should marry E—.' All but the initial of the name was erased. And the following day's entry: 'The thoughts of [blank] kept me awake all night. My dear Elizh was ill this morning [presumably she had not been told about E]. I am very fond of her which is not inconsistent with thoughts of E.' There is no clue as to who was E. No wonder that 'my plans & projects waver, I am very happy [with two strings to his bow], & a change might spoil all.'

He was in London in February and March while George IV, fortifying himself with brandy, held out for six hours one day against the advice of Wellington and Peel to let the Roman Catholic Relief Bill be submitted to the Commons. For the Iron Duke, sensing that continued opposition would inevitably bring about his government's defeat, had completely changed his tune. Late in the evening the King gave him and Peel permission to proceed with the Bill. In the Lords Devonshire spoke briefly on behalf of the Bill the passage of which caused the Whigs much concern throughout the summer. In between attending the House of Lords and buying a house in Kemp Town, Brighton, he was preoccupied with his womenfolk. He remained charmed by the appearance and conversation of the mysterious E while tolerating Dolly Lyndhurst's persecutions. That tiresome lady quarrelled with him over Eliza, whose drawing she tore in half. It made him so angry that he drove her from the house. However she was not the sort to endure ostracism for long. He may have declared that she bored him to death, but she almost certainly seduced him in the course of the summer after having first 'mutton brothed' with him as he put it. He really was going through a period of dissipation, a sort of crescendo of self-indulgence to which males are sometimes prone at the hectic approach of middle age. On 23 June he dined with officers of the 15th Regiment at the barracks in the Kemp Town vicinity. 'I got beastly drunk I lament to say & came home sick and ill.' That evening Eliza miscarried for the second time.

A major interest was the promotion of a marriage between his cousin and heir William Cavendish and his niece Blanche Howard, his sister Georgiana Carlisle's daughter. Before the two young people even knew each other the Duke had set his mind upon the match. William was an extremely intelligent, serious and reticent youth, without much charm. He was over-pious and lacked humour. But he was good. On 27 April the Duke with customary generosity towards members of his family gave him a twenty-first birthday party at Devonshire House. His coming-of-age present to William was a carriage. On 30th he took Blanche who was only 17 to a drawing-room at the palace. The following day he gave a ball for her. William was duly attracted by Blanche. The Duke was as much struck by the girl's unself-consciousness, humility and yet independence as by the boy's gaucherie. He felt apprehensive lest the suitor might be too shy to press ahead. But four weeks later William called to tell him he liked Blanche much better each time he saw her. Elected to Parliament for Cambridge in June, he gained enough confidence to propose. Without ado he was accepted. All the relations were happy except William's mother Louisa. Left alone with the Duke she gave vent to a violent rage of jealousy, upbraiding him for having engineered the engagement. Eventually the Duke pacified her and at a dinner attended by thirty-five people at Devonshire House for the affianced couple all behaved well, including Louisa. On 6 August the wedding took place. As things turned out it was a marriage of true minds as well as of true Whiggery. Both were deeply religious, and deeply family conscious.

Meanwhile improvements at Chatsworth continued apace. In September of 1829 the Duke was 'entirely taken up with Wyatville all this time'. The house was crammed with guests. All the resources of the house – horses, carriages, keepers, and so on – were at their disposal, and there was plenty of whist and *écarté* and loo. No wonder that another financial crisis was looming. The two Currey brothers, Benjamin, solicitor to the Duke, and Colonel William Samuel, agent at Lismore, were hovering nearby with dire forebodings. The Duke's excess of expenditure over income this year was £16,643. He agreed to give up his stud of stallions and even volunteered to sell his Staveley estate on the far side of Chesterfield to pay off debts. By the end of October the deed was done and on 27th the Duke wrote in his airy way, 'Happiest day of my life'. For another few years he need not worry. As though to celebrate the financial equilibrium he had a beautiful fur made up for Eliza. She was in ecstasy. Most exciting of all, his new house in Kemp Town was ready to be lived in.

The Duke had long been partial to Brighton. Not only did he gravitate there by virtue of the King and the Pavilion, but he found the fresh air beneficial to his health, particularly in midsummer when elsewhere he was tormented by hay fever. No. 1 Lewes Crescent was part of a vast new layout at the easternmost end of the Brighton development, called Kemp Town. The Duke believed that in winter there was less smoke there than in the heart of the town, which was probably true, and that the gentle breezes of Kemp Town compensated for the raging winds of Brighton proper, which was probably imaginary. An undoubted advantage was that in Kemp Town he could, particularly during the next reign, escape notice of the court if he felt inclined. The Duke spent large sums installing three water-closets, sinks and cisterns, enriching ceilings and cornices, and generally beautifying this 'nutshell' as he termed it. He also fitted the drawing-room and parlour windows with plate glass which he deemed the acme of good taste. As the years went by he continued tinkering with the structure, adding a porch with a little closet over it and even extending the premises by purchase of the adjoining house, 14 Chichester Terrace, on the west side. Of elliptical plan their combined shape was like a fan. The nutshell soon became his joy and toy.

The year 1830 opened well with the observation, 'Eliz my only thought now', which suggests that the anonymous E and Dolly Lyndhurst were no longer serious rivals. Also Blanche Cavendish fainted at chapel, which portended an heir to the family. And turning from domestic to public affairs, the Whigs were about to undergo a great revival. Spurred on by the revolution in France – great and glorious news to the Duke – which drove out the reactionary Charles X and replaced him with the bourgeois Louis-Philippe, the spirit of reform in England burned with a brighter flame. Wellington resigned the premiership to be succeeded by Lord Grey, whose government made the pledge that reform was to be a Cabinet measure.

The King's illness, on the other hand, indicated a close to the reign of that luxury-loving, art-absorbed dispenser of wit, fun and delight to those few of his subjects privileged by their rank and intelligence to benefit from them. The Duke of Devonshire was genuinely devoted to him. He viewed the decline of his health with great concern. A visit to Windsor in February was not reassuring. George IV was ghastly pale. The Duke decided that it was pointless to hang around the court merely awaiting the poor King's demise, so he spent April at Chatsworth setting up Schadow's bas-reliefs of *Castor* and *Pollux* in the sculpture gallery.

The most ambitious enterprise this spring, in fact one of the most extraordinary achievements among so many at Chatsworth, was the transportation of the large weeping ash tree from Derby to the newly formed north court facing the grand entrance to the house. The undertaking was entirely the ingenious Paxton's. When we consider that the tree was already forty years old, with roots extending 28 feet in diameter and branches measuring 37 feet from the trunk, that it weighed 8 tons, that it was brought down narrow roads on a machine specially constructed and drawn by a team of horses, we must applaud the miraculous *tour de force*. Anticipation at the house was fraught with excitement and apprehension. The tree was expected on Good Friday morning, but did not arrive. The Duke went to church instead. On Easter Saturday it reached the gates of the park at eleven o'clock. To let it through, the gates had to be taken off their hinges and the stone piers and parts of the wall to which they were attached removed. At three o'clock the tree appeared. The Duke was enchanted and made a sketch of it lying on its side, the roots overhanging the end of the waggon. Forty labourers under Paxton's guidance were mustered and planted it on the site which it embellishes to this day. Immediately all the world rushed 'to see my adorable tree'.

On 26th the Duke, having returned to London, dined with the Lyndhursts. When the Duke of Clarence who had been invited did not turn up the Duke of Devonshire was struck with serious alarm about the King's condition. In great anxiety he drove to Windsor Castle and saw the Conynghams who protested that the monarch was better. But the Duke considered his condition most precarious and his spasms dreadful. He was much affected. The Conynghams were gratified by his presence. He slept at Chiswick which was handy for Windsor. On 6 May he set out for the castle with his friend Lewis Sneyd. The King being too exhausted to grant an interview sent his doctor Sir Henry Halford to speak to him. 'I shall not go again unless sent to, for I am afraid of tiring him. I think very ill of the appearance of everybody.' The Duke moved to Brighton to keep out of the way, as he put it. On 26th the Newburghs and Blanche and William came to him with news of the King's death. The Duke bathed in the sea, and brought out his black-edged writing-paper. 'I am very low,' he mourned. At the funeral he was a pall-bearer.

It was the end of an era. It had been a short one, sandwiched between the reigns of the old, mad, blind George III and the dotty-conventional William IV, and highlighted by the chameleon monarch whom the Duke of Devonshire – alternately exasperated and charmed – persistently visualized as the gay Lothario dressing for the fight and the beloved confederate in his parents' youthful escapades. In these roles he was remembered and the vagaries and vanities of his middle age were forgiven.

5

William IV and Reform
1830–1837

W HEN KING WILLIAM IV walked up St James's Street one of two
boys asked, 'What's that?' The other replied ''E was the Duke
of Clarence, but now e's the Duke of Wellington.' So universally
familiar was the hero of Waterloo's name that a street urchin who had
never seen him might be excused for mistaking any Mr Smith for the
Iron Duke, provided he had a faint aura of gentility. As for the initiated
they recognized their new monarch by his coconut head on to which
in the excitement of his accession, so the Duke of Devonshire was
informed, he poured at luncheon a bowl of pea soup while declaring
that he was the Lord's Anointed.

The incident merely emphasizes the contrast between King William's
humour and his predecessor's subtler wit. In polite society it marked
a sad declension of civilized standards. The new King's high-ranking
officers were not impressed by his broad language. On meeting a group
of generals for the first time William's spurs all but threw him to the
ground as he got out of his carriage. So he hollered out, 'God damn
your spurs, God damn them I say.' The generals looked bewildered
without discerning that they were in any sense responsible. And the
Duke of Devonshire was shocked by the sovereign's too premature
delight at succeeding his unlamented brother. 'I'll be damned if it's
not just like the cable tear of a first-rate man of war,' he exploded
loudly when George IV's coffin descended into the vault at Windsor
Castle. But the masses soon warmed to their sovereign because he
descended to their level. Just like any Mr Smith he would meander up

and down the streets peering into shop windows. A common woman so taken with this easy behaviour attempted to kiss him while a passer-by called out, 'Go it, King!'

William IV may have been a boor and a buffoon. He may have been ill-educated, coarse, obtuse and philistine. But like other Hanoverian sovereigns whose mental calibre approximated to the lowest rather than the highest denominator he had a kind of horse sense which asserted itself when crises threatened the stability of the throne. He could thank his stars that the masses, whose opinion of the Crown is what counts in the long run, were entertained by and grew fond of the bluff, gross, loud-mouthed jack tar. His reign coincided with the rapid turn in Great Britain from a feudal to a democratic society. Reform which was in the air at his accession was not to be curtailed by anything he would do. This was thanks largely to the discernment and influence upon him of a few progressive-minded noblemen like the Duke of Devonshire.

William IV's reign witnessed important scientific developments of which steam power and its locomotion on land and water were the most far-reaching. Whereas in 1830 the Duke of Devonshire drove from Chatsworth to Devonshire House in a coach and six – there was no other means – before the decade was over he went from Chesterfield to Euston station by railway. Unlike the majority of his fellow land-owners he was a railway enthusiast. As early as December 1824 he received a deputation of Birmingham contractors about a proposed railway line in the Midlands. When able to travel by train he pro-nounced it a delightful, easy way and 'a delicious new sensation. I like it very much.' It was particularly thrilling 'when two trains passed each other'. More surprising still he positively wanted a railway line to run between Chatsworth and Edensor village.

In November the first serious riots against the anti-reform govern-ment of the Duke of Wellington took place in London streets. It was remarkable how little agitation there had been in the previous decade although Peel and other moderate Tories saw the inevitability of partial reform if there was not to be revolution. As for Wellington, although obliged in 1829 to give way on the Catholic Emancipation issue, he was adamant against constitutional change of any sort. Needless to say the rioters directed their violence against the recently established police force which was much resented by the lower orders. The Duke of Devonshire felt certain that if Wellington did not resign and a popular government were not formed there would soon be serious trouble. He was relieved to learn that Lord Grey was publicly rendering tribute to Canning's principles and uniting with Canning's friends. On 17 November the King sent for Grey.

On the following day the Duke of Devonshire received a letter from Lord Grey (the very man who years before had been his mother's lover and the father of her daughter Eliza Courtney) whose cause he had been fostering at court behind the scenes. Grey wrote that he was charmed with the King who was giving him his constitutional support and virtually *carte blanche* to introduce reform. Grey offered the Duke the Lord Chamberlainship and asked him to make any requests he might have a mind to. Instantly the Duke replied to Grey's letter, 'which has given me more pleasure and satisfaction than I can well express and I must in the first place assure you that I shall with all my heart and soul support your administration.' He readily agreed to accept the wand once again although an ambiguous entry in his journal shows that a resumption of this office was distasteful to him. 'I choose the least of 2 evils. I hate some things in this, but others are too gratifying.' Now the Duke, although easy-going, had a strong sense of duty. He knew that William IV was stupid and weak; and he believed that as Lord Chamberlain he might be able to influence him in the way he ought to go.

From now on he was constantly at court dining with the King and Queen and dancing attendance. He found the King very reasonable. On the surface monarch and Lord Chamberlain got on well together although there was little underlying sympathy. The Duke resumed the duties of inspecting the royal palaces. At St James's he was given by the King a portrait of George IV which he asked for, there being a dozen of them lying around unwanted; and he arranged for his pew in the Chapel Royal to be made comfortable with a rail and hangings round it. At Windsor he was saddened on entering the room in which King George died to see the floorboards covered with the stains of his medicines. He gave orders for them to be planed out. He also directed that the private rooms of the King and Queen were not to be shown to visitors. A friend who was allowed round the castle in the previous reign had noticed a shirt of George IV drying on a chair before his bedroom fire. Another regular duty was connected with the stage. Expected to censor all London productions the Lord Chamberlain also had the right to veto performances of opera and ballet (but not oratorios) on Wednesdays and Fridays in Lent. This sometimes led to tussles with producers, but owing to the Duke's well-known patronage of the theatre his edicts were usually accepted without protest.

The New Year of 1831 saw the restless Duke at Chatsworth with William and Blanche. He took to moving his books from the music room and drawing-room into the finished library. In this task he was assisted by John Payne Collier, a Shakespeare critic and scholar of note and some subsequent disrepute. But the Duke held Collier's scholarship in high esteem and was to pay him handsome tribute. This year Collier dedicated to his patron *A History of English Dramatic Poetry and Annals of the State*. The Duke gave him £100, entrusted his unrivalled collection of dramas to his care, and appointed him literary adviser. He soon employed him as librarian on an annuity of £200, a sum which was to be confirmed by the 7th Duke. Collier's duties were to include reading to his employer on lonely evenings. He undoubtedly made a large contribution to the rediscovery of Elizabethan and Jacobean playwrights but in the process committed several blatant forgeries, of which the first was emendations to and corrections of a second folio of Shakespeare (which he actually gave to the Duke), maintaining that they were contemporary. The 6th Duke was never made aware of these misdemeanours. It was after his death that the diarist Henry Crabb Robinson and the Shakespeare editor Alexander Dyce disclosed them.

In spite of his evident satisfaction with Collier as scholar and librarian the 6th Duke had certain intuitive reservations about his personality. The man was no companion when they were alone together. 'He was well enough' at Devonshire House where the Duke could escape from him, but at Chatsworth his company was 'impossible'. He was 'so simple and vulgar'. He improved slightly when relaxed. The poor man was clearly shy, and certainly tried too hard if his own diary is anything to go by. He was at great pains to relate on what familiar terms he was with his patron. Some of Collier's anecdotes are open to question yet all of them picture the Duke as a man of exquisite courtesy, high culture and eagerness to imbibe knowledge from his learned librarian.

Another permanent member of the Duke's household who appeared about this time was the pianist Charles Coote. He emerges as an endearing personality, an unselfconscious, earnest and dedicated musician. A slight figure of fun, he was teasable. For a long while the Duke never spelt his name correctly. 'Mr. Cotes played to me,' and 'Mr. Coates is a treasure playing to us.' Coote likewise was in receipt of £200 a year. Whenever his master needed diversion Coote was whistled up to play favourite airs from Rossini or to accompany Mrs Arkwright's singing. He would follow the Duke to Lismore where he conducted the band at the castle balls and became a great favourite with the neighbours. At the ball given on Queen Victoria's visit to Chatsworth in 1843 Coote composed for the occasion and accompanied a set of quadrilles arranged for the pianoforte. Humbly dedicated by special permission of Her Majesty they were subsequently published and sold at 4s. a copy. For the breakfast at Chiswick which the Duke gave the Tsar the following year Coote expressly composed a homage. For this effort he was rewarded by the grateful Emperor with the St Anne medal. By now the Duke referred to his protégé as 'the Paxton of Music'. And in 1852 Coote earned the heartfelt praises of Charles Dickens for his persistent politeness to the orchestra at the novelist's amateur plays, 'which keeps them grinding away in a manner wonderful to behold'.

Coote was not however the only executant pebble on the musical beach. Edouard Schulz, a Hungarian immigrant – his father had once played the piano to Beethoven – was of slightly higher calibre than Coote. Edouard's fine piano-playing had attracted George IV; and the Duke probably first heard him perform at the Pavilion or Carlton House. He was a favourite teacher of the English aristocracy to whom his excellent manners endeared him. He soon became a regular pianist at the Duke's houses and Coote never seemed to resent his presence. On the contrary the two combined to make music together happily. According to *Grove's Dictionary of Music* (1898) Schulz 'might have been one of the very first pianists had he not over fatigued his hands by too zealous practice of the then new technique of extensions.'

By March 1831 nothing was 'talked of, dreamt of, but Reform', Charles Greville wrote. 'Every creature one meets asks, what is said now? How will it go? What is the last news? What do *you* think? and so it is from morning till night, in the streets, in the clubs, and in private houses.' On 1 March Lord John Russell moved in the House of Commons leave to bring in his first Reform Bill. The prospect of the Bill's success did not look bright. 'We are going to be beat, and then go out,' the Duke of Devonshire wrote despondently to Harriet. 'I approve entirely of the reform measure – the country is with us – and in a year or two the question must be carried like the Catholic one.' On 1st he spoke in the Lords with good effect against the objectionable means by which the hereditary proprietors of boroughs secured election to the Commons of their friends and dependants; and on 18th presented fourteen petitions. On 22nd he was in Derby delivering a speech which was an extraordinary display of his radical sentiments. 'Members of the aristocracy have been sometimes considered in an unfavourable light by the people,' he began. He advocated wider representation in Parliament of small owners of property. It was high time for the aristocracy to be relieved of privileges detrimental to all parties. It was time for them to descend from their false positions. Let them by all means occupy their own lands and stand on their own merits, in which case 'I have no fear that the people of England will be unjust to the aristocracy.' But the property-owning middle classes must be admitted to the electorate. Thus the richest and one of the greatest land-owning dukes in the British Isles was publicly declaring the principle that he and his kind must henceforth allow competitors in the hitherto exclusive field of national government.

On 23 March he heard while travelling through Dunstable that the second reading of Lord John's Bill had been carried by one vote amid scenes of almost indescribable excitement. For a few days all was jubilation among the Whigs. On 19 April while the Duke was with the King at the opera house the Bill was thrown out in Committee. Harriet, esconced in the Paris Embassy, got to hear of it and wrote off in a state of tension to her brother:

> I am a little frightened. The Bill, my dears? And is it true that the King will not dissolve, and that if beat, Earl Grey bolts, and then what, where, who? and how will the country bear it? and shall you soon all come swimming over in a long boat? *Emigrés* to set off with us to take lodgings in Pekin?

Her fears were not of long duration. The levée at St James's Palace on 20th was an uncommonly painful affair. The King demanded time to consider whether he should dissolve Parliament. The Duke, aware of William's serious dilemma and indecision, took the bull by the horns on his own initiative. On 21st 'I went to the Palace early, asked for audience and stated my intense conviction that dissolution could alone save us. King heard me quiet and very kindly.' William IV responded and behaved gloriously. On 22nd the Duke wrote to Harriet an hour-to-hour account of affairs: 'An eventful week. We have conquered. The King has surpassed himself, and at the moment is preparing to go down in state to the House of Lords and dissolve the Parliament,' in the face of every Tory remonstrance concoctable, but '4 defeats them in his coach and cream colours.' He continued:

> St. James's Palace, where I am now writing, the King having gone to the House while I watch over and guard his palace (I begged hard to go in

the gold coach but I wasn't let) [another good point in William's favour] –
it's against the etiquette ...

The King's action, whether constitutional or not, was very cour-
ageous. Wearing his crown, to which strictly speaking he was not
entitled for he had not yet been crowned, he took the Commons by
complete surprise. There was uproar on both sides. Peel lost all self-
control and stormed. Sir Francis Burdett gesticulated. All members
rose to their feet and shouted wildly. The Speaker was helpless. Black
Rod entered and summoned the House to the throne room where the
monarch confronted and dissolved them.

The scene in the Lords was even worse. Lord Londonderry so far
forgot patrician etiquette as to brandish his whip and shake his fist in
the Duke of Richmond's face while several peers restrained him by the
coat-tails. Thus by a bold stroke did the Duke of Devonshire help
Lord Grey to get his desired dissolution. To the election cry of, 'The
Bill, the whole Bill, and nothing but the Bill', Grey's ministry was
swept back to power with a majority favourable to reform. In June
the second Reform Bill was put again by Lord John Russell and carried
through the Commons with a majority of 136 instead of 1. While
waiting for the outcome the Duke practically lived at St James's Palace,
and his duties were so exacting that he seldom had time to dine or
spend the odd night with Eliza.

In September he went with his friend Sneyd on a tour of Kent and
Sussex country houses. With the exception of Palladian Mereworth ('a
quadruple Ionic Chiswick') all were medieval strongholds like Knole,
Penshurst, Dover and Leeds Castles, which he found curious old
places, and on the whole bleak and comfortless.

On his return to Devonshire House his uncle Lord George Cavendish announced that he had accepted an earldom and wished to consult
him as to a title. It took the Duke a day to think it over and discuss
with his solicitor, Georgiana Carlisle and even Lord Grey. Whatever
he may have suggested the title of Burlington was chosen, a revival of
that held by Lord George's grandfather, the famous architect Earl
who brought so much property to the Cavendish family. The Duke
professed to be vexed on his heir William's and the county of Derbyshire's account, but may have resented Lord George's assumption of
what he considered his right of choice as head of the family.

The coronation took place on 8 September. As Lord Chamberlain,
magnificent in long robes held by a page, and carrying the orb, the

Duke outshone many of those present in the Abbey. In his own case he deliberately flouted King William's desire that the ceremony should be a muted affair compared to his brother's lavish and theatrical spectacle. In fact the Sailor King's coronation was deemed too drab by most of his loyal subjects, who called it a half-crownation. Nevertheless both King and Queen were satisfied and mightily relieved when it was over. The sovereign had shown his loathing of being attired like a Chinese mandarin and above all of being kissed by the lords spiritual. Mary Shelley, the poet's widow, present in the Abbey, was struck by the 'gentlemanliness' of the Duke of Devonshire who gallantly tilted the inkstand to enable the King, prodding with a quill, to sign his name. The Duke, having had a hand in the arrangements, seemed pleased that the proceedings went off without a hitch notwithstanding that several muddles followed, not the least being the inability of his coachman to drive up to the Abbey door when the service was over. The Lord Chamberlain was seen running, coronet on head, half way up Parliament Street looking for his carriage. In the end he was obliged to push through the immense throngs of good-natured onlookers and take refuge in a shop. He dined with their Majesties afterwards and the King laughed merrily at the vision of his Lord Chamberlain cast away in the mud. It was the sort of joke he relished.

The King's popularity was enhanced by the third reading of the Reform Bill passing the Commons by 109 votes on 21 September. But the barometer was not to remain fair for long. In spite of Lord Grey's 'beautiful' speech and Brougham's (for he was now a peer) 'superhuman' speech in the Lords the second Reform Bill was thrown out at seven o'clock in the morning of 8 October, to the accompaniment of darkness, rain and a thunderstorm. The ministry refused to resign. Gloom at Westminster was followed by riots in Bristol and the Midlands, notably Derby and Nottingham where the castle was burned by the mob. The Duke of Devonshire rushed to Derby where he found little he could do, the disturbances having momentarily subsided. Two days later the Mayor of that city came to Chatsworth in great anxiety with a deputation to ask the advice of the Lord-Lieutenant on how to act pending a renewal of trouble.

Even the delights of Chatsworth and walks through the woods with Paxton failed to disperse the Duke's lowness of spirits. It is true that never since the seventeenth century had Britain been closer to revolution than in the autumn of 1831. Meanwhile because Peel refused either to join him or compromise with reform of any kind, Wellington was rebutting the persuasions of the King that he should form a government pledged to a moderate sort of reform.

During the Christmas recess the Duke spent most of the festivities at court where a huge joint of beef from a Chatsworth ox weighing 240 stone figured on the royal table. Good Queen Adelaide gave him a hideous carpet which she had bought at a bazaar. It looked threadbare. Never mind, the thought behind it was kind. And the Duke of Sussex, a little elevated by mulled wine, pulled off his Garter star which he presented to him with a gracious flourish.

The fact that the country was going through a very grave political and constitutional crisis did not mean that social activities halted, or even slackened. The Duke of Devonshire gave a great ball at Devonshire House in February 1832. It coincided with one of the worst London fogs on record. Owing to its density many of the visitors were obliged to leave their carriages and walk in their finery from as far as Bond Street and Arlington Street. One lady on descending from her carriage was grabbed by a man who snatched her necklace, valued at 600 guineas, and escaped in the confusion. 'The lady, on reaching Devonshire House,' according to a press reporter, 'fainted away; and she remained in the porter's lodge for some time insensible.' At least she managed to get there. Another lady, escorted on foot by a link boy, was set on fire by his flambeau. Another dropped a huge diamond of incalculable rarity in the court which the Duke had filled with torches. The jewel had been lent her by a friend so the loss was doubly vexatious. Some days later the Duke discovered it in the mud and was able to return it to the relieved borrower.

'Such a night never was seen.' The fog got into the rooms and the men in their uniforms, having walked in their boots, dirtied the floors and carpets. Nonetheless the ball was a very gay and brilliant affair. On the other hand Lady Lyndhurst was unusually tiresome and restless and viewed every woman with a jealous eye. She kept up her game of quarrelling with the Duke in public, much to his embarrassment. Lady Louisa Percy remarked on 'their uncommon cleverness – their constant sub-flirtation – & the address with which they play into one another's hands,' which 'makes them more like a scene in a clever novel than any thing one ever saw before.' She had an inclination to laugh in their faces, they were so diverting. Dolly's tiresomeness soon turned to scorn and she actually announced to her lukewarm lover's friends that on her death she would leave all his letters to his greatest enemy, whosoever he or she might be.

On 23 March the third reading of the Reform Bill was passed by the Commons, but Earl Grey resigned in protest at a hostile amendment raised by the Lords in Committee. In May battle between government and crown over the Prime Minister's insistence that the King must consent to create peers in order to force the Lords to pass the Bill was joined in earnest. In spite of the gratifying prospect of endowing all his illegitimate Fitzclarence sons with coronets gratis the King was at first steadfastly opposed to such an encroachment upon his prerogative. The Duke of Devonshire supported Grey although sympathizing with the poor King's predicament. However, on Wellington failing to form a Tory government Grey remained in office. Whereupon William IV, anxious to conciliate the wishes of the country, gave way by promising to create as many Whig peers as were deemed necessary to pass the Bill. Fortunately, and not for the first time in similar circumstances, the sovereign was spared the indignity of having to implement his promise owing to the anti-Reform lords seeing sense and abstaining. On 4 June Wellington at the King's urgent request withdrew his opposition. With a hundred supporters he walked out of the House. The remaining lords forced the Bill through. That evening all the windows of pro-Reformers' houses were illuminated, and those which were not were broken by jubilant crowds. Queen Adelaide, who was known to be hostile to Grey, had her carriage pelted with offal on returning from a concert in Hanover Square, while her footmen were obliged to beat back the mob with their canes.

Thus the great Reform Act came into being. Further acts granting more extensive franchise were to follow throughout the century. But the Act of 1832 did away with the major abuses, including the rotten boroughs, redistributed seats and gave votes to a range of householders and freeholders who hitherto had never enjoyed them. It greatly enhanced the political weight of the middle classes. Until this historic event (according to F. M. L. Thompson) eight leading peers, of whom the Duke of Devonshire was one, had mustered some 50 Members of the House of Commons, 87 peers in all bringing about the return of 355 Members, and 90 commoners that of 213 Members through the disposal of hereditary seats. Moreover tenants had always voted with their landlords.

The majority of landowners sincerely believed that, in the words of Charles Greville, reform would 'introduce the principle of change and whet the appetites of those who never will be satisfied with any existing order of things.' The Duke of Devonshire on the contrary was in a small minority of landowners who had long regarded the old system as indefensible and wrong. It is to his credit that throughout the struggle he was an ardent pro-Reformer. Although the part he played in it was not prominent, behind the scenes it was considerable by virtue of his influence with the monarch who held him in respect and valued his counsel. It was he who had ultimately persuaded William IV to dissolve Parliament during the fateful constitutional crisis of April 1831. If Prime Minister Grey was slow to acknowledge the Duke's part on that occasion King William was not. As an 1833 New Year present he gave him some shirt studs ('very pretty ones', noted the recipient) in token of his profound gratitude.

Meanwhile Harriet's younger daughter Georgiana Granville, called by the family Dody, was in love with a man of small family and little fortune although eventual heir to fairly large estates in County Antrim. A. G. (Freddy) Fullerton was a young officer, charming, intelligent, well-read and companionable who had resigned from his regiment in order to become Lord Granville's attaché at the Paris Embassy. The Duke took to him and in his generous way did his utmost to promote Fullerton's suit with the Granvilles who did not think him or his prospects good enough for their daughter. The Duke directed his solicitor Currey to supplement by £2,000 a year the suitor's meagre allowance from his father and wrote rather sharply to Harriet.

> We none of us are disposed to be fine, & we have no prospect of being thrown over in the way of the F family. The man himself is gentlemanlike, high spirited and remarkably free from flummery and vulgar notions. The family I believe to be extremely respectable. I'm sure I respect them much more for living their own life than for putting their happiness on Almack's & drums.

'*Voilà, ma soeur, il est né ce monsieur,*' he wrote a second time. In defiance of the Granvilles he advised the young people to 'follow my advice which is to marry first and settle afterwards.' Then he had misgivings and consulted Eliza. Her advice, derived no doubt from experience of the English beau monde, was to enquire first how many daughters Lord Granville had. Two. 'Then it won't do,' she said. 'If he had six he would consent.' Nevertheless the Duke did not waver in his support and his niece and Fullerton were married a year later. How the husband managed to retain his jolliness throughout their married life is hard to conjecture. Dody, who entirely lacked the radiance and sparkle of her sister Susy, was dour to a degree, ill-dressed and rather slovenly (the

Duke was to complain of her failure to use a toothbrush), dedicated to good works and the relief of the poor. These laudable qualities were ill matched by aesthetic sensibility. Brought up in the Paris Embassy she was given piano lessons by Liszt, but her performance was so unsatisfactory that sometimes the composer would run about the room stopping his ears. She became a novelist of some note and, what mattered to her more, a Catholic convert and founder of a religious order, called the Poor Servants of the Mother of God Incarnate. She always remained grateful to her uncle Devonshire for his adorable kindness and support in what proved a happy marriage.

On Friday, 19 October, the Duchess of Kent brought her daughter Princess Victoria to stay at Chatsworth. A large house party was assembled to meet them. For a child of 13 it must have been a daunting experience. But she not only behaved impeccably, she enjoyed herself immensely. The Duke was enraptured. 'The Princess is the most engaging intelligent creature possible,' he told Harriet. Mother and daughter arrived at six o'clock in the evening. That night the Princess ate alone with her governess, the German Baroness Lehzen, while the Duchess dined in Wyatville's great dining-room which had just been fitted in a hurry for the royal visit. In fact the Duke had eaten in it the previous day for the first time by way of rehearsal, and was thoroughly satisfied.

The first day, Saturday, was spent admiring the statues in the gallery and the flowers in the conservatory, in planting a commemorative tree, watching a cricket match, driving to Haddon Hall which, though 'singular', did not please, and visiting the Duke's marble mills. That evening the Princess dined downstairs in the great dining-room; it was her first grown-up dinner party. What with thirty-five people round the table which was groaning with gold plate from Russia, the nosegays and the music, she nearly fell asleep. Yet she managed to keep awake to admire the cascade and waterworks illuminated by Paxton with blue and red lights. At ten o'clock charades began – scenes from Bluebeard, Tom Thumb, Kenilworth, King Nile, and so on. During the intervals a display of coloured Bengal lights, watched from the south front windows, excelled anything the Duke had seen in Russia.

On Sunday after a service in the chapel the Princess was driven to the Stand, or hunting-tower, behind the house. Unfortunately the pony drawing the royal chaise threw the groom from the box and galloped, kicking and plunging, uphill. When it slackened pace it was caught by the Duke who gallantly jumped from the chaise. In the evening Mrs

Arkwright sang 'quite beautifully and with so much expression', the Princess recorded. Monday was devoted to Hardwick which in spite of its antiquity was 'yet so *liveable* that it looks as if it is not as old as it is.' The people cheered as they drove through Chesterfield. In the evening the Princess sang her little song before watching fireworks from the small library. On Tuesday they went to Belper and Matlock to visit cotton mills. Victoria was interested in everything and took leave of all very graciously.

The year 1832 ended at court, St James's Palace and the Brighton Pavilion. Sitting at dinner next to the Queen the Duke squabbled with her. 'She is so spiteful against the French and attacked me about liking everything French ... On the whole she is very good-natured to me,' he conceded. On the whole too he was fond of the 'very excellent, amiable, well-bred little woman' as Harriet described her, in spite of her extreme Toryism. For 'Addy' was unaffectedly kind to all and sundry, not excluding the King's bastards who were odious to her. Admittedly her taste in clothes was deplorable. By no means handsome she habitually dressed in red velvet 'which did not vie with the many mulberries of her face,' wrote the Duke. Temporarily he was not in the good books of either King or Queen. His sovereign complained that the Lord Chamberlain did not wait on him enough. Yet, 'he is always most kind and praising. What does it mean? He might have fitter men of business but that is not wanted. As state officer I think myself very efficient. More I do not want or choose to be ... I only go when there is business to put before the King.' But kings often want unsolicited attentions. Did William IV sense that his Lord Chamberlain was often extremely bored? And that when he dropped broad hints that he would like to be invited to meals the Duke prevaricated? It is true that on one occasion the Duke had him and his entire family, bastards included, and court to dine in Kemp Town. They crammed into the dining-room of the little nutshell,

> and bore with great good nature the pressure, and the results of short notice having been given; and all were much diverted when the German clock struck up one of its merriest tunes in the midst of the repast, sounding like a street organ; and the polite birds, turning to each organ and opening their beaks in correct time, were compared to Mesdames Malibran and Sontag.

And now Harriet's elder daughter Susan became engaged to George Lord Rivers. In this case there was no hesitation on the part of the

Granvilles. At first the Duke did not care for the horsy suitor with a stammer who was also a Tory and anti-Reform. Within a matter of months though he changed his mind. He promptly settled £10,000 on Susan, and told the good news to the King and Queen on Christmas Day while dining at the Pavilion. That morning he had taken the Sacrament in the drawing-room of the palace. In the evening he played commerce with the King and Queen in the same room. Such a game would never be countenanced on this particular festival at the court of Queen Victoria.

The year 1833 saw more of the Duke at Chatsworth than previous years in spite of his duties as Lord Chamberlain. 'My happiness at Chatsworth is quite different from anywhere else.' 'I like nothing in the world so much. No, nothing $\frac{1}{2}$ so much.' His love of the place approximated to adoration of a person. And unlike a person this golden palace set in the most beautiful undulating park of all England responded to his lavish attentions with a seasonal constancy which he had learned not to expect from relations, friends or paramours. Chatsworth never let him down, never answered back no matter how he treated it, and was seemingly immortal.

Not so poor Agar-Ellis, now Lord Dover, who was to have an abscess in his side opened. Little hope. Before going to see the King he was told of Agar-Ellis' death. He went to Dover House in Whitehall and knelt by the body. He begged a lock of hair. George Agar-Ellis had been a friend of long standing. A generous and discerning patron of artists, he formed one of London's important private collections of British paintings. He had been a trustee of the British Museum and the National Gallery and in 1832 was elected President of the Royal Society of Literature. Appointed Chief Commissioner of Woods and Forests by Lord Grey, he was obliged through ill health to retire after two months' service. He was also a provider of fun; the Duke used nearly to die of laughter over his letters. His premature death cut short a life of prodigious promise.

Retreat to Chatsworth again afforded consolation. 'Sir Jeffry has arranged everything most happily.' The new state rooms were at last showing signs of completion. Then too there was Paxton. Joseph Paxton, now aged 30, was already more than mere head gardener at Chatsworth, exalted though that post was. He had become virtually garden adviser at Hardwick and Chiswick. He was also a companion, a fellow horticultural enthusiast. Together master and man visited other famous gardens including that of Windsor Castle and propagating nurseries. In July the Duke had Paxton down to Brighton to see the new conservatory being built at the Pavilion with a view to future developments of the sort at Chatsworth. At this stage of their relationship Paxton's successful propagation of rare species in the Chatsworth glass houses was undoubtedly whipping up the Duke's comparatively recent enthusiasm for gardening and planting. The journals are henceforth punctuated with horticultural observations such as 'new plant in blow. Hibiscus mutabilis. Lovely quite.' Yet young Joseph was still the pupil who had to submit to lectures from his employer on how not to overthin plantations and how to prune rose bushes; and also to reprimands for not being exact with his accounts.

The year 1833 was for the Duke overshadowed by a mysterious illness which was to incapacitate him for quite two years. His first mention of it was made on New Year's Eve. He confided in Clifford who recommended a specialist, Dr Price. Price warned him that he could not be too temperate. He must abstain from alcohol entirely. 'The ennui is too great if I don't drink a little at those dinners,' the unhappy Duke exclaimed in reference to his duties at court. Then Dr Nunney was called in. 'It's rather suspicious.' He must also diet. By February he was lame in the left leg as though gripped by cramp, and his leg swelled. Sorry for himself he sent for the King's physician, Sir Henry Halford who, though old-womanish, was comforting. The mistake the Duke made was to call in too many doctors, each with conflicting advice. 'I have a luxe of doctors, a regiment, they walk in a frightful procession.' Then in July on getting out of bed at 4 in the morning to look at the moon's eclipse he slipped his crutches and hurt his knee. It began to seem as though he would never get well.

What with 'crutching' himself about the house and being wheeled in 'the Buxton chair' he was in sorry plight. He made up his mind that the best hope for a cure was a complete change of scene. Come what may he would go abroad. He felt sure Naples and blue skies would be therapeutic. He was taking Dr Richard Verity and two young men, William Cowper and cousin George Cavendish. The former, aged 21, was the second son of the 5th Earl Cowper and his wife Amelia Lamb, who in widowhood was to marry Lord Palmerston. The Duke had met him the previous year and found him perfection. He was to grow extremely attached to him on the tour and take him into his confidence over Eliza Warwick and probably many other matters. A shared sympathy was Evangelicalism to which Cowper was an almost fanatical convert. It was largely owing to Cowper's brand of pietism that he finally parted with Eliza.

George Cavendish was likewise a newcomer to his cousin's affections. A younger brother of William he was 23. A boy of solid merit, he was delicate and subject to fits. He was also too pious by half and while on tour declined to set foot out of doors on Sundays except to church. Between them the two fledglings had a deleterious effect upon the Duke's state of mind which was beginning to waver between Regency hedonism and Victorian religiosity.

Before they left the country George's mother Lou made a dreadful scene about her son accompanying the Duke. 'How this ungracious woman manages to do everything without pleasing or obliging! From the first it was certain that George would go, but what a breeze about nothing!' The peace-keeping William induced his hysterical mother to give way. There were other farewells hardly less depressing. Eliz was extremely low at his leaving and one can hardly suppose much cheered by old Benjamin Currey the solicitor being dispatched to comfort her.

At Dover the Duke and young George stayed at the Ship Inn. Billy Cowper soon joined them. It was pleasant being 'with these two young men who are, I think, perfect in their way.' Dr Verity was of the company. On 3 December the party reached Nice. The Duke rejoiced in the drifts of cypress and olive trees, acacias with pods, jasmine entwined among orange trees, and roses. From Genoa he wrote to Harriet that it was a pleasure to see George and Billy so happy; and that the Doctor was grandiose, still in his fur and red comforters although the weather was like July in England. By now he was keeping a special travel journal in which he wrote that they were all rather depressed by the decay of Genoa and the splendid palaces turned into shoddy inns. They were buying rich silks and satins and being cheated left and right. They dined in a room that smelt of singed pigs and burnt feathers; in the next room were three men in bed chattering through thin noses and four English travellers across the passage smoking evil tobacco.

Via Pisa, Radicofani and Viterbo they entered Rome, where the Duke was assailed by a hundred memories, especially of the Villa Borghese with its poignant associations with the seductive Princess Pauline. On 16th they left for Naples. On arrival the Duke was in transports over the view from his window and the sunshine; but with Christmas came the rain, and in spite of a beautiful eruption of Vesuvius Naples was lugubrious. Things improved in the New Year. While on weekdays 'the lads' went gallivanting the Duke would take a cold dinner to Portici where he established himself in a pavilion in the royal park, whence he looked across the bay to Castellamare and Capri bathed in the setting sun. Until dusk he would enjoy the panorama and watch two small streams of lava descend Vesuvius. On his return one evening he learned of the death of George Lamb, husband of his half-sister Caroline and Billy's uncle. Billy, who was very cut up by the news, made him go to church. Portici became a favourite retreat, and with Cowper next day he took bread and two bottles of wine to 'my dining room there, and got, not drunk, but happy, overflowing with friendship and confidences.' And another day Madame Potocka, 'whom I will always love', was given the same treat. Having met her in the piazza on her donkey he swept her off to Portici where they consumed wine.

Death seldom comes singly. No sooner had the Duke returned with Madame Potocka than he was handed a copy of *Galignani's Messenger*. He had a nasty presentiment. It contained a paragraph announcing the death in Paris after a premature labour of Lady Lyndhurst, at the age of 39. 'How strange, how dreadful, with all her faults and thoughtlessness. May God forgive her as I have done with all my heart,' he wrote. The condescension in the forgiveness indicated no little guilt. For had he not egged on poor Dolly, flighty and coquettish and yet so intelligent, a strange mixture of good and bad, when she threw herself at him and bombarded him with letters? And to crown his unhappiness he received a letter with the information that Sir William Rumbold, the best friend of his extreme youth, had died in Hyderabad. True, he was always dull, boring and vulgar ('God forgive me'). But he had suffered adversity when his bank went bust, and old associates must be recorded with tolerance and affection. 'All these deaths remind one of our frail tenure of existence. How one should try to prepare for its close!'

The Duke settled to leave for Sicily, and Cowper to whom he had given the liberty of choice, decided to accompany him. So they boarded the steamer *Il Re Ferdinando* of 80 horsepower. The Duke had reserved two cabins and nothing could be more comfortable. How this can have been the case it is difficult to imagine considering that, besides himself, George, Billy, Count Karolyi who had joined the party in Rome, and Verity, there were Ridgway, Santi, Meynell, Royal, Giovanni the *laquais de place,* Karolyi's servants and Cowper's and George's one between them; also a Neapolitan landscape artist, Raffaele Carelli, who had lately been enlisted. The Duke was very pleased with Carelli's

accomplished watercolour sketches, of which several survive at Chatsworth. He 'makes everything exactly like and recallsome'. Being a
foreigner he was treated, albeit in the country of his birth, with the
utmost contempt by Meynell the valet. Whenever Carelli stopped to
make a sketch Meynell would shout directions at him loudly in a bossy
manner. 'Now put that there prickly plant in, or it will never be
believed in England that they are so big.'

Landed at Messina the party had difficulty hiring rooms. Eventually
they got four for fourteen persons and considered themselves lucky.
It was usual for four persons to share one room in Sicilian inns, and
often with but one bed. Few inns had glass windows. But the good
nature of the islanders made such inconveniences rather fun. The
carnival was in progress and an earthquake shook the city during their
first night. Next morning in calèches and on horseback they moved
off. The Duke was still suffering from his knee and had bad cramp in
the left calf. Yet he was better and, though weak in the legs, could
walk without sticks.

The road to Syracuse was bad even for mules. Cowper was disappointed with this town considered by Cicero to have been the most
beautiful of the Greeks', now shrivelled into a dirty modern-looking
place. He thought nothing of the temple of Athena its 'columns half
hidden in the walls of the cathedral, plastered over with whitewash
and compelled to echo to the nasal preaching of a Dominican friar.'
But he admitted that the monks were simple and nice, and clean for a
wonder. The Duke observed that 'Cowper made great hit with them.'
For a week they were held up in Syracuse by bad weather. The rains
and floods made it impossible to stir. Bridges were submerged and
roads washed away. Then Billy managed to leave for England.

At Biscari the Duke wangled himself somehow or other into a very
good house belonging to Prince Biscari. It had 'two looking-glasses,
piano-forte; two venerable leather armchairs with very hard bottoms,
and a handsome painted ceiling – and have had a most excellent
dinner – so much for travelling in Italy when you know what's what.'
The activity and zeal of the servants was beyond anything. 'What's
what' made him almost ashamed when he reflected upon the privations
which the rest of the party were undergoing. The poor doctor who
had been thrown from his horse had to make do with a dark alcove
and George with great skill contrived a bed out of a pair of sedan
chairs, his head in one and feet in the other.

Never had the Duke enjoyed a day more than at Girgenti. The

grandeur of the situation surpassed the miracles of ancient art. 'The heat was delicious: the carob trees, the olive trees, the wild flowers.' There was everything to intoxicate a middle-aged man on the brink of complete restoration to health.

> The huge bulk of the walls of the town containing tombs ... but above all the colossal remains of the temples of Jupiter and Hercules, dashed to the ground but imposing beyond the rest.

Of all the impressions made on him by places he had visited those of Girgenti were the strongest. The site was eternal and timeless. The temples looked the same as they must have done before the birth of Christ. He wanted to carry off a famous bas-relief in his litter, but the British consul would not allow it on any account. On they went to Selinunte slowly and surely.

There the Duke was enchanted with the ruins and the perfection of the stones' carving. He was deeply impressed and awed by the thick slices lying as they had been thrown by one tremendous earthquake hundreds of years ago. They reached Trapani having come all the way from Messina along the coast. From dull country they struck off inland into a series of gigantic wolds. Suddenly the temple of Segesta burst upon their sight. It was like the great temple of Poseidon at Paestum, only on the slope of a hill, its rush-covered sides glistening like glass. Steep rocky ravines protected it. Openings in the distant mountains of the most varied and fantastic shapes afforded views of the little towns of Alcamo and Calatafimi where twenty-six years later Garibaldi and his thousand heroes were finally to rout the Bourbon troops. Three hours were spent at Segesta in the company of strolling players from Calatafimi who were in possession when they arrived.

On 8 March they reached Palermo. In the Villa Butera, a *palazzetto* in an enchanted garden, where hothouse plants and exotic trees throve out of doors, a stream ran alongside and papyrus grew in abundance, they were in Elysium. 'The house more luxurious, more full of furniture and comforts than the most recherché Paris hotel or English drawing-room, to travellers fresh from muddy floors and staircases and case-mentless rooms there never was such a promotion.' The Chinese villa in the Favorita park with its stupendous views was visited; and in the dining-room the means of sending dinner 'smack up on the middle of the table by invisible agency' was much marvelled at. The decayed condition of the grotesque Villa Palagonia at Bagheria with its monstrous statuary and inlaid looking-glasses 'which no longer looked'

1. William Cavendish (Hart), Marquess of Hartington,
before he succeeded as 6th Duke of Devonshire in 1811.
By Sir Martin Archer Shee

2. Georgiana, Duchess of Devonshire (*left*), and Lady Elizabeth Foster (*right*) from a drawing by John Downman

3. Harriet, Countess Granville, younger sister of the 6th Duke. Lithograph by Johannes Notz, *c.* 1840

4. Lady Georgiana Morpeth (later Countess of Carlisle), the Duke's elder sister, with 2 of her 13 children. By John Jackson, *c.* 1805

5. Dorothea, Princess Lieven. Unfinished sketch by Sir Thomas Lawrence

6. Emperor Nicholas I of Russia. Bust by C. D. Rauch, 1821

7. (*above left*) Admiral Sir Augustus Clifford, Bt., half-brother of the 6th Duke. By Frederick Say, *c.* 1832

8. (*above right*) Lady Margaret Eyre of Hassop, styled Countess of Newburgh. Drawing, 1824

9. (*below*) The Hon. Richard Cavendish with Spot, the Duke's whippet, by Sir Edwin Landseer, *c.* 1828

10. (*above left*) Anne, Lady Hunloke, from a stained glass window at
Scarisbrick Hall, Lancs., *c.* 1865

11. (*above right*) Joseph Paxton. Portrait by Henry P. Briggs, 1836

12. (*from left to right*) The Duke, Mrs Arkwright (at piano), Lady Granville,
Trentanove's *Amore*, Lady Newburgh and Lord Granville. Drawing *c.* 1830

13. The carriage accident on the way to Boulogne, 22 May 1847. 'In
middle distance the Duke gesticulating.' Sketch by G. Carelli

14. The Bachelor Duke, recovered from indisposition, discards his crutches. Sketch by Carelli, Spring 1834

15. (*above left*) Antonio Canova, 'the most talented, the most simple, and most noble-minded of mankind', by Rinaldo Rinaldi, 1823

16. (*above right*) Pauline Bonaparte, Princess Borghese. Bust by Thomas Campbell, 1824

17. *Endymion:* sculpture by Canova, commissioned by the Duke, 1819–22

18. Hardwick Hall, Derbyshire – Entrance Front. Drawing by Blanche Burlington, *c.* 1832

19. Lismore Castle, Ireland, showing Paxton and Stokes's projected north-west tower, 1858

20. Chatsworth: showing the Duke's extensions to the north.
Architectural drawing by Sir Jeffry Wyatt, 1824

21. Queen Victoria and Prince Albert arriving at Chatsworth,
1 December 1843

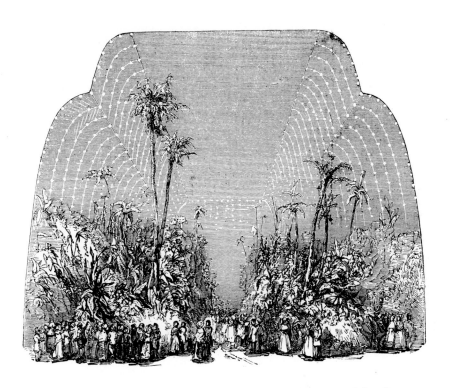

22. The Grand Conservatory at Chatsworth, illuminated for Queen Victoria's visit, 1843

23. The Breakfast given for Emperor Nicholas I of Russia in the Summer Parlour at Chiswick, 1844

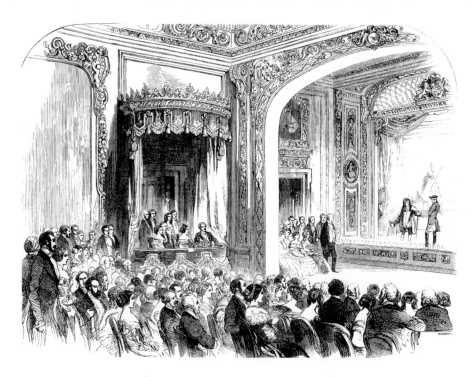

24. Dickens's production of Bulwer-Lytton's comedy at
Devonshire House, 1851

25. The 6th Duke, William, Lord Burlington (afterwards 7th Duke),
Lady Louisa Cavendish and (*standing*) her husband George Cavendish
between four Burlington children. By Charles Baugniet, 1852

was deplored. Under the guidance of the Duke of Serra di Fulco, an enlightened and distinguished antiquarian, they visited the catacombs of the Capuccini, 'the most disgusting exhibition of rotten vanity and mouldering bones I ever saw and I would never go on any account a second time.'

As was so often the case adverse winds and obstinate calms delayed departure by boat, and they were obliged to remain another ten days. Since the Duke was furnished with letters of introduction this did not much matter. All the Palermese dukes and nobles were overjoyed to entertain him. At last, having taken the ship's captain to the opera and afterwards to a party where he felt obliged to pull from his finger a newly bought scarab ring and present it to his hostess for her name day, he set sail. He had on board sackfuls of seeds and bulbs given him by the gardener at the Villa Butera for 'Mr Paxton' (note the Mr). It was high time to make for Paris and sister Harriet. In Florence he settled with the sculptor Bartolini for the recumbent *Bacchante* statue he had commissioned in 1822. The 'excessive beauty of it as a work of art' mollified his vexation over the sculptor's prolonged delay in delivery; and in his usual generous manner he gave him £100 more than the original contract stipulated.

A staccato entry in the journal dated 11 April 1834 and headed Hôtel de Bristol reveals the Duke's excitement on reaching the French capital: 'The Place Vendôme again! Curious! Cured! Dolly! Saw Harriet in bed. Called on Ly Cowper; told her all about Billy, and said nothing of any blame ... called Ly Hunloke. A ball. Mme de Caraman bewitching but I'll never be bewitched again.' Although there was but one ball there were numerous social engagements, all duly noted. Harriet took him to dine with King Louis-Philippe and Queen Amélie, who were both very civil. Late at night on 19th Paxton arrived and they went round Paris on foot. For a week he conducted his head gardener to a number of horticultural sights including the Jardin des Plantes at the Luxembourg Palace, to St Cloud and Versailles. With the Versailles gardens the observant and astute Paxton was pleased although disappointed by the waterworks. It was his first jaunt abroad with his master and every strange impression was indelibly recorded in his retentive mind. He missed little and wished to experience nearly everything, even a gaming house. Back at Devonshire House at the end of April the Duke was happy. He acknowledged that the trip had restored him to health.

In June the Duke was once again absorbed in books. On 21st he recorded, 'I am making great acquisitions at Heber's sale.' This was

Richard, half-brother of Bishop Reginald Heber, author of the popular hymn *From Greenland's icy mountains, From India's coral strand*. Richard Heber had died the previous year. His enormous collection of some two to three hundred thousand volumes had filled eight houses. It took three years of sales to disperse them. The early English poets and dramatists were of unrivalled importance. They had been catalogued by Collier who advised the Duke how to select from them. In August the Duke got Lewis Sneyd to introduce him to the Bodleian Library in Oxford where he looked through some unique manuscripts relative to the catalogue of his own collection.

As for plants, this interest was being hotly pursued throughout 1834. The Duke took Billy Cowper to Blenheim Palace to see the Duke of Marlborough's new rock garden and Powis Castle in Montgomeryshire to examine Lord Powis's plants. He was much disappointed by the large wood and glass building like a magnified barrel, neither store nor greenhouse and ill warmed by hot water which had been the ruin of all the fine Indian specimens sent to Lord Powis. He would do much better one day at Chatsworth. From Alton Towers he came away with a rare specimen in great triumph. If the owners of important gardens were absent then the head gardeners gladly bestowed choice plants and cuttings upon the genial Duke who treated them as fellow enthusiasts. In October the learned botanist William Hooker stayed at Chatsworth. In November the Duke with George Cavendish and Paxton visited the botanical parks of Liverpool, the first of such municipal parks to be founded, and Manchester. The Duke considered Liverpool's worth going a thousand miles to see. By now he 'had got fairly bit by gardening'.

In November King William, profiting from the difficulty of finding a successor to Lord Althorp, who on succeeding to the Spencer earldom ceased to be leader of the Whigs in the House of Commons, and to Lord Grey who in July had been made to resign from the government over the Irish Coercion Act, kicked out by his ministers. 'Rare news,' wrote the Duke of Devonshire. 'Release beyond measure for me.' He could with the return of Peel as first minister give up the Lord Chamberlainship which had become odious to him. What he now dreaded was pressure to return after inevitable Tory failure to remain in office. He thought the King's conduct in forcing Melbourne to be Prime Minister on Grey's resignation and within four months getting rid of him quite atrocious. The whole business sickened him. His active interest in politics was from this moment spent. He wanted never to have anything further to do with them beyond occasionally sitting in the House of Lords and becoming a passive witness of events.

The year 1835 saw the zenith of the Duke of Devonshire's horticultural mania. Not only did he go on further tours through England and even France with George Cavendish, Billy Cowper and Paxton to see famous gardens and buy plants from nursery gardens but he planned and subsidised expeditions by young botanists to Asia and the New World. His journal entry for New Year's Day opens with the line, 'I went to Clapton and agreed with Mr. Love [Hugh Love a well-known orchid and fern grower] about sharing his expense of sending to Mexico. £200. Another £100 hereafter.' This particular expedition came to grief. John Henchman, a young explorer described as very promising, had been inducted by Paxton to the hothouses at Chatsworth preparatory to his going to Mexico. To Paxton's great disappointment Henchman was obliged to return in October having contracted fevers. He brought back few plants. In March the Duke bought from a Mr Huntley of Chiswick, 'an intelligent & shrewd and *touchy* man', his collection of plants and orchids and in April settled with Paxton details of the journey to Calcutta of another young gardener, John Gibson, whom Paxton had discovered. Under the auspices of Dr Nathaniel Wallich, head of the Botanic Gardens in Calcutta, Gibson was to make a hazardous expedition to Cherrapunji in the Ganges basin in search of rare species, especially orchids.

At the beginning of April Peel's short-lived ministry fell and Melbourne resumed the premiership. At once Lady Granville took up her pen and wrote:

> Now my dearest brother, look on this picture and on that. On one hand, you and Paxton, sitting under a red rhododendron at Chatsworth, under the shade of palms and pines in your magnificent conservatory, with Arkwright and Harrowby in the evening, but no thought of your country's weal and woe. Now, walking up and down a terrace in the Phoenix Park, arm in arm with Morpeth [their nephew], your Secretary, saving that hapless country, adored and worshipped. Think of the gratification to them, of the power to you of doing good. Damp but glorious. I hear they want you to go to Ireland.

The sisterly cajolery was in vain. It was just what Hart had feared. He had absolutely no intention of going back on his resolution to keep out of political life. And no calls to duty would weaken him. A few days later he duly received a letter from Lord Melbourne requesting to see him immediately and help him form an administration. The Duke declined to go lest he be persuaded to accept office. Instead he asked Lord Mulgrave to call on Grey with a message that nothing would induce him to be Lord Chamberlain again and that the Lord-Lieutenancy of Ireland, if that were a positive offer, was also out of the question. He thought it not unhandsome of himself thus to ward off ministerial offices. Moreover he gained the double satisfaction of serving two friends. Mulgrave was appointed Lord-Lieutenant and Lord Conyngham, whom he cited as fit to be Chamberlain, succeeded him in that office.

On 25 May the Duke celebrated his forty-fifth birthday by going to the King's Theatre to hear the first performance in London of Bellini's two-act opera *I Puritani de Scozia*. He soon came to call it the most beautiful music in the world and would make Coote play it to him over and over again. He went to the second performance four days later. 'Oh! how I did enjoy it.' By now the Duke was well into middle age. White hairs, in spite of Eliza's ministrations, kept reappearing. On looking into the glass he was not as satisfied as he used to be by what he saw. What he saw was a sad, withered, decrepit beast. When Madame de Flahault dined with him he commented to Harriet, 'An ugly pair I thought we must have looked with our underjaws.' He dined with the Duchess of Kent and sat between Madame de Lichtenstein, 'a hateful Autricienne', and Princess Victoria who was charming. The little Princess talked all the time, and he could hear her quite well. 'Duke, Mama desires me to tell you that I talk so much she's afraid you won't get any dinner.' He pronounced her a love, 'and talk as she may will never commit herself, & yet is natural and pleasing.'

Then George Cavendish came to talk about his affairs. He fancied Lady Louisa Lascelles, a daughter of Lord Harewood and sister of William who was married to Caroline Howard. It was a suitable match for a younger son and the Duke could find no possible objection. It simply meant the loss of yet another male friend whom hitherto he could rustle up whenever he needed companionship. Having obtained his cousin's advice George proposed and was accepted. The Duke was somewhat consoled on the receipt of a heart-warming letter from the blissful suitor. 'If in so great happiness I have one regret it is to think that perhaps I shall see less of one who has ever been the kindest dearest friend to me, and that dearest Duke is you.' On reading this the Duke did 'nothing more nor less than roar.'

The George Cavendishes were married in July and the Duke

promptly went to Paris and Rouen to buy birds and monkeys. Some of the birds were doubtless destined for Eliz whose fondness for them was one of her sympathetic qualities. The Duke had already given her an aviary's worth and she in return gave him an owl, which was still alive at Chatsworth in 1848. The journey was a lightning one. On the way he stayed a night at Dover in The Ship Inn. 'O how the room reminds me of lameness and George and Billy Cowper! Verity and Spot.' The little Italian greyhound had also left him. 'My poor Spot quite worn out,' his comfort and faithful companion of ten years, was now dead.

Having made his purchases in Rouen, a strange and melancholy town, and seen Harriet and Lady Hunloke in Paris, the Duke on his return went straight to Compton Place. Here the monkeys broke loose. He caught them after dinner on top of the drawing-room curtains where they had become drowsy, and one bit his hand.

Eliza Warwick features less and less frequently in the journals, but in September the Duke stayed a night with her in Dorset Square and had the most violent attack of nerves which could only be cured by brandy and water. Relations between the two were by now on a muted emotional plane. The Duke recorded how on this visit Eliza was made uncommonly happy by his telling her about a bond of £1,200 which he had arranged so that she might feel in some degree independent of him. Presumably it was a supplementary gift because Eliza had for some time been enjoying quarterly payments of £1,600 a year which in 1834 were increased to £1,800, sums which noted in the Duke's personal account book do not recur after Eliz's departure in 1838. Her lover was an exceedingly generous man and it is inconceivable that he sent her back into the wide world inadequately provided for.

No sooner had Louis Philippe's second son the Duc de Nemours left Chatsworth than Dr G. F. Waagen, Inspector of the Berlin Museum and picture expert of international reputation, turned up. Armed with letters of introduction from the Prussian royal family Waagen had in the summer been admitted to Devonshire House and Chiswick. He found the Duke 'a man of noble demeanour whose features were expressive of so much goodness of heart, that I immediately conceived the most unlimited confidence towards him.' He was invited to a ball at Devonshire House where, since he knew none of the guests, he felt free to observe the constant stream of slender, sylph-like English girls of the highest classes of society in what gave him the impression of a fairy paradise. In *Treasures of Art in Great Britain* Waagen gives detailed accounts and exhaustive lists of the works of art contained in the Duke's three houses he visited. Of all the accumulated treasures that which bowled him over was the *Liber Veritatis* of Claude Lorrain. It contained some 200 drawings by the seventeenth-century artist of every picture he had painted. This priceless record had been acquired by the 2nd Duke from a dealer in Holland.

It seems that Waagen arrived at Chatsworth at random for his driver, perceiving a flag waving upon the belvedere tower, said it was a certain sign that his Grace was in residence. His Grace was in fact confined to bed with a violent cold. He sent the doctor a friendly welcome and ordered him to be shown into a room 'which combined in a high degree elegance with comfort.' Waagen had just taken a general survey of his surroundings when a servant announced that luncheon was ready. After eating alone he was ushered by another servant into the library where he observed the choicest bindings, exceeded by none in England except the library at Althorp. Soon the Duke joined him. His host, although very much indisposed, was overflowing with affability. He begged the doctor to stay as long as he pleased, and proceeded to display his literary curiosities, beginning with the oldest known edition of Homer on finest white parchment, the capital letters illuminated, and ending with a sumptuous edition of Camoens, privately printed but not unique, which had been presented to him by the Marquis de Souza. To mark his appreciation of the gift the Duke had had it bound in morocco leather with his initials and coronet in diamonds on the cover.

December seems an unwonted month to have gone with Clifford and Paxton on what the latter called 'a naughtycultural tower' in the home counties and west country. From Bath and Clifton they proceeded to Blaise near Bristol where the Duke thought John Nash's picturesque cottages formed the most perfect and benevolently planned hamlet. Maybe Paxton thought so too. Did they influence the eventual planning of Edensor village to which ingeniously conceived jumble they may be compared?

Striking north they visited Thornbury Castle ('very fine old ruin') and Berkeley Castle, 'a curious mixture of antiquity & vulgarity', and continued by way of Blenheim to Oxford. Finally in a very sharp frost they reached Latimers in Buckinghamshire, recently inherited from old Lord Burlington by his fourth son Charles Cavendish, where Paxton had laid out the garden. By 12th the Duke was snugly installed in Devonshire House.

The winter was extremely severe. On Christmas morning the Duke, wrapped in flannel and fur, walked to Dorset Square to lunch with Eliz. She, poor woman, still minded the frequent absences of her restless paramour. And now he had to break it to her that he was off to Paris in the New Year. To make some amends for not taking her with him he gave her a gem from Smith's the jewellers. 'She was very amiable before she got it,' the Duke remarked, 'as well as after,' which is hardly the language of fervent love.

On Christmas evening we are told that 'Mr Balf came ... and made music for me.' Michael Balfe was an Irish violinist and singer who had been encouraged by Rossini to compose opera. In October his opera *The Siege of Rochelle* had opened at Drury Lane. It had an instantaneous success. That Balfe consented to play the piano for the Duke on Christmas Day suggests that the newly risen star had previously enjoyed the Duke's patronage and help. Indeed the Duke was so much taken by one aria of the opera, 'And waft me home with thee to dwell/My love and cottage near Rochelle' (for which he facetiously substituted 'Bake-well') that he made Coote play and Lady Lou Cavendish sing it to him. Three years later Balfe produced his third opera *Falstaff,* which he dedicated to the Duke. Yet there is no record that the Duke attended the first night's performance. Of all Balfe's works *The Bohemian Girl,* composed in 1843, was the most popular.

The Duke was a genuine lover of music without being exactly a connoisseur. His tastes were for the simple and tuneful. As a boy he had a selection of music scores – Mozart's jostling with those of Princess Charlotte, sister Lamb, and Mrs Arkwright – beautifully bound with *Hartington* embossed on the covers. In later life Bellini, of whom he had a bust made by Dantan le jeune, was his favourite composer, with Mozart, Donizetti, Mayer and Rossini close runners-up. He could play the piano tolerably well, although he never did so before others. After all he had Coote and Schulz in permanent service, and he was a man who modestly recognized his own limitations. From the moment he succeeded his father the 6th Duke delighted in giving musical parties – in 1821 five concerts at Devonshire House alone, and thereafter seldom less than four a year. He not only engaged the best-known performers and singers of the day but made friends with many. The 'divine' Malibran, her sister Madame Viardot ('too hideous'), Madame Vestris, Madame Grisi and Jenny Lind who wrote him arch little letters, Giuditta Pasta and, as we have already noted, Henrietta

Sontag, frequented his parties and even dined alone with him in Devonshire House or at Chiswick.

Someone as exalted, romantic and seemingly unattached as the Duke of Devonshire inevitably attracted female pen friends. And contrariwise literary ladies of a certain age and spinsterishness had a morbid fascination for him. Mary Russell Mitford, well-known novelist and dramatist, employed a valid gambit for addressing him. Might she take William Wordsworth to see Chiswick? The ageing now Tory poet had already been to Chatsworth which he lauded in a sonnet beginning, 'Chatsworth, thy stately mansion, and the pride of thy domain, strange contrast do present,' while referring to the estate tenants as displaying 'every semblance of entire content.' This sentiment was a long way removed from those once held by the young radical Wordsworth who saw the landed gentry as tyrannical oppressors. On 4 June Miss Mitford wrote a gushing letter of thanks for the concession granted. The poet had pronounced Chiswick a 'triumph of art and nature'. Never, she volunteered, had painting and architecture been so triumphantly conjoined. And she begged for a cutting of one of the Duke's geraniums. It was dispatched with the mild rebuke that what she really meant was a cutting of a pelargonium. The gift elicited a further rather whimsy letter:

> Flowers are a tribute which the humblest cottager may offer to one who is more than a prince; and I cannot resist the temptation of sending to your Grace a few cuttings of geraniums [she was impenitent] not at present to be purchased ... together with some seedlings, actually raised in the little garden belonging to our own poor cabin. I have even had the presumption to call the two best of my own seedlings by the name of the Duke of Devonshire and Lady Granville.

The Duke deemed Miss Mitford precious but clever, was amused and asked her to stay at Chatsworth when she next passed by. She availed herself of the first opportunity. He grew fond of her over the years and correspondence was maintained until her death in 1855.

About the same time Miss Agnes Strickland, authoress of the very popular *Lives of the Queens of England,* met and so interested the Duke with her talk about Mary Stuart who had spent some months a prisoner in the old Chatsworth house that he invited her and her sister Elizabeth to dine at Chiswick. He made a delightful impression upon Agnes who was much flattered that he had hastened all the way from Brighton to receive her. After 'a delicate French dinner' Agnes related, the Duke dispensed with the attendance of the footmen in the dining-room, summoning them when required by striking a knife upon a tumbler. Before the sisters left he offered Agnes the freedom of Devonshire House, Hardwick and Chatsworth. 'It is in the highest circles', Agnes proclaimed, 'that I feel most at home.'

Another literary lady, younger, married and of different background with whom the Duke became more closely involved in 1836 was the poetess and wit, Caroline Norton, one of three beautiful and clever granddaughters of R. B. Sheridan. The Duke had known her since the 1820s and their relationship had always been of the flirtatious order. All men found Mrs Norton seductive, and most women viperish. Georgiana Carlisle called her 'a lady who speaks her mind which I think terrible', and Harriet Granville 'somebody impossible to like and ungracious to dislike'. She was thoroughly outspoken, flamboyant and affected. Yet she was original, good-humoured and vastly entertaining in a sophisticated way.

Caroline's husband was the beastly, brutal and impecunious George Norton whom she supported by her pen. So desperate was the couple's need of money that in June Norton brought a criminal action against Lord Melbourne, accusing him of being his wife's lover. It had in fact been a toss-up whether he would not have brought the charge against the Duke of Devonshire. But Norton decided that he stood a greater chance of raising scandal and funds by way of pay-off if his victim were the Prime Minister, whose weakness for women was public knowledge, than if he were a duke, who though admittedly richer, was less in the public eye. However Norton's evidence was so manifestly weak and his accusation so politically motivated that the Prime Minister was immediately acquitted. The furore was nevertheless tremendous; the King actually postponed a levée to be held on the day of the trial; and the Duke was made the target of vile anonymous letters. These were by no means the first he had received in his life. By now he professed to be callous to them.

And there was Eliza Warwick hovering in the background. It is difficult to keep track of the Duke's amours or to decide how serious they were at this time owing to the erasures in his journals. Who was responsible for the erasures? Probably the author himself when he re-read the journal in later years. Had his successor, the pious 7th Duke, come upon them at all he would surely have destroyed the lot. He would not have been content merely to expunge passages in his eyes discreditable to the Cavendish dynasty. That the 6th Duke was the perpetrator is strengthened by the fact that the ink of the erasures is exactly the same as the ink of the script.

As for Eliz, she was always on the watch, on the wait for slights. On 5 May, during the height of the London season, the Duke jotted down, 'Eliz going on. Eheu!' And on 10th, 'Eliz ill & mis.' Which suggest recriminations. Two months later there appears under 7 July the journey entry, 'Eliz came [to Chiswick] and sent away her carriage – a maid here does for her. So comfortable. She was very pleased again and I quite happy, tho' giving up Ly —.' Who was Lady —? Amongst the 6th Duke's papers is a small sheet belonging to this year on which is written in a woman's hand the date 8 July and the words, 'I cannot express to you how happy I have been for two days in your society to live on for a short period in this state.' Who was the author of this *billet doux*? Eliza Warwick? In which case it is the only known fragment of her writing. Or the mysterious Lady —? We may never know. The Duke was nothing if not devious where his private life was concerned.

At the end of October 1836 an immense house party was assembled at Chatsworth. Among the guests was the Hungarian ambassador to France, Count Antoine-Rodolphe Apponyi. In a journal entitled *Vingt-Cinq Ans à Paris* he left a glowing account of the splendours of Chatsworth and a not uninteresting summary of the political motives which he believed to underly the Duke of Devonshire's almost frenzied entertaining. Having expressed amazement at the palatial magnificence of the house, the panoramic landscape setting and the garden adorned with statues, urns, fountains and terraces, with stairways approached through iron grills of exquisite craftsmanship, painted and gilded, Apponyi described the evening:

> After dinner, that is to say at half past nine o'clock, because the men remain at table after the women have withdrawn [accounted a barbarous custom by all Continentals] coffee is served, then, an hour later, tea, and throughout the whole evening in the Duke's chapel opera by Rossini, Mayerbeer, Carafa and Bellini are performed with great perfection; nevertheless the company talked, even shouted because the Duke is deaf; as for me I shouted louder, so the others said, than anyone else and in spite of that he did not always hear me.

Apponyi slunk off to bed at one o'clock in the morning. Not so the Duke. He went to the washerwomen's ball in the back regions, dragging with him neighbour William Thornhill of Stanton, Derbyshire's High Sheriff, poor Coote who had been conducting in the chapel, and

George Cavendish who, having just been elected MP for Derby, was the hero of the house party. Apponyi had complained before going to bed of being obliged to read George's interminable speech as reported in the local press. The Duke thought the washerwomen's ball great fun, almost like a *bal masqué*, with Paxton, Robert the footman and other male servants in fancy dress. 'I danced & gave lots of happiness to my servants,' he said. It was the sentiment expressed in this phrase and indeed made most manifest on the occasion to which Apponyi objected for he went on to write:

> The Duke of Devonshire, Lady Granville and Lady Carlisle – in fact the whole clan – sont *affreusement* whigs; in spite of clinging to all the privileges which they owe to their birth, such as the rank they enjoy in the world, their wealth, their titles, etc., they are whigs not by principle, but through vanity, to render themselves popular, to make themselves adored in the English manner, that is to say to be applauded whenever they show themselves in public, to be in the lead of the party which is in the majority in their district, in that some members of the family must be in Parliament, and sometimes out of feebleness, sometimes fear. If this is not the case, how can we explain their mania to cling to the party which has no other aim but to take from them what they hold most dear in the world: rank, fortune, power?

The Count was giving to their sense of duty and their generosity little credit for honesty of purpose. He was accusing the Chatsworth tribe of self-interest in promoting the radical principles of a political party pledged to destroy them in the long run. There was only a small measure of truth in his stricture. In a corporate sense the Cavendishes, the Granvilles and the Howards never for an instant questioned the right they inherited as great landowners to be social and political leaders, in short the élite of their country. They had been brought up to believe so, had imbibed the incontrovertible notion with their mothers' milk. Nor were they wholly wrong. The English squire-archical system of regional, and in large measure of national government, culminating in the early nineteenth century, was still the fittest which European civilization had so far evolved.

Apponyi, however, like most Continental noblemen of the 1830s failed to understand or appreciate the genuine paternalism, even when aloof, and the positive striving of most Whig representatives after better conditions for the masses. After all it was they who brought about the Great Reform Act, the emancipation of slaves and the equal status of Roman Catholics and Jews. As for the Duke of Devonshire he was in the very van of progressive English landlordism. He was a passionate champion of popular rights and equal opportunities, albeit hoping that the aristocratic supremacy would last out his lifetime because, he would argue, sudden reversal of the established order would mean revolution and general chaos from which no one would benefit. Certainly he derived pleasure from his acts of beneficence. Vanity was one of his endearing human weaknesses.

In a summary of the bad and good conditions of the year 1836 the Duke jotted down under the first heading, 'My wickedness: Ineffectual attempts to diminish expenses,' and 'Threat of being cited as co-respondent'; and under the second heading, 'Better health than I ever had,' and 'Attention much more turned to religion. Ear cornets which enable me to hear Beamish.' This is the first mention of the name of a somewhat sinister cleric whose sermons he listened to with the aid of a new make of hearing aid. The name did not escape his sister Harriet. Always on the qui vive concerning her brother's welfare, material and spiritual, she wrote, 'I am more delighted than I can say at your going to hear and liking to hear Mr. Beamish, so is the Duchess [of Beaufort].'

The Revd. J. C. Beamish was incumbent of Trinity Chapel, Conduit Street, in the heart of Mayfair. He became an influential preacher and by his sermons great ladies like Lady Granville and the Duchess of Beaufort, and even susceptible members of the rougher sex became enthralled. Soon the aristocracy were flocking to Trinity Chapel and rallying to raise funds for the impecunious minister's wife and quiverful of children. Indeed superfluous children were a main outward and visible sign of evangelical sanctity. The Duchess of Beaufort had eight daughters, all ardent converts to the fashionable schism. It seems that Beamish was manipulated by the Duke's nearest and dearest, namely his sisters and nieces and William Cowper and George Cavendish, sometimes at odds amongst themselves, as the fitting instrument to bring the erring head of the Cavendish family back from the paths of iniquity and out of the clutches of the scarlet Jezebel Eliza Warwick. Not that the Duke was an unwilling sacrificial lamb. Over the past few years his thoughts, as we have seen, had been gradually veering towards godly behaviour and public worship. It was already a long time since he had confided to his journal that he could not go to church on Christmas Day because the wind was in the east, or, 'I must not dissemble to myself that my only motive for going to church is for the sake of example to others.' No, he had definitely seen the light since then. But Beamish certainly provided a convenient solution of his tormenting doubts and indicated a term to his mistress's reign.

On New Year's Day of 1837 the Duke twice heard Beamish preach at Trinity Chapel, after which he went with Billy Cowper for a walk in the cold. Next day 'My good angel paid me a visit and I trust did me good,' the ambiguity of the verb 'trust' being explained by his having called on the formidable Lady Harriet Baring for whom he had lately formed a mild infatuation, but serious enough for him to write, 'with her and Growler [his new dog] I could pass my life.' Thenceforward good angel Billy Cowper seldom left his side. Together they went for interminable walks in London's parks by day; and far into the night they discussed the meaning of the Evangelical movement, which laid special emphasis on personal conversion and salvation by faith in the atoning death of Christ, and which induced in its disciples a profound apprehension of the contrary states of nature and grace, the one meriting eternal damnation and the other eternal bliss. The Duke got so worked upon by Billy, Beamish, sister Harriet and the Burlingtons that he could talk of nothing else but theology and the salvation of his soul. Joseph Paxton who was more in touch with his master than any other servant did not fail with his quick intelligence to notice and deplore it. While travelling with the Duke in June he spoke his mind freely. To his wife Sarah he wrote:

The Duke is become a ranting, canting saint. We battled about religion almost all the way from Chatsworth to London. I am fearful he will not relish what I have said to him, though he took it all in good part. It is in everybody's mouth here, and all deplore the fall, for I can call it nothing else, of so magnificent a man. Some think it is a species of insanity. However, I agree with none of them, for I am sure he is well enough in that quarter. ... Young Cooper [*sic*] and Lord Burlington have the credit of having changed him, but more particularly the former, whom you may remember as a wild harum-scarum youth. They both verify the old proverb that 'Great Sinners make great Saints.' What do you think of the Duke and young Cooper? After having gone twice to Church and taken the Sacrament once that they should not have had enough without going to a chapel at Turnham Green in the evening, which is held in a schoolroom, and sitting themselves on forms among all the rag-tag and bob-tail of the place. There's dignity for you. That almost breaks my heart. My attachment to the Duke is so great that nothing can make me dislike him, but my love for him is now mixed up with some gall and wormwood. I can write of nothing else, for this is the subject uppermost in my thoughts.

Sarah's reply to this effusion was no less forthright:

> The contents of your letter have upset me not a little. I can easily imagine
> how you feel. . . . Going to Turnham Green caps the donkey. I fear he is
> quite lost, and what a dreadful thing it is for such a man to be lost to the
> world, spending his time in singing and praying with a vile set of canting
> hypocrites. Oh dear, pray use what little influence you possess over him,
> and explain the folly he is now running into . . . I fear we shall have cause
> to regret it much, and so will many others. You will have to build a chapel,
> I think, instead of a stove.

The Stove, or Great Conservatory, mentioned by Sarah, was her
husband and the Duke's enormous project, then in hand in the Chatsworth garden, to which reference will be made shortly. Meanwhile
the cynical Paxton's opinion of young Cowper was to some extent
shared by at least one dissident member of the nearest and dearest clan
pressurizing the Duke along the Evangelical path to salvation. Blanche
wrote in her diary: 'Uncle D's excessive love for W. Cowper . . . makes
one tremble for fear he should not keep up to all he thinks him, for
fear he should fall back.' Uncle D's happiness depended too much on
W.C., she opined. He was 'too exalté, too poetical'.

Carried away though the 6th Duke undoubtedly was by conversion
to Evangelicalism he never allowed enthusiasm to transcend his sense
of the ridiculous. 'That nice, modest little man, though bald', and a
'nice small potato', were his maturer assessments of Dr Beamish. Even
during the honeymoon of February 1837 he dared to write to Harriet,
'Condole with me that Beamish has fallen in my estimation. He is
grown so violent political and orange & ultra.' By 1849 the minister
was to become 'swindler Beamish', but that was still ahead.

The nearest and dearest clan and George Stanley Faber's *Difficulties
of Infidelity* proved too strong a force for poor Eliza to contend with.
The dissolution of the tie was rapidly approaching. Under 18 February
we read: 'Swollen neck. D of Marlborough called. Queer original. Eliz
dined with me. *contento non oggi.*' On 12 March: 'Shut doors to all but
W. Cowper who staid all day with me, & we read.' Which leads to the
next day's not surprising entry: 'Poor Eliz very unhappy & I too.
Scruples. She wrote me a very touching letter.' He dined out. 'It was
all very well but I drank too much – then Eliz – all vanity and vexation'.
16 March: 'I miserable now *à mon tour*. Quite ill, depressed & exhausted.
Sent for Cowper and had long talk all day.' Eliza's chances were clearly
doomed.

On 9 May Blanche was staying with him at Chiswick. He told her everything and mentioned his resolutions. No words could express her happiness to see her 'dearest beloved Uncle D' awakened to a sense of spiritual things and seeking the one thing needful. He confessed that until his forty-seventh year he had lived without God a life of sin; he had read infidel books about Voltaire and Frederick the Great. It was then that Cowper had remonstrated with him. There came the deepest sense of guilt. He lived in fear of lapsing, telling her, 'I had rather live in a mad house all the days of my life, & never see Chatsworth or anything I love again, than lose the impression I now have.' No wonder Paxton was worried. The Duke told Blanche he was going to take the Sacrament for the first time since he was quite young – which was simply not true. He told her that if ever he relapsed he would never see her again. He was playing up the innocent and guileless Blanche. 'We talked', she wrote, 'on the subject of his marrying, with the most touching and affectionate kindness to William and me.' He made her read the 51st psalm (*Miserere mei, Domine*) in order to convey to her respectable understanding what the nature of his great sin had been. Several further meetings ensued. The bond between them became extremely close.

There was a dreadful scene with Eliz; she was very out of temper, which so upset the Duke that he vowed it must not be repeated. Cowper counselled him not to visit her again. He disregarded this advice. For a man in a state of high religious ecstasy he chose to hear and see Mozart's opera *Don Giovanni*. And from Drury Lane he went straight to Dorset Square. When his carriage came for him to depart Eliz worked herself into a scene even worse than the last one. She attempted to stab herself to death with a supper knife. Having composed her the Duke left her in the care of her maid and sent for a surgeon. He felt disgusted and worn out. After this abortive attempt at suicide Eliz wrote him two rational letters to which he replied. Much shaken he was obliged to drink to keep up his spirits.

The Warwick worry was intensified by the very rocky state of his finances, the disclosure of which was accompanied by his agent Ridgway's recommendation that he reduce his annual expenditure of £141,000 by one-fifth. Ridgway pointed out that this could be done by his Grace's resolution and co-operation in fixing a limit to each head of expenditure and not exceeding it. The Duke summoned Currey to Devonshire House and put before him his two immediate problems. Being a virtuous man Currey expressed unfeigned delight that Eliz was to be dismissed. His feelings about the financial resolution are not recorded, but can be imagined.

For his master's birthday at Chatsworth Paxton took it upon himself to fetch from Sutton Scarsdale dear Mrs Arkwright, 'the kindest of friends and nurses', to cheer him up. She was an unfailing panacea in his recurrent perplexities both of heart and health. His sufferings were not lessened by the announcement that Eliza's mother intended calling on the morrow. 'I am very angry but must behave well, considerately, and with Cowper to hand.' The interview was less disagreeable than expected and the Duke managed to get said all he wanted to say. One wonders with what feelings the poor woman drove away from Chatsworth. It must have been made perfectly clear that her daughter would never be reinstated.

On 6 June the Duke retreated, with Cowper, to Kemp Town for some invigorating air. 'O man, what is thy reason?' he wrote. 'I am as dust before the wind carried to & fro & easily driven away by every light temptation. O help me Lord.' On the next line of the journal he complained of the terrible, the terrible boredom of Brighton in the off-season.

6

Early Victorian Duke
1837–1843

BY THE END of May 1837 William IV was failing. He recovered and relapsed. Princess Victoria, just 18, was in a state of nerves and tears over the prospect of responsibilities to be borne. At half past three in the morning of 20 June the King expired. The young Queen with extraordinary self-control pulled herself together and assumed a composure and dignity which she was to retain for the ensuing sixty-four years of her life. It is true she began her reign with the advantages of her sex and youth since total lack of experience and need of protection, signifying virginity, freshness and innocence, appeals at once to the hearts of older men and and even some women. 'Such a little love of a Queen,' Harriet wrote without condescension from the Embassy in Paris. 'Lord Melbourne must take care to throw a something paternal into his manner.'

She need not have worried. The gallant and tender-hearted old cynic took the cue without Lady Granville's exhortation. His fatherly wisdom and man-of-the-world attitude was precisely wanted to release from the rather prim and prudish carapace, with which a narrow upbringing had invested her, the natural wilfulness of his royal charge. The Duke of Devonshire, sensing that the Duchess of Kent, whom he liked, would soon feel bereft, wrote her a tactful letter of congratulation mingled with sympathy. It evoked a charming reply: 'Few things could grafity me more than your letter, your friendship for me has led you to express yourself in terms and with a feeling *that quite* overset me. I gratefully accept all your good wishes for our dear Queen and *my beloved child* ... Pray take care of your precious health ... Your Grace's very sincere friend.'

In July the Duke went up to London for the Queen's first Chapter of the Garter at which she made her half-brother Prince of Leiningen a knight. Henceforth the Duke dined several times at Buckingham Palace. He found the palace gaudy and the ceremonial stilted and Germanic. 'Stockmar & Lehzen rule this devoted land,' was his laconic comment on the royal mentor and governess, for in spite of his unnatural submission to Dr Beamish's evangelical influence the flavour of the new court was antipathetic to what he was accustomed to in good King George's raffish reign. Perfect the little Queen was, he conceded, in grace and unconcern, but nevertheless 'perfectly ugly too'. He was always placed beside her and found difficulty in making conversation. After she had remarked that she thought her blue riband 'looked very well' he dried up. In fact to get through an evening creditably he was obliged to indulge rather more freely than was suitable to the abstemious environment.

He was far more interested in the news now pouring in from Dr Nathaniel Wallich, head of the Botanic Gardens in Calcutta, Lord Auckland the Governor-General of India and his sister Emily Eden about the phenomenal successes of John Gibson's expedition to Cherrapunji. In March Gibson had embarked for home via the Cape of Good Hope with over 80 species of orchids and, more exciting still, *Amherstia nobilis*, described as one of the most striking trees in the world when it blooms – its large flowers of a bright vermilion with yellow spots. Of this delicate specimen, which could be raised in England only in stove conditions, Gibson brought two cuttings, one for the Duke and the other for the East India Company. In July the triumphant traveller landed with his precious cargo at Plymouth. But on investigation it was discovered that the *Amherstia* reserved for the Duke had died *en route*. Instantly the Duke wrote to the directors of the East India Company who most graciously complied with his request to be given their *Amherstia* which had arrived in a flourishing condition. Paxton on hearing of the dispatch of the Duke's share of the plants to St Katharine Docks hastened to collect them. There he learned that they were already on their way to Devonshire House, so he turned back. Before he could unload his luggage from the cab Meynell put his head out of a window and told him not to go near the cases but come immediately to the Duke. It being nine o'clock his Grace hurriedly dressed, and then, Paxton related, came the solemn introduction of him to my long cherished love the *Amherstia*. I cannot detail how this important introduction took place; suffice it to say the Duke ordered his breakfast to be brought into the Painted Hall where the plant stands, and he desired me to sit down and lavish my love upon the gem, while he had his breakfast by it, after which I had to be personally introduced to the remainder of the beauties ...

Amherstia nobilis was soon transferred to Chatsworth but notwithstanding the attentions of Joseph Paxton, who, the Duke assured the directors, was the only man in England capable of handling it, failed to flower. Before this lapse could be detected John Gibson's triumph went to his head and gave him such airs that, according to Mrs Paxton, he proved himself a grievous puppy. The young man's conceit was perhaps excusable in that, albeit indirectly, he laid the foundation of the largest orchid collection in this country to which the number of species named after Devonshire and Chatsworth testifies.

Straight away work was begun on a fitting repository for the exotic plants amassed so abundantly by Gibson in India, and, it was confidently anticipated, for many more about to result from a further expedition, this time to South America. The Chatsworth Stove, or Great Conservatory, was the brilliant brainchild of the Duke and Paxton with the practical help of the architect Decimus Burton. The Duke claimed it would be the assembly place of the floral poetry of the world. Certainly it was the largest glass building in the world before the Crystal Palace. It was 277 feet long, 123 feet broad and rose to a maximum height of 67 feet. The prodigious edifice was sited away from the house and due east of the Canal Pond. Paxton had to clear and level a large area of ground out of the hill and wood before he could raise the steel skeleton in two curved stages so as to form a nave and aisles. His engineering skill was matched by astonishing aesthetic assurance. He clothed the skeleton with over three-quarters of an acre of ribbed glass panels in what he called the ridge-and-furrow technique. In March 1840 the last scaffolding was removed to reveal what the Duke called the most glorious building of modern times. Harriet Sutherland went further. Nothing, she maintained, could match it save St Peter's, Rome. It was heated by seven miles of iron pipes fed by an elaborate system of eight underground furnaces supplied with coal brought by tramway. The stupendous undertaking was completed in 1841. At the same time Paxton was busy contriving an aqueduct to carry water from the upper moorland reaches beyond the garden wall to feed the fountains.

In September occurred a break in the long and well-tried friendship with the Arkwrights. The cause seems to have been political for the Arkwrights, as opposed to the Duke's irreversible Whiggism, were fanatical Tories. For reasons which he does not specify resentment turned to conviction that Mrs Arkwright had acted falsely towards him and had somehow let him down. Whether it was that in the past she had bottled up her political opinions in order not to offend him and then could no longer contain them, is not clear. The Duke's journal gives vent to snide observations such as, 'Mrs. Arkwright is much spoiled by the world and Toryism', and 'Mrs. A is difficult but a dear'. At any rate when visiting her and Squire Robert at Sutton Scarsdale during election time he was so overcome with their 'vile ingratitude' – their son standing for Parliament in opposition to his interests – that he had the greatest difficulty disguising his feelings until he could decently leave the house. All he could do was to induce them to take him into the church to be shown the new tort stove installed by Mr Arkwright. Under pretext of admiring the ingenious heating apparatus the Duke prayed over the altar for strength to keep his temper, 'to return good for evil, and to say nothing painful to them, & I succeeded and came home happy'. He even mentioned the disagreeable incident to the pianist Schulz, there being nobody else available in whom he could more properly confide. Schulz's reaction was hardly to be expected. He suggested to the Duke that he was breaking Mrs Arkwright's heart. The Duke riposted that perhaps she had not got one to break.

If Fanny Arkwright was temporarily out of his life Eliza Warwick was about to disappear for ever. Since the ugly scene over the supper knife their relations were on a different footing, polite and distant. It is quite clear that, having completely abandoned any prospect of the Duke making her an honest woman by marrying her, she was looking for consolation elsewhere. A jocular allusion to a German admirer having failed to move him Eliza hinted about her 'secret'. 'I know it already,' the Duke noted. Then in March 1838 she wrote about her probable marriage. This news likewise failing to move him the Duke with Currey's assistance composed in reply a letter of which no copy survives. Whatever he wrote her reply incensed him. He flew with it to Currey for further advice and noted in his journal that 'she behaves very ill and very wickedly'. Even so on 10 August he called with the Colonel. He found her fat and well but tearful because, she explained, her sister was threatening to become a nun.

And that was the final farewell. He never saw her again. Her name no longer appeared in the Marylebone rate book or the Royal Blue Directory as resident at 22 Dorset Square.

A new influence on the Duke's devotional life, in that it was less puritanical and narrow than the Beamish variety, was that of the Revd Francis Hodgson who in 1836 had been appointed by Lord Melbourne Archdeacon of Derby. Hodgson was a close friend of the Arkwrights between whom and the Duke he had vainly endeavoured to patch up the rift. Failure did not prevent the Duke offering him the gift of Edensor parish church into which he was inducted in February 1838. Hodgson being then in his fifty-eighth year was ready for a parish whose duties would not be too exacting. Moreover he knew the district well having been vicar of Bakewell from 1816 until he moved to Derby. And he knew and liked the Duke. He was a scholar and poet, and his greatest distinction was his close friendship with Byron whom he first met in 1807 while he was resident tutor at King's College, Cambridge. Byron admired his translation of Juvenal and invited him to Newstead Abbey where they drank champagne and caroused incontinently. Byron became fond of Hodgson and respected his utter integrity and devotion. He also made loans or rather gifts of money to enable him to clear his debts and marry. Yet he much enjoyed mocking the Reverend's efforts to convert him to Christianity. 'Talk of Galileeism? Show me the effects –' he wrote. 'Are you better, wiser, kinder by your precepts? I will show you ten Mussulmans shall shame you in all good will towards men, prayer to God, and duty to their neighbours.' Hodgson, instead of being shocked, revelled in being a repository of the great poet's confidences, including Byron's love for the choirboy Edleston. Besides it was through Byron that he got to know other men of letters, Rogers, Campbell and Tom Moore. In after years Hodgson would look back upon these green salad days of fun and frolic with the famous and his strong addiction to wine with slightly guilty, but delicious nostalgia. He either gave or left the Duke by will his bust of Byron by Thorvaldsen.

The Duke of Devonshire's renewed, howsoever chance link with his Harrovian schoolfellow Byron through the Old Etonian Hodgson was fortuitous. And just as Byron relished teasing the Archdeacon because of his faith so the Duke enjoyed mocking him on account of his sentimentality. He called him a goose. 'Very out of patience with Hn for his twaddle and love at 58,' he wrote. The first Mrs Hodgson having died, the portly and poetical Archdeacon was madly smitten by and courting a daughter ('a brown mouse of 31') of Lord Chief Justice Denman. Although irritated by his lovesick ways and excessive absurdity the Duke also became very fond of him. When Hodgson and Miss Denman finally married he lent them Hardwick for their honeymoon. In fact he treated the Archdeacon as his confessor and engaged him in such long debates about happiness in the next world that the Archdeacon gently directed him to concentrate more on his duties in the present one. Nothing loth the Duke turned to discussing how best he might relieve the distress of the handloom weavers in Derbyshire. As well as virtual confessor the Archdeacon was virtual private chaplain whom his patron obliged to read prayers to the Chatsworth servants each morning. 'Nothing, no nothing has made me so happy.' The Duke himself even started delivering to them a short exposition on the Sermon on the Mount until emotion nearly made him founder. 'Stuck fast at one time, but with great effort got on ... But I suffered a great deal.' Yet in spite of this unprecedented access of piety the Duke never lost his sense of values. 'Early Sacrament,' we read. 'Not very temperate alas. devil & mulled ale on egg flip.'

Naturally restless, loving travel, and a little shaken by the break with Eliza which involved on her side reproaches and tears and on his guilt and remorse, and by the Queen's gentle reproof over his absences from the House of Lords ringing in his ears, the Duke of Devonshire set off on what was to prove the longest of his foreign tours, its ultimate destination Constantinople. On 17 August 1838 he left London in the britshka with the King Charles spaniel Bony, who had taken the place of beloved Spot in his heart, and a new doctor, by name Condell, the ubiquitous Meynell and second valet Cornelius perched on the box; a cook, courier Theodore, a third sub-valet and Robert Royal the footman followed separately. Condell was in high favour, a sort of dandy of 35, handsome, gentlemanlike and quiet. 'He must have been when young very attractive.' At the Ship Inn, Dover, the Duke was given the very room which in 1816 he had shared with Nicholas. It gave rise to sweet reflections, and lament that those carefree days were long past.

For the first part of the journey the Duke was in an odious mood and cross with the servants. As for Theodore, the courier, the very sight of him sent the Duke into a frenzy. 'Oh wretched heart and mind ... Now this is perfectly detestable in me ... But I am only too vile altogether! O why can I not feel more deeply that love which ought to prevent all grovelly nerves and passions?' Beastliness to subordinates was behaviour he reprobated most in others.

On 30 September the Duke noted in his journal, 'No letter from Paxton. Why?' The following day Paxton turned up in Geneva, bringing letters. From that moment the Duke's bad mood lifted. He was no longer cross and disagreeable to his entourage. Had the gardener's arrival been prearranged before the Duke left England, or had he been summoned on the spur of a moment's desperate loneliness during the travels? At all events Paxton duly wrote to Sarah who was on the verge of giving birth to another child and was not happy at losing her husband on such an occasion. He told her he had had some difficulty finding his master who had changed his address three times. All the retinue were delighted to see him.

> Meynell would have it that I should have something to eat (no bad thought), as he was sure the Duke would keep me a long time. The Duke received me most kindly. He was more than astonished at the rapidity of my journey. He was pleased to say that no one but I could have done it in the time. His Grace has been in a terrible stew for want of me for some time. He would reserve some of the great sights of Switzerland until I came, and they all say how he has worried himself.

In additional letters to Sarah Paxton he throws further light on the situation. The Duke very much dislikes the courier who is a terrible liar and has no finesse. 'Sometimes the Duke breaks out at him with a rattle.' Paxton manages to relieve the tension while thoroughly sympathizing with his master. And scarcely a day passes 'but we meet with something that the Duke wishes me to have imitated.' And he adds:

> You cannot think how very kind he is to me. He doesn't think half so much of pleasing himself as he does in gratifying me. Whatever sights I want to see, I have only to hint half a word and the thing is done.

No doubt the information that her spouse was being treated so liberally and given an unprecedented experience of the countries they passed through was some compensation for Sarah's deprivation of him. Not once do either husband or wife complain about their separation. That they had an understanding to write cautiously is likely. The Duke delighted to read Sarah's letters to Joseph and learn the Chatsworth news and gossip from below stairs. Any hint of Sarah's discontent would be noted by him; and he would be saddened by it.

The cavalcade continued to Chamonix. Now Paxton was seated with the Duke and doctor inside the britschka; and now walking with the Duke to the confluence of the Rhône and Arve; and now buying the Duke a pair of stout shooting shoes. Paxton was struck by the old willow trees, the ground arbutus and even the fruit of the elms. There was little he did not notice and in his eager search for knowledge jot down in a pocket book. His company revived the Duke's interest in life and all life's creatures and vegetation. His master's content was but slightly marred at Domodossola by Meynell waking him at midnight to announce that the Queen of Greece had arrived unexpectedly and was demanding his room at the inn, and even his horses. He considered this a little too much and was put out. Nevertheless such was his respect for royalty that he complied to the extent of vacating the room. Then he rushed off to the Simplon vowing that he would not get up again in the middle of the night for a Queen or anybody else. Had Her Majesty sent him a message direct and not through her doctor he might have been disposed to surrender one horse, but all – no.

They crossed the Alps into Italy and were enchanted with Isola Bella on Lake Maggiore where Paxton paid much attention to the plants and wrote to his wife:

> I have seen wonders upon wonders; we get up every morning soon after five and often earlier and continue upon the move until seven or eight o'clock at night. The Duke is a most excellent getter-up. I have kept him in excellent humour much to the satisfaction of all about him. I understand he was so cross before I came that the people were about to petition him to read prayers in the morning!!

Paxton had some reason to be pleased with himself. It was not everyone who could change overnight the Duke's mood from caprice to sweet reasonableness. Now the Duke was as happy as a sandboy. At Milan they met up with the Burlingtons and their children, and for the only time in his life the Duke was not particularly pleased to see them. They were an interruption to his days of walks and botanizing. And they separated him from Paxton.

In Venice he took Paxton to dungeons and prisons enough to break one's heart; and to Murano and S. Michele, those two islands of glass and tombs. They met the famous English resident Rawdon Brown who spent half a century researching amongst the reports sent home from the Venetian ambassadors to London. In Bologna Rossini and Mrs Sagan sang to him and he gave the composer a magnificent

Dresden box as a present, which did not mean that he liked him as a man. He remembered how over-familiar the fat, sallow creature had been with George IV at the Brighton Pavilion and how the King, to the indignation of his courtiers, politely deferred to his genius.

By the middle of November they were in Rome. The Duke was greeted by dearest William and Blanche, the Sutherlands and numerous London acquaintances. After introducing the doctor and Paxton to his favourite monuments and viewpoints the Duke launched himself on the familiar round of card leaving – deciding 'whom to keep down at first makes the burden less' – entertaining and being entertained. He then returned to that popular pursuit of his cultivated countrymen, visits to sculptors' studios. He began with Canova's. All the great sculptor's works were of course gone, which was depressing. Indeed those galleries where the old sculptors he had known were still oper-ating seemed to him uninspiring. Tadolini's figures, for example, displayed a tiresome affectation. Then there were his countrymen's. 'How little the British sculptors do get on in 14 years,' he observed tartly. Paxton however, who had not previously indulged in studio-crawling, was delighted with what he saw in Gibson's gallery, including the artist himself. The congenial natures of gardener and sculptor at once coalesced. The Duke too was so fond of Gibson that he commissioned from him a copy of Algardi's *Doge*, and a relief of Hero and Leander. Also he could not resist persuading shy Bony to sit to Joseph Gott – the folly of it, but it would be pretty.

The Duke's notes made on sculpture, not only modern but Renaiss-ance and Baroque, during this visit, are more mature, more informed and the result of more intensive scrutiny than those kept when he first fell under the spell of this particular medium of art. For example, he now reserved praise of Michelangelo's *Christ* in S.M. Minerva Church, of which the head struck him as slightly insipid; on the other hand he discerned great beauty in Bernini's *S. Teresa* in S.M. della Vittoria, which he never could have done in 1819, and which indeed few of his contemporaries would have done in 1838. He had truly become one of the best judges of sculpture of his time. In Italian painting, of which he professed ignorance and in which even scant interest, his taste was, apart from Raphael, for the Bolognese school, Guido Reni, Guercino and Domenichino, artists who were universally admired by his con-temporaries until Ruskin wiped them off the slate in *Modern Painters*.

From Naples a smooth passage of twenty-two hours brought him to Palermo where Paxton was in raptures over the botanical garden.

After two days the party re-boarded the steamboat in a glorious sunset for Messina whence they sailed to Syracuse; and from Syracuse to Malta. In Valletta harbour they were met with congratulations from old, gouty Lord Howe, acting as Chamberlain to the dowager Queen Adelaide of Great Britain, then resident on the island. The friendly, kindly Addie sent word that she hoped the Duke would consider her table his own. Twice he dined with the Queen whose reception of him was as touching as the blue waters of her eyes. Yet he did not care for the island which was treeless and bare, so he leapt at the offer of a berth in a government boat HM Steamship *Acheron* to Constantinople. He immediately ordered Paxton to get everything ready and accompany him the next day. Paxton was obliged to inform his wife that go with him he must. There were no two ways about it.

On 26 February they disembarked at the Piraeus. The Duke spent hours on the Acropolis of Athens, ruminating, marvelling and just looking, while Carelli sketched the Theseum. Athens city was like a new settlement. Seven years before not a house had been left standing. Now a splendid new city for King Otto was being erected. On 1 March he dined at court, the young King, whom Paxton deemed rather soft, and the Queen being seated on raised chairs.

On 7 March they reached Constantinople, a city enveloped in a haze of blue and gold. They stopped a few minutes off the Grand Seraglio to have their bill of health examined, before sailing gently up the Bosporus five miles beyond Terapeia, making for the residence of John Lord Ponsonby, the English minister, and the Duke's cousin. Having sent a *caique* with eight rowers, two guards, a footman and a guide to fetch them Ponsonby expressed immense surprise to see the unheralded visitors. His house having been destroyed by fire he could not invite his cousin to stay. Paxton was dispatched to look everywhere for lodgings, but they were all so dirty that he advised his master to sleep on board. The Duke, disenchanted by the filthy streets of Constantinople, readily agreed to take this advice.

For two days he declined to stir. He then strode through the bazaars, and contented himself with the outsides of churches and the doors of the Seraglio, having no permit to enter. 'I suffered from heat, crossness, nervous prostration, etc., but commanded my temper well, and came home to my ship. Out only after dark. Thoroughly disgusted with the place, people and climate. Very glad to have seen it.' Mr Paxton however made friends with the consul Kennedy who entertained him. For several more days the Duke remained on board, sulking like

Achilles in his tent. Humour took him to write to Mrs Arkwright, hoping not to make matters worse. His cabin was very cold and the fire in it smoked, fit to poison him. The weather was foul; it snowed; he pined for Athens. When he eventually sallied forth into the city all the inhabitants pursued him like flies.

On 15th he watched from a shop, where he drank coffee and smoked, the Sultan's return from a mosque. A pasha had evidently forewarned the Sultan where the great English nobleman might be sitting, for His Imperial Majesty in passing gazed at him in a marked manner. The Duke noticed that he was handsome, small and made up. He guessed him to be some five years older than himself. He then moved off to watch the dancing dervishes slash themselves in religious frenzy with knives, 'which was a sad, melancholy spectacle indeed – poor creatures'. He thought them degraded and without an honest pretext for such an exhibition. While Carelli sketched the courtyard of the Beyazit mosque the Duke walked all over Pera trying desperately to keep warm in spite of wearing a fez, two shirts, a great coat, worsted stockings and flannel drawers.

Only the hope of being granted audience with the Sultan kept him in Constantinople, for no matter what foreign capital the Duke visited he expected to be received by the reigning sovereign. So he spent the days in the bazaars, much entertained, walking very fast in his shooting shoes, making all sorts of bargains, and buying a bit of marble brought from Heraclea. The weather continued foul but when the sun did shine the waters of the Golden Horn turned to the yellow of a polished guinea. At last a summons came from the Sultan. March 22 was fortunately the finest day so far vouchsafed. The Duke landed at Seraglio Point; he had a quick look round at the marble baths, the gaudy rooms in bad taste, the hall of the throne, awesome in its darkness and yet glimmering with precious stones. He saw where the sultanas, tied in sacks, were chucked into the sea. He was much harassed by the crowds of officials whom he could not refuse to let come with him. He returned on board *Acheron* where he dressed for the forthcoming audience in his best clothes. Having met Ponsonby by prearrangement he was received by Nourri Effendi Pasha in whose room, plied with coffee and sweetmeats, he smoked. Duke and minister were then ushered into the presence. Upstairs the Sultan was seated, his back to the light, in a sort of bow window with the blue sea behind him. Mahmud II had succeeded his brother in 1808, and borne the brunt of the Greek War of Independence. An enlightened and charming despot, he never recovered from the defeat of the Turkish fleet by the European powers, including Great Britain, at Navarino in 1827. The Duke described him as 'a fine royal creature . . . the most royal looking person in manner and appearance', with an expression of intense cleverness. His manner was gracious and cautious. At first he talked to Lord Ponsonby of whom he seemed fond, laughing a good deal. The Duke, who had been advised by his dragoman that he must at all costs begin the conversation, was under no constraint. The Sultan confirmed that he had seen the Duke the previous Friday from his barge. He offered him every facility for sightseeing and hoped he had enjoyed what he had so far seen. In front of 'a good imperial fire' more pipes were produced for smoking, more coffee was drunk and then a sort of currant jelly was eaten. Finally tea, one of the Sultan's innovations, was produced.

The Duke was delighted with his reception and succumbed to the Sultan's affability. He left with Ponsonby in a caique. Within three months Mahmud II, a disappointed and disillusioned sovereign, his reforms having come to nothing, was dead.

On 24 March the Duke sailed back to Malta on HM Steamship *Acheron*, passing Mount Athos and landing at Smyrna on the way. Here the party were lavishly feasted by the Turkish governor and Paxton sampled forty-seven dishes. At Valletta twenty dismal days of quarantine in the *lazzaretto* were threatened because they had come from the Orient. After reading some joyous letters from Rome and Naples the Duke's heart sank. He feared lest ostracism in a dingy prison, stinking of fumigation, might not be a price worth paying for having seen Athens and Constantinople. As it happened he was lodged in a charming palace with a large garden to walk in, wild flowers abounding, and a tolerable kitchen. He passed the time reading Byron's poetry and Gibbon's *Decline and Fall*, and sorting through his drawings. But he was confined. Even Bony was not allowed outside the precincts.

It was clear to the Duke that after seven months' absence from wife and children, not to mention supervision of the Great Conservatory at Chatsworth, Paxton should be released. He reproached himself for his great selfishness in having kept him so long – 'my own wretched unworthiness staring me full in the face' – and wrote to Hodgson that he could not have managed without him. Paxton packed up three dozen orange trees with the help of *Acheron*'s captain, and put them with other purchases on board. On 18 April *Acheron* bearing Paxton, who by then was in floods of tears, left Valletta for England. The

Duke waved until it was out of sight. At last on 26 a ship, *Sesostris* – 'such a gentlemanlike captain' – wafted the Duke, the doctor and Carelli to Naples, on the first leg of their journey home.

They arrived back at the end of August, having been abroad for just over a year. Poor Eliz Warwick was by now almost a forgotten ghost of the past, only occasionally haunting his conscience. On 28 August he wrote: 'Unbounded gratitude to God – to my beloved Saviour for unparalleled mercies to unworthy wretched me. Every day of my life to be devoted to his service.' Dinner that evening with the Queen was undoubtedly regarded as a praiseworthy act of self-oblation. 'Her love of Melbourne is dégoutant ... I think the dinner at Palace too unbearably long, dull and odious.' Not till 7 September did he go down to Chatsworth where he was delighted with the rooms of the west front and the Conservatory, now glazed.

In spite of an ostensible renunciation of politics the Duke could not remain in the country, even at his adored Chatsworth, for more than a few weeks at a stretch without craving for House of Lords debates and court gossip. He had to frequent London if he was to feel in the swim of current affairs. On 23 November he attended a Privy Council at Buckingham Palace to hear the Queen announce her engagement to Prince Albert of Saxe-Coburg and Gotha. It was a very bullish assembly, the Queen entirely alone among 150 men, not even a lady-in-waiting at hand. Nearly every Councillor was present including a superfluity of Tories ('they never do fail in a palace'). In a black spotted gown and with nothing on her head, 'small and pale and ugly looked our Sovereign'.

On 10 February 1840 the Duke was privileged to attend Victoria's wedding to Prince Albert in the Chapel Royal, having a 'famous' place seated between Georgiana Carlisle and the Duke of Bedford; and afterwards he watched from his sister's house the pair drive to Windsor. The spectacle interested and amused him. His attitude to the Prince Consort was always slightly patronizing. He admired his ability and dedication to duty; yet was slightly repelled by his earnestness which was a bourgeois and not a patrician trait. On a first meeting at the Duchess of Kent's the previous June he described Albert as 'a very fine young Prince, who is perhaps our future fancy King'. He conceded that he was handsome in a barber's block way, and when Victoria was gruff could be affable. Yet he had no small talk and in conversation was sticky. He had none of the graces of the Regency period in which the Duke had been brought up to divert and shine.

Between 1838 and 1841 Edensor village, a mile from Chatsworth and west of the River Derwent, was all but entirely rebuilt. The Duke's motives were to promote a model village on up-to-date lines and informal plan, yet of uniform material, namely the local honey-coloured sandstone. He had been immensely struck by John Nash's hamlet at Blaise outside Bristol and the deliberate way in which each cottage was treated as a unit, apparently unrelated to its neighbour, and at the same time part of a homogeneous community. In this respect and no other can the new Edensor village be related to Blaise hamlet where each dwelling is in the *cottage orné* style. A more likely influence, advanced by John Kenworthy-Browne, is the village of Harlaxton in Lincolnshire, which Squire George de Ligne Gregory was building in the 1830s. There the cottages run through a gamut of architectural styles in almost crazy eccentricity. Whether the Duke of Devonshire made a point of studying them when he visited Mr Gregory at Harlaxton Manor on January 1833 he did not record.

The Duke of Devonshire's rebuilding of Edensor has been attributed to a dislike of seeing the old village from the Chatsworth windows, but this is not at all in accord with what we know of the Duke's character. He was not like the typical Georgian landowner who sought to dissociate himself and his immediate environment from his tenants. On the contrary he liked to share his demesne with his neighbours just as he made a point of being acquainted with all his cottagers. It merely happened that the old Edensor which straddled the busy road running north to south from Baslow to Beeley had been partly visible from Chatsworth. The old Edensor was in his eyes a ragged conglomeration of nondescript buildings unworthy of a well-run estate. In deciding to demolish it the Duke chose for the new Edensor an adjacent site protected from the public road in a sheltered dip and bounded on the west side by the hillock which conceals it from Chatsworth.

The new village that arose has survived to the present day with remarkably few alterations. After some initial work carried out by the Duke and Paxton together the first architect (if he can be so called) to be engaged was a relatively unknown John Robertson of Bayswater, originally a draughtsman to the landscape-gardener J. C. Loudon, famous for his *Encyclopedia of Gardening*. Robertson's role was definitely that of subordinate assistant to Paxton, who was not himself a trained architect. It is hard to discover how many of the villas and cottages of Edensor are to Robertson's design, or Paxton's, or indeed the Duke's. It is certain that the derivation of several came from current pattern books and in the process of erection were given an extraordinary idiosyncratic twist towards the robust, the solid and sometimes the incongruous. The 'Robertson' architecture strove to be a serious attempt at correct interpretation of a variety of styles of the historic past.

Loudon in *The Gardener's Chronicle* of 1842 pronounced, with a suspicion of banter, his pupil's village to be 'a perfect compendium of all the prettiest styles of cottage architecture, from the sturdy Norman to the sprightly Italian.' Indeed this is so. His opinion, favourable enough, was not shared by his contemporary, the diarist Mary Frampton who found the village ornamental but insufficiently rustic. The truth lies somewhere in between. But can a strict assessment of Edensor's architecture be made? And is it really called for? It is surely enough to be amazed, amused and delighted by the Castellated Lodge, the Norman Villa, the Swiss Cottage and the Tudor Cottages with their curvilinear dormers, oriels and porches, to which may be added Wyatville's peripheral half-timbered lodge and the later octagonal villa, Dunsa, under a large central chimneystack, which the Duke was to lend to the egregious Mary Thornhill. As for the superb landscaping, the planting of trees, layout of lawns and meandering paths, they complete a unique specimen of the William and Adelaide Picturesque, contrived under the direction of Paxton and the 6th Duke of Devonshire.

A sad loss to the Duke was Wyatville's death. The old architect had stayed at Chatsworth over the New Year of 1840 but was very weak. When he left, the Duke knew he would never return. Sure enough six weeks later news came that Sir Jeffry had succumbed to a disease of the chest. The Duke on reading Genesis at prayers lamented that the 'old rogue' was not present for him to appeal to over the meaning of an ambiguous passage. Architect and client had served each other well. Sir Jeffry owed his highly rewarding commission at Windsor Castle to the Duke; the Duke owed the successful reconstruction of Chatsworth to Sir Jeffry, declaring that the place would be incomplete until it contained a memorial to him by Lawrence or Chantrey. In fact no memorial by either was forthcoming. On the other hand the Duke was to pay him a glorious tribute in the *Handbook*.

At Chatsworth the thoughts of him are so connected with every part and every stone, that, forgetting their inability to express themselves, I had a sort of impression that everybody must know as much of his share in the work as I did. Success was his great merit here, as at Windsor ... His aim was to restore in the character of the place he improved. The compliment he liked best was, that people should point out one of his creations, and say, 'they well remembered that, ... that part is old', etc.

It must however be submitted that notwithstanding Wyatville's vaunted respect for old buildings, a respect which the Duke did not share, his treatment of them was often remarkably cavalier. At Windsor it was brash. The exterior of the castle was literally rebuilt from top to bottom, and looks it. At Chatsworth Wyatville's endeavours to synchronize his architecture with Talman's for the 1st Duke of Devonshire were far more sympathetic in that he had greater affinity with the classical than the medieval style. In spite of a certain blandness and newness of texture here which has not yet subjected itself to the patina of time his creative architecture, as distinct from his restoration work, marries happily with what went before.

In view of a forthcoming death, to be even more grievous than Sir Jeffry's, a reunion with Mrs Arkwright, who when all is said and done invariably turned up to comfort him in times of distress and loneliness, was gratifying and timely. It was brought about tactfully by Hodgson while she and her husband were visiting the Rectory. The Duke was showing his sister G and some of her children round Chatsworth when quite unexpectedly Mr and Mrs Arkwright were announced as having arrived at the door. The Duke rushed downstairs. 'Explosion. I roared for joy & kissed her hand and said it was a happy day to see her here again. She was calm,' as well she might be in feeling her way. He returned the call at Sutton Scarsdale in March, and had a long talk. Mrs Arkwright was no more than civil at first, but warmed up before he left.

He went to Paris for Easter. Before crossing the Channel from Dover he dropped in at Compton Place on the Burlingtons. Blanche's appearance filled him with a terrible foreboding. She was clearly very ill. He wanted to stay but rather than cause alarm went on his way. 'All my happiness is embarked there,' he confided to the journal. Since her marriage eleven years before she had come to mean more to him than any single soul. He told Georgiana Fullerton that Blanche alone held the inmost place of his heart. And he knew that his adoration was reciprocated. Among all the Howard relations there was but one opinion of Blanche. She was gentleness and goodness personified. Her sister Harriet Sutherland, whom she closely resembled, was better educated, more scintillating. Blanche, unlike Harriet, was utterly unworldly. And her religious faith, excessive though we may find it, was the greatest solace to her uncle during the crisis of his love affair with Eliza Warwick. She was the one person to whom he could unburden himself; the only person he is known to have addressed as darling.

Life at the British Embassy in Paris was highly social, but overcast by anxiety about Blanche. A letter announcing imminent danger decided the Duke on 26 April to pack up and return to England there and then. At Boulogne a newspaper declared that Lady Burlington was better. 'Such a relief. God's will be praised.' But on reaching Chiswick next day he learned that all was over. She had died at Westhill Park near Wantage. Without hesitating a moment he dashed there. Lord Burlington recorded in his diary: 'We hardly spoke and his look was one of extreme misery and wretchedness. He wished to see her and I went in with him and uncovered her face. We both knelt down and I trust our prayers were heard.' The bereaved widower dreaded what might be the consequence to his uncle; he might even return to his former irregular ways of life.

William Burlington's brothers George and Richard Cavendish and the Duke's old friend Margaret Newburgh rallied immediately to comfort him. He retired to mourn by himself at Chiswick, and reflect upon the irreparable turn of events which had deprived him of supreme happiness in the knowledge that Blanche would inherit and delight in his houses and possessions. Now that was not to be. An avenging God had visited him. So in the extravagance of his misery he composed a letter to William that proved to be a signal mistake. He prefaced it by boldly reminding this godly man how 'circumstances combined in his younger days to prevent my marriage'. What these circumstances were he did not particularize. 'But for ten years of my life I formed a connection which occupied and gave me interest' – surely a faint compliment to Eliza Warwick. He went on: 'When from motives of conscience I broke that off, my happiness in your union with Blanche, and her attachment to me, one I must say of unusual strength, were sufficient – though at times I felt the pressure of my lonely life.' Then he came to the gist of his letter which was that William should get rid of his London house, and unite his and his children's lives with the Duke's at Devonshire House, Chatsworth and Hardwick. Having obtained the approval of Currey before posting the letter he sent a copy to Georgiana Carlisle. He waited. Meanwhile in great anxiety he discussed the subject with Hodgson, Richard and his old schoolfellow

Lord Clare. Ten days later the reply came. *Refusal from William* was underlined in the journal.

Lord Burlington's rejection of the proposition reflected as much credit upon him as upon the spirit of the offer. It was affectionate, if not wholly sensitive. William pointed out that Holker Hall in Lancashire was his real home, created for him by Blanche. Living with the Duke would involve loss of his independence. As it was he wished his sister Fanny to act as the children's mother. The Duke's scheme, if adopted, would commit him, the Duke, to not marrying and having children of his own. Alternatively William suggested that his children might visit their great-uncle more frequently than they had done hitherto at Chatsworth and Hardwick, and even stay at Devonshire House on occasional visits. The Duke chose to detect some underbelly barbs: namely that William did not care for Chatsworth enough ever to make it his principal home (indeed he never was to) and did not relish anticipating a premature burden of the place when the Duke should become old and ailing; that William's sister Fanny was married with two baby sons of her own and so unlikely to have time or inclination for her brother's; that William realized perfectly well the Duke would never at his age marry and have children; and that William had hitherto prevented his children from visiting him because of Eliza's presence in the background. 'Wretched me, and vile,' was the Duke's disappointed reaction to the snub as he saw it.

It is noteworthy that the first thing to give the Duke any pleasure after Blanche's death was the acquisition from a reluctant nurseryman called Mollison, by dint of presenting him with a blank cheque, of the epiphyte moth orchid *Philaenopsis amabilis*; and that the first person whose sympathy positively revived him was Mrs Arkwright. She came post-haste at his summons and added her tears to his.

A resolution to go abroad in the late summer of 1840 for a long spell and to close down Chatsworth and so save money did not amount to much. In fact it amounted to a short visit to the Granvilles in Paris. Back in England he promptly set forth on a tour with Paxton of houses and gardens in Derbyshire and Staffordshire. Then, on the spur of the moment, the Duke decided to cross with Paxton to Ireland, and on 23 October he reached Lismore. It was the Duke's first visit to his Irish seat for eighteen years and he found the place embellished a hundred fold; he was also delighted with the young agent Francis Edmond Currey who had recently succeeded his father Colonel William Samuel. 'My agent is dead, long live my agent,' he wrote to Harriet. Francis

Edmond was nephew to old Benjamin Currey, still the Duke's auditor and solicitor in London. This change in the agency may have been the reason which induced the Duke to attend to the long-neglected property. The chance visit was a huge success. He revelled in the beauty of the romantic castle perched above the Blackwater and became inspired to make still further improvements. He was undoubtedly encouraged by the extraordinary fervour of Paxton who instantly fell in love with the place. Paxton at once saw endless scope for his architectural talents as well as great horticultural potential in the soil and climate. 'Plants grow like trees,' the Duke observed to Harriet. 'Frost is almost unknown, so myrtle, arbutus, hydrangeas, fuchsias, clianthus, erythmia flourish out of doors. Salmon to be caught under the windows almost by whistling to them.' Paxton too was as keen on fishing as he was on everything else. Together they roamed round the garden, vaguely planning great extensions, the Duke restraining his companion's ardour only out of nostalgic fondness for the old walks and not by any reluctance to spend money. This visit was a mere preliminary to a future of a great activity at Lismore.

The last months of 1840 were chiefly remarkable for the Duke's determination on his doctor's advice to restrict drink to two glasses of wine each day. The effects induced Meynell to insist that this abstinence would merely kill him. At the same time the Duke made a resolution to be up and dressed by nine o'clock each morning, paying Meynell a shilling a day for so long as it lasted. The chuckles with which the valet pocketed the money, which he was putting by for his boys, were a constant irritant.

In April of 1841 the Duke went, accompanied by Richard Cavendish, to Leamington Spa where Augustus and Lizzie Clifford, perennially on the move, were now lodging. Richard had been enlisted in the role of part-time companion, since he was the only one of Burlington and his brothers to be and to remain unmarried. Delicate, suffering from spinal trouble, and formerly the least popular of the brethren, he was much improved in health and manner, though always restless and fidgety. But he was attentive and now seemed genuinely attached to the Duke. Altogether Richard had come to suit him well. The Cliffords were in great distress because their daughter Betty was dying. Her uncle brought a little agate cup for the child. 'She smiled and liked it, but I saw death in her smile.' The company of the omnipresent Bony gave her pleasure. And to Leamington the post brought bad news of Lord Granville's severe illness in Paris. 'How much I feel the want of energy and youth [he was rising 51 now]', the Duke wrote to Harriet, 'and other causes of not being equal to set off directly to see my sister.'

On 19 June the Duke of Devonshire gave a breakfast for the Queen and Prince Albert who had expressed a desire to visit Chiswick. A dreadful storm spoilt the arrival and cast a gloom upon the meal. But the rooms looked grand and the sun came out to allow walking in the grounds. Like most royal persons the Queen was intensely curious and wished to see everything. There were roses everywhere, and children everywhere. But because the Duke was still in mourning for Blanche the guests were limited to his relations and the two Secretaries of State Lord Normanby and Lord John Russell, whom he felt obliged to include. The occasion was very formal and stiff. When it was over the host felt tired but mightily relieved.

Richard Cavendish was ordered by the Doctor to sample the waters of Salzburg for his spine, which was still weak, and the Duke decided to cancel his customary autumnal house parties at Chatsworth, the prospect of which he suddenly loathed, and follow his cousin abroad. Attendance at a reception of the Queen at Woburn in July confirmed the rightness of his decision. The strain of the *état de béatitude* in the royal presence, as Dorothea Lieven put it, the tremendously long dinners and hot rooms, the cold food, the dessert an age coming, the music shocking bad, the band playing nothing but 'God Save the Queen' over and over all evening, with variations 'like music at a fair', Her Majesty out of spirits and the presence of six other dukes in residence turned him smartly against a courtier's existence. As usual the Duke wanted to escape from himself. And so he accompanied Richard Cavendish on yet another European tour which lasted nine months and proved less rewarding than many previous ones.

The summer of 1843 was a particularly hot one and the Duke took refuge in his house in Kemp Town before dashing up to Derbyshire. At a cattle show in Derby he had to make a speech. The applause from the guests was tremendous 'and did my heart good, tho' undeserved'. At Chatsworth he had leisure for reflection. 'What a brilliant time it was at Derby! What respect! O Chatsworth too – new fountain, plants. Why cannot I be satisfied, and who should if I not?' It was the same old story. He had everything this beautiful world could offer, and there was little left to covet. Amplitude had its drawbacks. There were the ever-recurrent financial anxieties. In June 1843 he sold some extensive properties in Kennington, Kensington and Hampstead. Bought in 1825 they had been considered adequate security. He invested large sums in building residential houses on them. The times had turned against such property and he lost all the money spent on the purchase as well as £12,740 on the development.

In the autumn of 1843 the customary annual visit to Bolton Abbey was resumed after a five-year interval. This time it was presumably prompted by the death of the agent, William Carr, who had also been the rector, the last of four successive Carr incumbents of the Abbey church since 1726. His guests were Harriet Granville's two sons, George (or Gink to his family), styled Lord Leveson until he succeeded his father as 2nd Earl Granville in 1846, and Freddy Leveson Gower. Both were beloved by their uncle, but Freddy was the favourite. He was as yet unmarried and on leaving Oxford University to study law in London became a supernumerary companion, on whom the Duke grew greatly to rely. Together they went to the theatre and opera for they shared a love of the stage and music. Tall, oval-faced, with small eyes and a largish nose Freddy's appearance like his manner was genial and endearing. He was popular with all his uncle's contemporaries and Meg Newburgh positively loved him. Soon the Duke was to write, 'I dote on him, and hardly can bear his going.'

In August, while the Leveson Gower brothers were having good sport on the moors, the Duke was instructing Paxton, whom he appointed to succeed William Carr as agent for the Bolton Abbey estate, to draw up plans for extensions to the house. He was well aware that the most ambitious would not be realized, as is indicated by a surviving list of '*Grand Projects for Bolton* which I am prepared to be over-ruled in, on account of expense'. What was permitted and completed within less than a year was Paxton's new north wing, bathroom and all that the heart of man could want. Paxton wrote to his Sarah, 'I am already here as at Chatsworth, not a thing can move but I must be consulted.' The Duke took Paxton up to the famous Strid, the extremely narrow gully of rocks no more than a yard wide through which the gathered waters of the Wharfe rampage with frightening volume. It was here that the novelist Trollope made Lord Lovel induce Lady Anna to leap into his arms, a feat which nearly succeeded in inducing her to jilt her lover, the tailor, in his favour. The result of the Duke's walk with Paxton was the creation by the latter of a duplicate Strid in miniature in the garden at Chatsworth.

In October 1843 the Grand Duke Michael of Russia, the Emperor Nicholas's younger brother, stayed at Chatsworth. The visit was a great success for the charming prince brought back to the Duke memories of the warm-hearted young man who had entertained him at Pavlovsk in 1826. He professed to be enchanted by Coote's music, the little ball held in his honour in the billiard room and a day spent at Hardwick. The Duke wondered if his imperial guest would ever be followed by another even more welcome. Instead a royal visit was imposed upon him which called for an immense amount of preparation, effort, trouble and expense about which he grumbled inordinately. Yet one cannot help wondering if the Duke's complaints were entirely genuine. For what other purpose than to entertain on the grandest possible scale did he, a bachelor, transform Chatsworth from a country house into a palace without parallel in England? For the benefit of his heir and descendants? For self-aggrandizement? Unlikely. He had no need of kudos. His cousin Charles Greville, a guest at the time of the Grand Duke Michael's visit, looked back with regret to the house in its unfinished state when the family lived in three spacious cheerful rooms on the south front. Now these rooms were quite useless in the ordinary run, being gorgeously refurbished with velvets and silks and adorned with marble tables and precious inlaid cabinets, but unoccupied, the windows closed and the curtains drawn lest the sun should spoil the finery. Greville thought that the comfort enjoyed before was ill exchanged for the magnificence which subsequently replaced it. In consequence the house was made so enormous that the Duke could barely afford to live in it and never stayed in it above two or three months in the year. There was a degree of truth in these allegations, for the Duke admitted to feeling happier and far cosier (his own word) in his nutshell at Kemp Town. A greater measure of truth possibly lies in his overwhelming pleasure in the anticipation and memory of entertainment on the grand scale, rather than in the actual participation. Many entries in his journals made this plain.

On 9 November a letter was handed to the Duke at Devonshire House from Colonel G. E. Anson, the Queen's secretary, announcing that, should it accord with His Grace's convenience, it would be very agreeable to Her Majesty and Prince Albert to receive an invitation to visit Chatsworth at the end of the month. 'Ah! a deal of trouble,' the Duke committed to his journal, 'but it's better over, and now is a dull time tho' taking a pleasant bit out of my year.' To Colonel Anson he replied that no event could give him greater satisfaction.

From Paxton and Ridgway he received expressions of dismay. Paxton was appalled by the Queen coming at such a season and Chatsworth being in a state of disorder. However if she could not be put off he would make the best of it. Of course all the garden walks would have to be put right and the approach roads tidied up. Ridgway pointed out the unfinished state of the new wing. Must the Grand Conservatory be illuminated? In that case innumerable lamps would be needed. 'Your Grace's band with additional talent will be better than an expensive military one. 10 coach horses should be hired.' A suggestion relative to the housekeepers raised by the Duke would not be advisable for they would never *unite in harmony*. 'Pray don't visit Chatsworth at present is the wish of Paxton as well as myself. Your Grace's presence would retard what may be necessary to be done.' Ridgway had not been in service for over forty years for nothing and he chose to speak his mind on occasion.

The Duke wrote again to Anson begging to know when his guests would come, how many persons they would bring with them, how long they intended to stay, and also how they would arrive. Furthermore should he submit for approval a list of the members of his family he proposed inviting to meet them? Colonel Anson replied that the Queen and the Prince would arrive on 1 December for three nights only. They would be coming from Drayton Manor, Sir Robert Peel's house in Staffordshire, by train to Chesterfield. They would be attended by one lady-in-waiting, one maid of honour, one state officer (Lord Jersey), two equerries and himself which was not many in the circumstances. The Queen did indeed wish to study a list of the proposed guests and hoped Lord Melbourne would be among them. The Duke duly sent the list of proposed guests who included the Bedfords, Buccleuchs, Rutlands and the Duke of Wellington; the Normanbys, Levesons, Waterparks, Beauvales; Lady Portman, Lord Morpeth, Lord A. Paget, Sir A. Clifford, and Cavendishes galore.

Then Colonel Anson wrote that the carriage the Queen expected to be met by must be a chariot with room behind for two heavy footmen with pistols in their holsters. Lord Jersey wrote on behalf of Anson that he, the Colonel, expected that his apartment should not be far from Prince Albert's. The Duke informed the Colonel that his cousin George Cavendish's wife Lady Louisa must be considered first lady of the house; he hoped she might receive the Queen and be taken in to dinner by the Prince; the Queen's and Prince's rooms would be on the west front with a private staircase to the breakfast room, the library and sitting-rooms and close to a door leading to the pleasure grounds. Finally the Colonel informed the Duke that Her Majesty preferred that His Royal Highness should sit on her other side at meals and not opposite. They would arrive for luncheon. They would like dinner the first night at seven o'clock, and thereafter at eight o'clock. The Queen wished to travel from the station in the Duke's coach-and-six without the royal servants in attendance. Two carriages should follow the Queen's. One inspector and one sergeant of police would accompany and guard the Queen at Chatsworth.

John Gregory Crace, the well-known interior decorator whose father and grandfather had worked for the Prince Regent at the Brighton Pavilion greeted the Duke on his arrival at Chatsworth, which he had deferred till 27th of the month in order obediently to keep out of the way, with the request not to go into the ballroom till the following day. In fact the Duke was positively not wanted either by his own staff or the tradesmen. Nor, once arrived, was he allowed out of the house lest he disturb the tidiness of garden and park. The greenhouses and the Grand Conservatory were likewise put out of bounds. Through the window of a top room he must be content to gaze upon the pearly gravel walks, immaculately raked. The park was indistinguishable from the pleasure grounds in that not a leaf or speck was out of place on the verdant green. The fountains were dancing at an unwonted pace. And Paxton, looking extremely stern, avoided his eye. No wonder the Duke was shunned for when he peeped into the Queen's bedroom he made a scene. The furniture was all wrong and ill arranged and the bed too lugubrious for words. He worked himself into a turmoil of excitement, and made the servants take everything out and move down from one of the Leicester rooms the green satin French furniture and bed which at least looked cheerful.

On the last day of November the relations and friends assembled in good time for dinner. There were thirty-two of them and George Cavendish acted as chief aide-de-camp, never leaving the Duke's side. The Duke of Wellington while driving through the arch to the house recognized a Waterloo medal on the breast of one of the special constables. He immediately accosted the man and asked the name of his regiment. This condescension caused universal pleasure, and appreciative comment by the press. The constable happened to be the only man left alive who had accompanied Wellington to Portugal in 1808. Lord Melbourne looked frail and almost shy. He drank ale at dinner, which his doctor specially recommended him not to do, observing that it was 'an insult to come to a fellow's house & not taste his malt.' There was general concern about the weather.

On the appointed 1 December, Friday, the Queen duly arrived

at Chesterfield station. The Duke in his britschka headed the royal procession to Chatsworth. The cavalcade was cheered by a crowd collected in the park and saluted by a battery of guns established at the Stand. At two o'clock the Queen and Prince Albert lunched alone in the Red Velvet Room which was part of their suite on the west front. Afterwards they met the house guests and received the four county MPs and other local dignitaries in the drawing-room. The Queen was grieved by the sad vacant look in Lord Melbourne's eyes. Sad it undoubtedly was, but nostalgic rather than vacant. The old man was reflecting upon those brief years of his premiership when the virginal Victoria had submitted her every thought, problem and resolution to him, as she was now doing to Albert. After luncheon the party proceeded through the orangery and walked into the garden. Past the not-yet-completed rockery they came to the Great Conservatory, which the Queen declared to be the most stupendous and extraordinary thing imaginable. She at once made a note of its measurements while Paxton imparted technical information to the Prince.

At dinner in Wyatville's dining-room the Queen was quite radiant and merry with the Duke; but poor Lady Louisa Cavendish had an uphill task making small talk with the Prince. After dinner they marched to the ballroom where Crace had put finishing touches to the ceiling enrichments only the day before. The Duke called it 'the room to make a row in', especially when playing charades. On this occasion it echoed to the chatter of the house party and eighty neighbours who had come from near and far for a ceremony which lasted a bare two hours. Before supper the two ex-premiers, taking advantage of their age and renown, retired to bed. The Queen, according to Morpeth,

> was moved to indecorous laughter by the Duchess of Bedford, who has a bad cough, but does not consider it right to indulge it, so she nearly chokes, & the effect was heightened by her head-gear, a velvet military Polish military cap with a diamond egrette which was all of her that remained visible above the folds of her convulsed napkin.

The Queen then retired, and the rest of the company supped at two buffets. Morpeth hoped they did not think they had too little food for their pains. Some had come above twenty miles, only a few dared to dance, and not many were presented to the Queen. One of them was the diarist Mary Frampton who was staying at the Rectory. She observed sourly how unbecoming was the Garter ribbon round the

Queen's plump little figure when she danced. On Saturday evening the efforts of the Duke and Paxton were put to their severest test; and they surpassed anything of the sort displayed at Chatsworth before. The Conservatory was illuminated by 14,000 lamps arranged along the gallery and the ribs of the serrated glass roof. A local newspaper compared it not ineptly to a fairy palace of some eastern tale. The Duke of Wellington was heard to exclaim, 'This is really wonderful – astonishing'. Lord Morpeth on the other hand was critical. While admitting that the illuminations enhanced the size, he thought the beauty of the Conservatory was thereby somewhat diminished. The fabric assumed a too regular aspect and was Vauxhall-like both in sight and smell – what with the exotic flowers and the large house party combined. To everyone's admiration the Queen and Prince were driven, with their host and Lord Jersey seated in the rumble, through the Conservatory from end to end, while the band played the royal anthem. When the party left a large number of ticket holders were admitted. Unfortunately some riff-raff managed to edge a way in, and a few members of the house party rash enough to mingle with the crowd were relieved in the Conservatory of their gold watches. Of the house itself the plate glass windows were left uncurtained so that the public could view the great people reassembled within. The Duke of Devonshire's 'gallant, graceful and manly bearing' which realized the press's 'highest conception of a high born nobleman' was thus visible to thousands.

Dinner in the grand dining-room was much the same as on the previous night with the additional presence of the High Sheriff and gentlemen who presented addresses from the county of Derby to the Queen and Prince. At the second course four enormous castles made of sugar, complete with loopholes and battlements, were placed on the table. At ten o'clock came the climax of the evening. The Queen was led to a window of the state drawing-room at the east corner of the south front to view the spectacle prepared for her in the garden. She stood on a stage which elevated her to the height of her husband standing behind. Three thousand Russian lights had been attached to trees. The Cascade, a staircase of tumbling water, was lit like a ribbon of descending fire. The fountain in the canal pond was brilliantly illuminated. And while cannonfire echoed from the hillside fireworks were visible to thousands in the park and pleasure grounds. The Duke of Devonshire, deeply moved by his own handiwork and the resource of his head gardener, exclaimed, 'Paxton has outdone himself'. The

Duke of Wellington kept repeating with emphasis, 'I have seen Versailles and La Granja the Queen of Spain's, but I never in my life saw anything so beautiful as this fête'.

That night every vestige of debris was cleared away by Paxton who supervised an army of two hundred employees. The old Iron Duke out walking in the garden at seven o'clock the following morning met Paxton still at work and said, 'I came out to view the field of battle, but I find that all the slain and wounded have been removed'. No wonder that he told his host, 'I should have liked that man of yours for one of my generals'.

The Sabbath was a day of happy anti-climax. Moreover the sun condescended to shine fitfully. The Duke had wished the Queen to attend the simple village service in Edensor church, but she chose to worship in the chapel instead. After luncheon the Queen walked, wearing a poke bonnet of purple velvet, to the kitchen garden through a crowd of sightseers. Paxton showed her the small greenhouses, the collection of orchids and *Amherstia nobilis*. With much pride he ushered her into his own house where he presented her with a copy of his *Magazine of Botany*. After dinner for forty-seven covers the band played military airs in the statue gallery and in the music room sacred music, it being Sunday, which the Queen did not much care for. On Monday morning the party broke up. Altogether the visit had passed off without a hitch.

7

Literary Duke
1844–1847

THE YEAR 1844 opened at Devonshire House with the Duke in poor
health. The fogs were bad and his breathing suffered. So he bought
a respirator, an ugly sort of mask, to protect himself from the soot,
smuts and germs that circulated in the cold air. When the bitter weather
abated he called on some Derbyshire neighbours, the Joshua Jebbs, in
Hyde Park Square, accompanied by his bear. The family was at luncheon. The children, particularly the little Gladwyn, were enchanted and
screamed for joy to see the bear's tricks. Not all the bear's outings
went so well. In March the animal slipped its chain and was lost for a
quarter of an hour in the middle of Brighton.

On 10 January the Duke received out of the blue a letter from the
essayist, critic and poet Leigh Hunt. Hunt was undergoing one of the
gravest financial crises of his life. He was all but destitute and in want
of bread. 'There is an old gentleman', the letter ran,

> (the father of my dear friend Shelley) at whose death, which has been twice
> expected during the past year, I shall receive ten thousand pounds; and
> what I would beg of your Grace (if I do not presume too much on your
> sympathy, or on my own very doubtful, I fear, right of addressing you) is
> that the before-mentioned sum might be lent me, upon the understanding
> of returning it as soon as Sir Timothy dies ...

He asked for £200 immediately. The Duke, who received countless
begging letters of the sort, was sympathetic. The very next day he
walked to Edwardes Square in West Kensington where Hunt was

living. There he met for the first time a clever, nervous man, not unlike his nephew Morpeth. The Duke gave him £200 outright and informed him that he had arranged for Ridgway to dispense the £10,000 by four cheques. He took to Hunt who told him how, while awaiting from hour to hour a reply to his letter, he was scared by the liberty he had taken; and confided that he was expecting arrest for debt. 'I was deeply interested in him,' wrote the Duke after walking home for luncheon. Next day a grateful letter from Hunt reached him. 'Poor honourable noble man,' was the Duke's sentiment. By this act of generosity a literary friendship was forged.

When Lady Palmerston wrote congratulating the Duke and Paxton on their arrangements for the Queen's visit to Chatsworth she said, 'How pleased Paxton must be at his success. I hope it won't turn his head – but I believe nothing can.' She was abundantly right. Nothing did. And when the Duke told Georgiana Carlisle that Paxton was so dreadfully busy that 'he rather snubs me in my talk', he meant to indicate on what easy terms master and man were. Paxton was engaged on immense works to the gardens at Chatsworth, setting up the Queen's Rock, producing models of the Strid rocks, laying down pipes and shifting over 100,000 cubic yards of soil to make a new reservoir behind the Stand Wood. A conduit $2\frac{1}{2}$ miles long was dug across the moor to drain water into it. The Duke was half frightened by the immensity of the project, which was to release into the Canal Pond a jet of water to a height exceeding by 80 to 100 feet that at Wilhelmshöhe near Cassel, then the highest in Europe, which he had seen in 1817. After work on the great Chatsworth reservoir had begun rumours reached the Duke at the beginning of May that the Emperor of Russia was expected in England. He was tremendously excited by the possibility of Nicholas visiting Chatsworth. Paxton too was so enthusiastic to finish the monster fountain in time that he pressed on with the work by night as well as day.

At the beginning of June the Duke of Devonshire was at Chatsworth, hoping to rest awhile and inspect at leisure work on the great fountain which he had already dedicated to the Emperor. Suddenly he was greeted with the astounding news that Nicholas had, without further warning, landed in England, and with a letter from the Queen bidding him stay at Windsor Castle to meet the Emperor. After witnessing a quick, initial trial of the fountain which darted higher than 260 feet into the twilit sky he immediately hired a special train from Chesterfield to London. He must at all costs see his beloved autocrat before the formal meeting at court and settle his visit to Chatsworth. On learning in London that this was not to come about he at once wrote informing Paxton of the disappointment which he knew would devastate him after all his efforts. He told him to come to London instead and take a look at the Emperor there.

A couple of days later the Emperor's secretary called to announce that His Imperial Majesty expected the Duke to breakfast with him *'amicalement'* at three o'clock. The Duke went to the Russian Embassy, where the Emperor was staying. There he found Madame Brunnow, wife of the chief gentleman of the Emperor's entourage and 'a confounded old jinglepot', her daughter, the entire Russian suite and two English courtiers deputed by the Queen to shepherd the Emperor. While the Duke was listening to Madame Brunnow's trivialities the door opened and the Emperor strode into the room. 'The joy that he deigned to show on seeing me – his frank noble and cordial reception enchanted me; go, Chatsworth; all was forgotten.' The Emperor led Madame Brunnow into the dining-room while the Duke followed with 'Miss Olga' Brunnow, a good but not pretty girl. Nicholas made a sign that his friend was to sit next to him. At first the Duke felt rather shy, but shyness soon wore off. 'It was no longer the Sovereign of Moscow, it was the Grand Duke Nicolas – the same manner, the same delightful conversation.' The days of their youth together and their happiness, in fact every minute of them recurred to him in overwhelming waves of emotion.

Whether the middle-aged autocrat looked in the eyes of the 54-year-old Duke the same man he was when the Duke commissioned the Prussian sculptor Christian Daniel Rauch's startlingly handsome bust of 'the finest head in the world,' he did not say. On the other hand his cousin Charles Greville, observing him at close quarters, wrote:

> His appearance on the whole disappointed me. He is not so tall as I had heard he was – about 6 feet 2, I should guess; and he has no remains of the beauty for which he was once so celebrated, and which at his age, forty-eight, need not have so entirely faded away; but the cares of such an Empire may well have ravaged that head on which they sit not lightly. He is become bald and bulky, but nevertheless is still a very fine and grand-looking personage. He accepts his age and its consequences, and does not try to avert them by any artificial appliances, and looks all the better for so doing.

A less critical male guest, Lord Malmesbury, described his magnificent features, perfect profile and dark olive complexion with slightly inflamed eyelids over a stout body. But the Duchess of Sutherland, always susceptible to manly looks, referred to his brow of great expanse, eyes as two large lakes and his chest as wide enough to support the globe. She derived the same sort of satisfaction in gazing upon him as she did from contemplating a statue by Michelangelo. The sophisticated and formidable lady hesitated and stammered in his presence; and was intoxicated by his voice. Queen Victoria was seldom abashed by a man, whether emperor or peasant, even when she admired him. With her percipience however she was at once struck by the sadness of Nicholas who 'seldom smiles, and when he does the expression is *not* a happy one.' This view was corroborated by the French Marquis de Custine who added that whenever the Emperor did manage to smile with his lips he could not do so with his eyes, 'a disharmony which denotes a perpetual constraint.'

After the breakfast at the Russian Embassy the Duke dined at Windsor Castle and after dinner managed to snatch an opportunity of eager and more or less private conversation with the Emperor, until they were interrupted by Prince Albert requesting Nicholas to move and sit with the Queen. 'There then was your Eagle,' wrote the Duke to Princess Lieven, 'chained down in an armchair for the whole evening, he between the wife and husband, having to listen to Herr Joachim [the great violinist then not yet 13] and the Queen's fiddlers playing pure Mozart.' Having separated the friends Prince Albert presented the Duke to King Frederick August II of Saxony. This descendant of Augustus the Strong was so very small that few could see that he was there at all. He appeared surprised, fidgety and awkward.

Next day, Tuesday, while the Emperor was driven to Ascot races, where he was received by the public with much enthusiasm and desire to get near him, the Duke remained in his room at the Castle issuing invitations to a forthcoming reception on the Saturday at Chiswick in lieu of the imperial visit to Chatsworth. As soon as he could decently leave Windsor the Duke rushed to Chiswick where in spite of threatening rain the lawns were burnt as brown as chocolate. He went through the usual forty-eight hours of agony for a host which precede all big parties, this one a thousand times worse on account of the special guest. A hurricane of wind blew over everything at Chiswick and the gardeners were driven nearly out of their wits.

In retrospect the Chiswick breakfast was acclaimed a huge success, and by no one more so than the Duke. The day was Italian, blue sky and soft, delicious air. The first question asked by the Emperor on arrival was, 'Where is the elephant?' in reference to the strange beast which had much interested him in 1816. 'Sire, she is dead but there are four giraffes.' Seen from the windows these shy creatures aligned along the edge of the lake made a subject of talk for everybody. Later in the afternoon one giraffe wandered across the water to mingle with the company and caused intense amusement. Coote's little orchestra, so much admired the previous October by the Grand Duke Michael, then struck up a pot pourri which contained tunes intended to awaken old recollections. The Polonaise of the Fiançailles of the Grand Duke Nicholas at St Petersburg was duly recognized and appreciated. Some of the bolder ladies present took courage and advanced to be presented or acknowledged.

Breakfast was held in the Summer Parlour. To create this large apartment the Duke had been obliged to break through a wall separating two lesser rooms and remove a whole chimneypiece. The Summer Parlour was made to resemble a tent, striped red and blue and bearing the emblazoned arms of Nicholas and Victoria. On sloping ceilings the Romanov double-headed eagle was displayed. From the cornice Ns and Vs in crimson and gold stood out above large hanging tassels. Flowers there were in profusion. Footmen wore the rich yellow Devonshire livery. Considering the short time allowed for the elaborate preparations much tribute was due to John Gregory Crace for their contrivance.

The meal did not last long and was very animated. The decoration of the Summer Parlour was universally approved. On leaving the tent the party assembled on the lawn in bright sunshine. In the middle of a large circle enchanted and respectful, stood the Tsar of All the Russias, gracious, attentive, obliging everybody. His attitude was throughout informal, and, according to the *Illustrated London News,* 'somewhat sailor-like.' He lent on his cane or flourished it, such was his enjoyment of the *al fresco* party, in a jolly jack-tar sort of way. As for the Duke he told Princess Lieven, 'I felt that in my life I had never beheld so interesting a sight. A strange event for me! that suddenly, like a meteor, this week of my life should have happened, and certainly the thing I should have most wished for in this world.' And yet throughout practically the whole of this week he was unable to speak more than a few words to his beloved Nicholas, and only once did he see him alone for less than five minutes. Can the reunion have been all that satisfactory?

When time for the Emperor's leavetaking drew near the Duke conducted him to his sitting-room where a book was ready to receive the imperial signature. Some appreciative words were added to it. 'He went away – the departure was very fine but a trial for me. I felt my heart full – but I trust without letting that be perceived.' It was perceived to some extent. The press reporters noticed that on parting the Duke took the Emperor's outstretched hand in both of his; that they then embraced, 'apparently under strong emotion'; and that beady-eyed Prince Albert witnessed the scene with interest.

At four o'clock the next day, Sunday, the Duke went to Buckingham Palace where the Emperor received him quite alone for a few precious minutes. 'He said things so flattering to me, that with all my egotism I cannot trust myself to repeat them. He seemed well pleased with England – the Queen so kind to him, and he praised her warmly and spoke with good will of Prince Albert. Then came Congé, and farewell.' It was their final parting.

In a postscript written years later to the copies he kept of his two diary letters to Princess Lieven, who he knew to be more devoted to her sovereign master than any of Nicholas's countrymen and who to some extent understood his infatuation, the Duke recorded that during the Emperor's short visit to England neither age nor time had deadened his 'feelings' for him. These 'feelings' for the Emperor were necessarily idealized. Whereas Nicholas's affection for his friend had throughout the years always been very genuine but absolutely straightforward, the Duke positively hero-worshipped Nicholas. He admired his Apollonian looks and revered his autocratic instincts which he liked to suppose were exercised in a spirit of liberal benevolence. He saw in their relationship a sort of biblical tragedy, that of twin souls which had they belonged to ordinary mortals would have been indissolubly linked together like those of David and Jonathan. As it transpired, responsibility, in Nicholas's case to a vast empire, in the Duke's to his principality, kept the twin souls far apart, geographically as well as ontologically.

After the Emperor's departure for Russia the Duke of Devonshire meandered home to Chatsworth, feeling restless, unsettled. Some consolation was provided in finishing touches to the monster fountain. After all it had been prepared for Nicholas; it was dedicated to him; it was his entirely, though he never saw it. 'It is a glorious success, the most majestic object and a new glory of Chatsworth. O Paxton! He gave me his statements which I devoured in the evening.' These were less edifying than the splendid works that had incurred them. Indeed another financial crisis was brewing. For four days The Emperor (as the fountain was known) played full out, exceeding 260 feet at times, to the amazement and plaudits of a house party, and the silent astonishment of the neighbourhood assembled without invitation. It was as though every drop of the water was a gratuitous drain upon the Duke's monetary resources. It was extremely worrying.

In June the old auditor Benjamin Currey had presented his employer with a statement showing the degree to which expenditure had exceeded income. The Duke was £1,000,000 in debt. He had passed on Currey's statement to Paxton who by now enjoyed his exclusive confidence in all monetary matters. Hence Paxton's careful and extraordinarily perspicacious summary of Currey's account of affairs. It showed that nearly half his patron's income was absorbed in paying interest on old debts, inherited mortgages and loans which had been accumulating ever since his succession. Paxton blamed the Duke's advisers at the time of his succession for not having paid off those frightful liabilities, including his mother's gambling commitments which had fallen to her son to settle. Paxton's recommendation was that enough of his several estates as would wipe away every farthing of interest owing should be sold; and he suggested the Yorkshire and Irish estates for immediate disposal. He also deeply regretted that he had been partly responsible for the Duke's extravagances, the excuse being that he was wholly unaware of his liabilities.

The Duke settled to go immediately to Ireland preparatory to a sale of Lismore. It was only his second visit in twenty-two years. Ireland was on the eve of the great potato famine, a period of near starvation, poverty and dire distress for hundreds and thousands of the inhabitants. Feeling among the peasantry against absentee English landlords was extremely bitter. The Duke was brave to confront his tenantry at such a time and knew that he would be called upon to show utmost sympathy and lenience and to exercise his personal charm to the full. On 24 July the Duke embarked with Paxton for Kingstown where he landed the following morning. Descending on a beautiful day to the broad valley of the Blackwater, he was struck by the first view of Lismore Castle towering above the swift river. It was so picturesque that his heart had grave misgivings. He dined that evening with the agent Francis Currey, his wife and his pretty sister-in-law, Sophie Hamilton. Coote was obliged to play the piano and a good time was had by all. Poor Currey was ignorant of the fate hanging over him.

On 27th the Duke confided to Currey his intentions. Currey showed great good sense and a quiet intelligence, though doubtless obliged to hide his feelings. The next few days were spent walking with Currey in the woods and visiting Belmont and Dromana, while Coote played to the ladies indoors. On 31st George Cavendish, who was one of the Duke's trustees, arrived by the mail cart from Waterford. His cousin took pleasure in conducting him round the property. Slow, steady old George was pleasant to everybody. With a ball which lasted until three in the morning and several calls on neighbours, the Lismore visit was a success.

It was a success also because George did not at all approve of the Duke selling Lismore. Nor now did the Duke. The beauty of the place, the carefree atmosphere, and the fun associated with it struck him this time more forcibly than ever before. The idea of parting with Lismore had become unbearable, and by the end of the month agreement on all points was reached by Currey and Paxton that Lismore should be kept, but that the Londesborough and Baldersley estates in Yorkshire should be sold to liquidate the Duke's monstrous liabilities. Although Paxton was obliged to give way over Lismore, credit for the general solution of the financial crisis was his, just as the ingenuity in finding a purchaser in George Hudson, the railway king, was his. Hudson was his close business associate. Avid to become a country gentleman he paid without batting an eyelid £100,000 for Baldersley and £475,000 for Londesborough. Six years later he went bust. It is worthy of note that the Duke, on receiving his agent's report that the Londesborough estate was in a high state of cultivation and financially flourishing, gave orders that his tenants should be reimbursed with all the capital they had contributed to this end and that he himself would not appropriate any of the benefit thereby accrued.

Paxton, now formally promoted assistant auditor of the Devonshire estates, was so depended upon in all serious matters that his advice was necessarily sought by the Duke in trivial ones. Meynell the valet, a thorn in the flesh of everyone in contact with him except the Duke was again in trouble and causing embarrassment to his master. On the Duke's journey from Bolton Abbey to Chiswick in early September, they stayed a night at a customary inn in Derby. 'Snug dinner and all comfortable when lo the innkeeper Cuffe, with a complaint about Meynell sending for a woman.' The reprobate valet had, it turned out, established an old love, a barmaid, in this respectable establishment some years previously. Summoning her on this visit Meynell was put out on being told that she had been dismissed in the interval. He made a scene. The innkeeper took exception and complained of the valet's conduct to his master. He talked morals, 'and I cd not help thinking Pecksniff. I said M (which is true) is the best of servants and married men, how could I believe such a thing. Cuffe wanted to prove. I asked what? Has it just happened? I said it was his business to keep improper persons out of his house. Meynell rather elevated said truly they were a pack of fools.' Overhearing the word 'fools' Cuffe was furious. The situation became ridiculous and involved the Duke in a row for which he had no heart. 'Poor Meynell is I support frail and weak, but surely I cannot be supposed to know that, and if I did, can *I* take the high moral line and begin to purify my house by parting with him?' The other servants thought he could, and should. Such is the cant and self-righteousness of subordinates who readily compound for sins they are inclined to by damning those of their fellows they have no mind to.

No one could reproach the Duke for self-righteousness. In this particular case he deplored the inn's treatment of the barmaid and considered that more indulgence would become the virtuous Cuffe. The story illustrates how the Duke always took the part of his servants until they overstepped the limit which even an employer of his lenience could no longer tolerate. Meynell's final transgression of the Duke's lenience was yet to come.

Much of the autumn of 1844 was spent by the Duke of Devonshire in compiling what came to be called the *Handbook of Chatsworth and Hardwick*. This delightful book is a minor classic and in a sense the progenitor of those social histories of country houses so popular with our own generation. Indeed few such present-day histories can vie with it in extraneous information, humour and anecdote. In the opinion of many of the Duke's literary contemporaries it was a great pity that such a master of evocative rendering and also of graceful prose had neglected until so late his true vocation of belletrist. His discerning sister Georgiana had long ago pointed the way in a letter to him.

> Your details ... the way you tell me all I wish to know and nothing I don't, the pound of flesh, no *parler après avoir dit,* the best style of writing with no manner of doing it, makes your correspondence one of the greatest pleasures in the world.

In the summer of 1837 he had confided in his niece Georgiana Dover that the idea of what he called a Chatsworth book had long been germinating in his mind (inclusion of Hardwick and the house at

Kemp Town was supplementary). The *Handbook* positively radiates the
Duke's benevolent disposition, idiosyncrasies, high spirits – and charm.

The two men chiefly consulted before publication were Sir Denis
Le Marchant, a Liberal MP whose editing of Horace Walpole's *Memoirs
of the Reign of George III* had much impressed him, and the author's
librarian John Payne Collier who made comments and read the proofs.
His new literary friend Leigh Hunt was not sent the proofs but was
lent an advance copy in January 1846. In returning it the poet confessed
to have written comments in the margin, but in pencil so that they
might be rubbed out. They are nearly all laudatory, being mild criti-
cisms under trowelfuls of flattery, which make one wonder what his
friend Shelley, that rebel from the ranks of the aristocracy, would have
thought of him had he been alive.

> I fear I have given way to a hundred impertinences, many of which it may
> tax your patience to peruse ... What I think of the book, in general and
> in particular, you will there see abundantly set down; but I must here be
> allowed to add, that it seems to have made me domestically intimate with
> a character as delightful to my particular personal predilections for its
> cheerfulness & powers of enjoyment, as it was already dignified in the eyes
> of my respect, & engaging to my heart & my gratitude. How much would
> that word say to you, which you forbade me the other day to write. What
> volumes of *daily* feelings! – Your Grace's most affectionate servant, Leigh
> Hunt.

Poor Leigh, it was such an uplift to be on intimate terms with a duke.
Yet his gratitude and friendship were absolute as his subsequent letters
faithfully show. He would have been so gratified to learn that his pencil
marginalia were not rubbed out, but on the contrary were inked over
in red by the recipient.

The *Handbook* is made intensively lively by being unashamedly
subjective. It is written in the first person and addressed to the Duke's
sister Lady Granville, 'as if you had asked me for it, thus enabling me
to do the job easy and ennuieless,' he says in a letter to her. And in
the first paragraph of the book under the date 18 July 1844 he starts
off with, 'Dearest Harriet, my plan is to suppose that you are just
arrived, and that I show you every room and corner of the house,'
which they had both known and loved since early infancy. The success
of this technique is demonstrated in there not being a boring sentence
throughout. The reader feels warmly invited to share the author's
memories, his jokes and his simple sense of wonderment.

At once the *Handbook* plunges into reminiscence both feudal and familiar:

> The Sub-Hall was the kitchen in my grandfather's time ... It led to the rigours of the inner courtyard ... What arrivals and departures this room recalls to me ... The charity children engaged at their plum pudding, inspected by our grandmother, Lady Spencer, from above.

He tells what existed before he took the house in hand and launched upon dramatic improvements. The Painted Hall used to be dark and dismal with deal wainscot, painted yellow, where now are lower windows. Memories occur to him of the house when frequented by the generation of Regency bucks. And lovingly he recalls some of the old servants like Hannah Gregory, the housekeeper whose rooms on the south-east side he sensitively refrained from tampering with, being unwilling to disturb the old woman. In the present Stag Parlour she lived and died. In the Plough Room formerly lodged Mrs Bunting and her dog Toujours:

> the most prim, and regular, and punctual of ladies' maids, walking as if she went upon wheels, generally in a riding-habit, passionately fond of horsemanship, and a hard rider. It was supposed by some that she was not averse to manship either; but that, I am persuaded, was a mistake, arising from her zeal in teaching the groom his catechism.

The Little Dining-Room was in his youth the tea-room from the door of which, under a wooden staircase, gave the closet where Mary Austwick, the swarthy, venerable and cross housemaid, reigned. 'Peace be to her soul!'

Considering how susceptible he was to the memories, smells and touches of the past it is somewhat strange that he was quite ruthless when it came to alterations and improvements. He had no pious inclination to preserve rooms because eminent men and women of history had frequented them, no sense of the sanctity of architecture and decoration, or even furnishings of a previous age. He gave away to his friends, Lord and Lady Dunfermline, a whole cartload of Samuel Watson's carvings. This indifference to what he had been brought up to believe was the work of Grinling Gibbons even provoked Leigh Hunt's veiled remonstrance: 'Ay, This it is for a man's heart to be larger than his house.' Everything had to succumb to his taste of the moment and to the greater convenience of living. He tore out sash-bars from window frames and replaced them with sheet glass, a practice he had observed and approved of in Russia, calling it the greatest ornament of modern decoration. It is a wonder he did not eliminate the first Duke's magnificent state rooms on the second floor. He referred to them as 'this dismal, ponderous range of Hampton Court-like chambers,' which he was actually tempted to turn into bedrooms since they deprived him of the most habitable part of the house. Instead he graciously spared them as a museum of old furniture of a poor period and as somewhere to walk about in bad weather. Yet he tampered freely with these famous apartments. He removed the green velvet hangings from the State Bedroom and State Music Room, substituting stamped and gilded leather which, contrary to his view, certainly does not enhance their gaiety.

His desire for cheerfulness was paramount. Dullness and gloom in decoration must be done away with. In spite of this conviction he created the Oak Room on the ground floor out of panels of carved woodwork, the fittings of some German monastery and the wainscot of an old-fashioned pew, than which no apartment in the house looks more dark and melancholy. Convenience was another matter. This he achieved in numerous respects. The three corridors on two floors of the inner quadrangle were fashioned out of open colonnades which he deemed bleak and dreary. His new inner corridors, wider as well as covered, were an undeniable asset in comfort, and afforded passageway hitherto reached through living-rooms and bedrooms.

The *Handbook* reveals the Duke's meticulous attention to detail, repeated attempts to get things right, and good-natured willingness to admit mistakes and even failures. For example he had a dedicatory inscription for the Painted Hall composed by his friend the Provost of Eton, not without first submitting the Latinity to his mother's friend Henry Luttrell, wit and poet, for approval. As for the multi-coloured pavement of the downstairs North Corridor he went to infinite pains with the design which had to be nicely calculated to divert the eye from the inequalities of the inner court. The marbles were provided by one Leonardi, whose workshop stood inside the Forum at Rome. Through the good offices of Ralph Sneyd, then in Rome, the Duke sent minute instructions. He enclosed a plan made by his clerk of works who wanted two feet added to the width of the ornamental part. He stressed that attention should be given by Leonardi to the principal centres by making a prominent circle or square opposite the steps leading from the Sub-Hall to the corridor. He wished to know whether the pavement should be fixed on slates and polished before it could be laid or whether it would be sent in bits. As for the Billiard Room walls they necessitated several experiments. At first he covered them with white scagliola but that turned out lustreless; then he took to paint and varnish, rubbed down like a coach panel. This looked all right but it soon turned yellow, breaking into small crevices, like an old coach in fact, and had also to be scrapped.

As for Hardwick Hall the author of the *Handbook* warns his sister that, 'though it appears old and unaltered, there has been a great deal done in my time to the house that Bess of Hardwick built.' This was by no means all to the bad. The house was crying out for repairs when the young Duke succeeded. He answered it in a generous and tactful response in nearly all respects. Exceptions were the blocking of a few windows in the gallery and replacement of certain window quarries with larger panes. He had much of the Elizabethan needlework mended and 'revived like magic' by John Gregory Crace. He did a good deal of shunting of pictures and tapestries to and from Chatsworth and introduced from that house state beds, chairs and stools, notably into the High Great Chamber where he remembered an eccentric neighbour once working herself into believing she was the Queen of Scots. The Duke's records of work done at Hardwick have been of inestimable help to the National Trust custodians of the house in their recent endeavours to reassemble the historic contents.

The Duke was devoted to Hardwick which he associated very largely with his mother Duchess Georgiana who spent some of the happiest part of her harassed life there, and with his niece Blanche Burlington who likewise revelled in the romance of the ancient structure and picturesque setting, and recreated the flower garden. 'Not having lived with her,' wrote her bereft uncle, 'it is the only recollection she has left me, and in all places her irreparable loss is equally felt.' His visits to Hardwick were never for long stretches. The cold, no matter how many fireplaces were made to blaze, was an almost perennial deterrent.

No. 1 Lewes Crescent, Kemp Town, was a very different affair to the great hereditary palaces. It was the Duke's refuge when the burdens of Chatsworth, Hardwick, Chiswick and Devonshire House became too oppressive. It was his toy thing, his exclusive creation, albeit on a small scale, his marine residence; his Petit Trianon, filled in its turn to overflowing with treasures all amassed by their owner. At Kemp Town he could momentarily forget his state of health and his duties, political, charitable and social. Pursued by stifling hay fever he could find midsummer respite in the refreshing breezes that blew along the top of the cliff. 'Are we to despise it because it is so small?' he asked Harriet, and answered for her, 'I have never repented the selection of it.'

'Hail to the volumes that are to come,' wrote Leigh Hunt as he closed the *Handbook*. Volume II was to concern Chiswick and Devonshire House, and be dedicated to sister Carlisle; and volume III to concern Bolton Abbey and Lismore Castle. Alas, although the second volume was sketched out, neither was written.

The Duke of Devonshire had never cared for the Duke of Wellington, quite apart from their political antagonism. In the House of Lords they sat on opposite benches, regarding each other as foes. Yet circumstances, especially at successive courts, had constantly brought them together. When both were dining at the Pavilion the Whig Duke had often found it difficult even to be civil to the Tory Duke on account of his retrogressive views. Yet they attended each other's parties and held one another guardedly in mutual respect.

In January 1845 the Duke of Devonshire was invited to stay at the Duke of Wellington's Hampshire seat Stratfield Saye for three whole days. 'How I am to bear them patiently I don't exactly perceive,' he wrote. 'But it is very kind of the Great Duke to ask me, and I will behave well.' He drove from Devonshire House by way of Basingstoke in time for luncheon on 20th. At once he was writing, 'No, nothing was ever so cordial and kind as the dear old Duke.' As so often happens visits most dreaded turn out the most enjoyable. The Queen and Prince Albert were the guests of honour. Of his host's family Lord Douro the eldest and Lord Charles Wellesley, the second son, and his wife had been summoned. The Bedfords, the Ashburtons and '2 gents unknown' both county MPs, were staying. At dinner they sat down thirty, waited upon by thirty very fat men. The food was good, but the dining-room, which is not large, was so hot and glaring that Devonshire nearly died of it. At luncheon next day the Queen who was 'adorable, in great beauty and much grown,' sent for Winterhalter's prints of her two eldest children, which she gave to him. The Duke had to admit that he enjoyed himself a good deal. When he got home to Chatsworth he felt like a condemned man in his cell.

His eyes were giving trouble. The doctors advised that a change and trip to Paris would do him good. He had not been abroad for three years and was getting stale. On reflection he decided that his constant carping signified a sad difference befallen him since the previous winter. Rapid old age was clearly possessing him. The weight upon his eyes too was accentuated by a heavier one upon his spirits. Yet there was no apparent reason for the latter. His affairs were going well; Paxton, the mainspring of his life, was perfection: 'To me a friend, if ever man had one.'

In Paris he renewed a number of acquaintances with old friends, including Dorothea Lieven, now rather blind. And of course Lady Hunloke quickly fell into line. A grand event was his introduction to the Palais de Luxembourg as a permanent Fellow of the French Senate by the Duc Decazes, Louis XVIII's old minister. Although greatly honoured to become a member of 'Le Cercle' the Duke of Devonshire professed that it was but the reparation of many years' neglect; and he wondered whether previously he had not been blackballed. Decazes made a fine speech of inauguration, but an immense blunder in referring to the Comte de Paris as the Duc de Bordeaux which was the title of the legitimist claimant to the throne, Henry V. A no less important though less enjoyable event was a visit to Stevens the dentist, who snapped off the old grinders close to the gum and supplied him with new. Even so he managed to dine out, 'most imprudently, refusing nothing. My own imprudence is enough to kill me sometimes.' He was punished by a bad cold which obliged him to stay indoors and reflect upon old sins committed in the environment of the Place Vendôme.

> Be still, old nerves, only now profit O my soul from all these warnings – and if I should recover, mend. I saw the blaze and the tops of the candles and girandoles [of the Hotel du Rhin opposite] from the back room of my apartment – and I knelt down, and thought of former times – and prayed that an impression might be made upon me before it is too late.

Rashly the patient rose from his sickbed to dine with the Duc Decazes and twenty-five celebrities in honour of his permanent membership of 'Le Cercle'. He was made a great fuss of and complimented by Victor Hugo on his French. Suffering from a bad cough and wearing his ludicrous respirator he braved the east wind to gaze at the Luxembourg lilacs in their full glory. He decided that one more Paris party and he would be finished off.

In the 1840s the Duke became closely involved with railway matters and speculation. Always a positive enthusiast for new ventures he was ever ready to profit from their development. In this he was unlike the majority of his landowning friends, who abominated the very idea of trains, those ugly, puffing iron monsters violating country estates. 'I am in raptures with your enthusiastic account of the railway,' he told Georgiana Carlisle. 'O wonderful triumph of mind and skill, O happy we to have lived to see the dawn of such brilliant achievements.'

In May of 1845 a company called The Manchester, Buxton, Matlock and Midlands Junction Railway was formed, of which George Cavendish, MP for North Derbyshire, was chairman and Hudson and Paxton were directors. The engineer was George Stephenson, inventor of *The Rocket* steam engine and founder of the railway system. The purpose of the company was to complete communication by rail between Manchester and the eastern counties by building a trunk line to join the existing Midland line from London to the north of England. Ambergate, north of Derby, was to be the junction. The proposed double-track line was to run through either the lovely Wye or the Derwent valley. Surprisingly the Duke of Devonshire in the company's prospectus gave his unqualified approbation for the line to run for several miles through his lands, which would have meant the Derwent valley and the Chatsworth demesne. The neighbouring Duke of Rutland, whose Haddon Hall was situated in the Wye valley, was however strongly opposed to either choice. When Stephenson sought to get parliamentary sanction for the Wye route, Rutland raised such vociferous objection that he got it turned down. He then offered to support his neighbour Devonshire in opposing the Derwent alternative. He was amazed to receive that duke's response that on the contrary the company were 'welcome to come through any part of his park' they chose. Furthermore, to give positive support to these sentiments, he offered a subscription of £50,000 to the company.

We may take it that the Duke of Devonshire was not swayed by Paxton's considerable interest in the venture for he was never the man to allow others to make up his mind for him. Certainly he earned tremendous popularity among the local villages for his promotion of the railway in this remote part of Derbyshire. Nevertheless in permitting the railway to run between the house and Edensor village he stipulated that it should not be within smell of the house. It must accordingly go underground at strategic intervals in a series of short tunnels with a station at the north (Baslow) end and another at the south (Rowsley) end of the series, so that he might use whichever suited his own journeys' arrival or departure. By this ruse he need never go through the tunnels which he held in abhorrence.

The cunning Duke of Rutland, seeing how favourable terms and compensation seemed a likely outcome of negotiation with the company, changed his tune and tried to get back the Wye valley route underneath Haddon. The MBM and MJR company's scheme, after appearing before Parliament four times, was passed in 1848. There was great rejoicing in the towns of the upper Derwent valley. But because of a shortage of capital the Ambergate section of the line got no further north than Rowsley where in 1863 it branched north-west to Buxton, passing indeed under Haddon Hall and up the sublime Monsal Dale. It must not be assumed that the Duke of Devonshire was indiscriminately in favour of trains passing through beautiful landscape and spoiling the parks of country houses in order to curry popularity with the masses. This was far from the case. During the very summer when he was pressing for a line through Chatsworth's park he opposed for all his worth a projected Newark-to-Chesterfield line intended to pass by Hardwick Hall. Through his forceful opposition it was thrown out, which shows once again the authority which great landowners could still exercise in matters concerning their own interests. The news was brought to him and Paxton by George Cavendish while they were playing billiards at Chatsworth and caused much jubilation.

In September the Duke paid a first visit to Cullercoats, a small fishing village or hamlet near Tynemouth, Northumberland. To Cullercoats Mrs Arkwright used to be taken when a child by her Kemble parents on the rare occasions when the theatrical manager and his actress wife could afford a holiday among the rocks and sands. She always had a great affection for the place and when sad and delicate in old age her husband Robert bought for her Cliff House overlooking the small harbour and the smacks. The Duke was at once captivated by the tranquillity and invigorating air of Cullercoats. He passed the days walking to Tynemouth, visiting the Benedictine priory, returning along the shore, or bathing in the sea from a tent. So deep an impression did Cullercoats make upon him that in an appendix to the *Handbook* he contrasted the animation of Tyneside with the tranquillity of the tiny resort where Mrs Arkwright had her house. It is a highly evocative passage written in a prose style limpid and unadorned.

> The immense traffic of the Tyne, the steamboats and steamtugs coming, going, towing, propelling; the foreign fishing craft, and, above all, the daily preparations of a fleet of herring cobles, containing a hardy enterprising race, watched by devoted women from the cliff, give endless action to the view: low tide displays reefs of rocks, on which the waves rage or sport with a brilliancy of light and colouring unseen elsewhere: – the purest sea, the boldest outlines of stony, projecting, rambling places. To step

from one rock to another, to repose on them, to watch the varieties of animated and inanimate nature, are perfect enjoyments, undisturbed, scarcely remarked, in the midst of a primitive and well-disposed population. To describe the beauty of the rocks in sunshine, with liquid pearls trickling and sparkling over their seaweed vegetation, is impossible.

He was sorry when after a fortnight he had to leave this isolated spot for Castle Howard, but happy that the visit had restored the fragile friendship, that *amitié amoureuse,* lost to him so he thought over silly politics and Mrs Arkwright's lamentable diversion into Toryism. Henceforth he was to see much of her at Sutton Scarsdale, which was but a stone's throw from Hardwick.

On 7 January Lord Granville died. After retirement in 1841 from being ambassador to Paris he and Harriet had wandered round the Continent and rented a château, La Jonchère near Versailles, before returning to settle in London. The Adonis of extraordinary beauty who for twelve years had been the love of Lady Bessborough and in whose 'eyes I have looked my life away,' as she wrote beneath his portrait, passed his last years, half paralysed, racked by gout, and ministered to by his adoring wife. Harriet, once so sprightly and acerbic, retreated into an agonizing grief round which like a cocoon she wove a mesh of such intense piety that even her brother, himself prone to religiosity, was never able to penetrate. Indeed he admitted a year later that her engrossment had made his old age very different from what he expected. Swathed in black and seldom leaving her room where she pored over biblical texts behind drawn blinds Harriet turned into the paradigm of a mid-Victorian widow. Her children and her brother remained consistently good to her but only the memory of her lazy and not very bright, vain and self-satisfied husband was a solace to her.

On 4 August 1846 a plaintive chord is struck in the journal: 'Torn to pieces about my plans.' The Duke had decided to travel again, and his ostensible reason was to save money. In what he called 'the first year of reform' at the instigation of Currey and Paxton which led to the sale for a huge sum of the Yorkshire estates, his annual surplus of expenditure over income did not allow him to raise the £8,000 needed 'to brush up and restore poor old Devonshire House,' which had become 'so very dingy and out of repair ... But by abstaining from Chatsworth entertainment for an autumn and by resolution not to purchase anything on my travels I shall save much more than that sum.' It was the usual hallucinatory estimate of the manic spendthrift.

At first Fullerton agreed to go abroad with him. On 8 August he chucked. On 10th the Duke wrote, ' I am all excited because there is still a chance of Romilly meeting me at Brussels.' Frederick Romilly was the sixth son of Samuel, the great jurist and philanthropist. He was a 36-year-old officer in the Scots Fusilier Guards. Although he declined to be the Duke's secretary he consented to accompany him to Germany and Austria until October when his leave would be up, 'for which [wrote the Duke] I feel the sincerest gratitude . . . and if his nature corresponds with his sublime outside, and people say it does, I shall think myself very lucky.' A Dr O'Grady from Paris, a *maître d'hôtel* Kulbach from Switzerland, a French chef Aberlin, the valet de chambre Meynell, and two footmen Henry Bland and John Hardy, had to 'suffice' as modest retinue and, oh, the Skye terrier Bob and mongrel Tom, both perfect in their ways, must not be overlooked. To save money – for after all the Duke knew the proposed route so well – he engaged no courier. A travelling post-chaise, a britschka and a fourgeon composed the vehicles.

Having decided to go to Italy, he wrote, since Romilly's engagement was not going to last, to a Mr Erskine, who had been recommended as companion, to join him at Milan. In Munich he met by appointment Paxton who was on a two months' railway tour of Germany and Austria with three companions, George Stephenson the great inventor and founder of railways, Richard Barrow and John Cottingham, a cousin of Sarah Paxton and now the Duke's agent at Hardwick. From Munich the faultless Romilly left for home and was much missed. '*En revanche,*' the Duke, forgetting his resolution made in England, plunged into an orgy of spending – an altarpiece, a statuary group, entitled *Swan Song,* of a girl with a woodman by the leading German neo-classical sculptor Ludwig Michael von Schwanthaler, and quantities of glass for Chatsworth.

Sure enough he was invited to an audience of the King of Bavaria on 17 September, followed by dinner next day at one o'clock. He arranged that Paxton and Stephenson were also invited. The latter, who was extremely shy at meeting the King, did his best to avoid it. His modesty and charm however captivated the monarch who both questioned and buttered him much. The Duke sat next to the King's eldest daughter Princess Mathilde, Hereditary Grand Duchess of Hesse and by Rhine. There were present, amongst others, the Emperor of Austria and the King's old sister, the Duchess of Leuchtenberg. No wonder Stephenson felt daunted by the plethora of royalty. He was nonetheless gratified by King Ludwig asking for his and Paxton's autographs; and furthermore by the attention of the Duke of Devonshire, who greatly admiring escorted him downstairs and handed him into his carriage. The next day the railway trio were conducted round the Botanical Gardens and the King's palace while the Duke drove to Berchtesgarten and bought £50 worth of wash-hand basins and jugs at a glass shop. On parting with Paxton and his companions the Duke felt flat.

In Milan the 26-year-old Mr Erskine arrived from England. Henry D. Erskine was undoubtedly very gentlemanlike but proved a poor alternative to Romilly. Inoffensive and insipid he lacked enthusiasm; was apathetic and unbearably taciturn. On receipt of a letter from Francis Currey that the Irish distress over the potato crisis was abating the Duke rejoiced. Whereupon Mr Erskine made his first joke which was not a success. He hoped that 'having got over the potatoes we shall soon get over the Po.' The passage over that river proved execrable. En route for Pisa the Duke ran into good Francesco Bienaimé in a street at Carrara. With the sculptor-dealer he settled for four additional statues for the west front at Chatsworth, namely *Telemachus, Minerva, Adonis* and *Flora.*

In Pisa he found not a single house undamaged by a recent earthquake. Three weeks were spent in Florentine society before Rome was reached on 3 December. Here he found the rooms engaged for him too high and not at all to his liking. 'Must try and get command of myself.' He felt unwell. Of this visit he kept a scrapbook of exquisite water-colour drawings by Carelli, prints, billets-doux and non-doux, and a long list of the English and foreigners he consorted with. He drove to the rebuilt basilica of St Paul's-Outside-the-Walls which he had known before the disastrous fire of 1823, and thought the enormous new columns of Egyptian alabaster glorious and beautiful beyond words. He went to the studio of 'my old Gibson' whose sculpture had improved wondrously, and to Carlo Trebbi's shop where was 'a Phocas column and an alabaster table that I must, must have. Ahi!' Needless to say he did have the giallo column and not one, but two alabaster tables for £150.

On 9 December he was granted an audience by the Pope which he recorded in detail:

Was ordered to Quirinale *alle 7 ore,* so we dined at 4 and then I went in black evening dress, cocked hat, to see Pio IX. Up an early circular staircase to a long gallery with Landscapes of sea ports. There waited several men in violet silk; a gilt embroidered diplomat with a paper in his hand & Prince Doria came and had his audience first, I being ten minutes before my time. Next when I into the room, the Pope seated with his back to the wall, a table before him with very strong light from shaded lamp which made the rest of the room dark. He rose on my coming in, and advanced a little way. His hand was out but I did not attempt to touch or kiss it. He then sat down and posted me the chair opposite to him. *Saint Père,* said I, *j'ai le malheur d'être extrémement sourd.* He smiled and then began to talk in the purest French, and pitching his melodious voice so well that not a word escaped me, or had to be repeated by him. Still I put my hand to one ear, and leaning on the table hardly sat to be sure of hearing him. Noble manners of the world, benevolent spirited countenance, knew I had been here formerly, talked of the Duchess of Devonshire, asked my plans here – Naples, said I, bad times for travelling, hope to remain unless obliged to return by parliament [?merely] in office of Ireland.

He asked with much interest about Ireland, that is about the distress and whether the Government would not be able to relieve it. I said this and the last were of accord. There could be no politics on such subjects of money. He asked about emigration to America, and soon, much too soon, ended the short interview which he stopped with excessive grace at about the same time that Doria's had lasted. It appears to me that I talked too much. I go on contented because it is a subject I have clenched and am unwilling for another to be started.

Below this succinct but vivid account the author drew a little pen-and-ink sketch of himself, almost leaning from his chair, left leg stretched behind him, left hand flourishing the cocked hat, right elbow propped on the table top, ear straining to catch every word of the Holy Father wearing the calotte facing him. 'I did not go out again. My day had tired me, and the rain came down in floods,' he concluded.

'Sad floods. The *Corso* full of boats. Higher than this has not been known for 35 years,' was an entry of the following day. Nevertheless he managed to watch the Pope officiate at Mass and was struck by the devout expression of his face on looking up. He was impressed by the apparent sanctity of this able but most temporal of nineteenth-century pontiffs. On New Year's Day of 1847, with a roll of bread in his pocket, having missed breakfast, he accompanied Madame de Flahault to a window in the Quirinal Palace to see Pius IX receive congratulations from all Rome. There were processions and countless crowds and everywhere signs of cordiality. Although there had been rain the moment the Pope made his appearance the sun came out.

From 10 to 26 January he was in Naples. One fine morning he hired a private steamer for an expedition to Capri. It was a signal failure. Firstly, Kulbach the butler fell into the sea from the pier as they were starting and had to change clothes on being fished out. Secondly, Lord Kinnoull had such a belly ache that he had to be put ashore. Thirdly, near Capri a violent storm of rain set in which made it impossible to approach the blue grotto. They were consoled by the excellent luncheon in the cabin provided by the incomparable Aberlin, prince of chefs.

On leaving Naples the Duke took Gabriele Carelli, who cherished a great desire to install himself as resident artist at Chatsworth, back to Rome for the horrible carnival. And so, after witnessing Signor Arban rise in his balloon from the piazza Terme di Diocleziano, he set off at the beginning of March for home, spending a month in Paris on the way. There he dined with King Louis-Philippe and Queen Amélie, and visited the painter Winterhalter's studio, which resulted in a commission. On the way to Boulogne in May the britschka was upset off the road, falling on its side against a tree. The doctor was much cut and hurt, John Hardy's foot bruised but Meynell unhurt. 'Never shall I forget the horror of seeing the carriage upside down, far below, and not knowing if the occupants were killed.' It was a mercy the accident was not worse. Carelli had time to do a detailed sketch, with key to the figures involved, on the scene.

8

Vicarious Triumphs
1848–1850

———————◆———————

WITH ADVANCING AGE the Duke of Devonshire in spite of declining health and decreasing friends was carried away on a spate of entertaining and being entertained. A sense of unease had been brought about in English society by threats to the stability of the July Monarchy across the Channel. The news from Paris was distracting. If the Citizen King Louis-Philippe was to lose his throne in favour of a republic, what next? In March 1848 the poor King and Queen fled from a back door of the Tuileries, crossed the Channel to Newhaven disguised as Mr and Mrs Smith and were given sanctuary by Queen Victoria at Claremont. Dorothea Lieven and her lover Guizot, the French historian and statesman, escaped with them. The Duke found the couple in London lodgings, the Princess lying on a couch, the minister retired into a corner with the newspapers. She narrated their adventures as Mr and Mrs Roberts, an artist and his wife, her diamonds sewn in her bustle. It was sad to see this proud lady in her fallen state.

At first the Duke was overcome by certainty that this revolution portended an end to rank and property in England. He even feared for his beloved Chatsworth's security. He had forgotten that social upheavals on the Continent did not necessarily have an echo in these islands. He had reached that stage of life when the horrors of the future are too readily magnified. Yet he was not by nature one to throw up the sponge. He was one to go down fighting with flag at full mast. So the year 1848 which toppled thrones and shook the foundations of noble dynasties in Europe was marked on the Duke of Devonshire's calendar by a superabundance of balls, dinners, routs and breakfasts. It was *après moi le déluge* in defiance. On 7 January comes an entry in the Duke's journal, 'My second ball and dinner'; on 21st 'my fourth and prettiest ball'; and on 27th of the same month the description of a musical evening he gave at 1 Lewes Crescent, Kemp Town, which began with an overture by Coote and included extracts from Verdi, Rossini, Bellini, Meyerbeer, Markull and Mendelssohn. It is no wonder that in this whirl of social activity an ageing Peter Pan got swept off his feet by the prettiest young lady he had ever encountered.

Florence Anderson's father had been a clergyman and her widowed mother was a daughter of Lord Teignmouth. With Mrs Anderson the Duke engaged in a discreet flirtation which was a blind to inclinations elsewhere. When the mother realized their real target she politely but firmly refused to let her daughter accompany the Duke in his carriage to a *matinée musicale* in Brighton. But he was not to be put off and made his nephew Freddy Leveson Gower chaperon him on several calls at 'nice' Mrs Anderson's dwelling. The trouble was that in order to gloat over Florence he was obliged to sit up till four in the morning at young people's balls. And this proved exhausting as well as unprofitable. Florence's engagement to Lord Alwyne Compton who took holy orders (he was eventually to be Bishop of Ely) came as a nasty shock. The Duke pronounced him a stick, and a dullard, and derived secret *schadenfreude* in assuming, what turned out to be the case, that their marriage would be unhappy.

Domestic troubles relentlessly harass people who spoil their employees. No sooner had the Duke rebuked and forgiven his Chiswick gardener for maliciously and untruthfully accusing his fellow servants of selling 'my bouquets' for £2 each (surely an exorbitant price for 1848) than the following disclosure relating to the Swiss master of ceremonies was brought to his attention.

> I got a letter from Kulbach's son Edward who sends to beg to see me and tell me about some disgraceful transactions. I consented to see him thinking it must be the bouquets continued; but, alas, it was to accuse his father of bad conduct towards him, his brothers and sisters of having a house in BJ Square full of prostitutes, and last of all, of having debauched at Paris his own daughter from school. The last accusation enraged me to such a degree that I wd hear no more and refused all belief of such an absurd and horrible story.

But the incredulous Duke was obliged to believe it. He sent for

Kulbach senior who after much prevarication and denial confessed. 'I was exceedingly shocked and told him so – and that of course we must part.' After confiding the dreadful affair to Freddy he charged Kulbach with a letter to Benjamin Currey, who, he assured him, would be indulgent and advise him what to do. Currey came bustling down to Chiswick. It was agreed that Kulbach should go abroad with permission to say to the other servants, by way of face-saving, that he was obliged to do so on family business, and that his return being uncertain he had to leave the Duke's service. How many employers in a case of this sort would have behaved so temperately and considerately?

On 11 March the Duke talked with Benjamin Currey about Erskine's permanent engagement as secretary. He had got used to the man's taciturnity and recognized his good qualities which were kindness, staidness and reliability. Currey's advice was usually sound. He approved of Erskine being taken on. He was a wise old man, obstructive at times as was the nature of a conscientious agent who must often put his employer's interests before his employer's desires. On 13th the journal records: 'A dreadful day! Currey struck with apoplexy at 12 – died at 4 in H of Lords. Oh! cruel, ruinous event. Was to have dined with Dow Bedford – O impossible. George, Cav, Erskine very kind to me.' The bitter grief, although genuine enough, was not unflavoured with a touch of self-pity. On 15th Paxton arrived, showed noble, disinterested conduct and relieved the Duke's mind by his warm praise of the deceased's son. William Currey was duly made auditor and solicitor in his father's place.

Good Friday was spent in bed with a sore throat, reading through all his journals kept since 1821 and scratching out 'the worst bits' – whatever these were –

> but they are very useful to me some times. When I'm dead it will not signify much who reads them, if anybody should have patience enough. They are not like letters. I *can* write good letters – but a journal is very different. You cannot realise your object in [re] touching.

He was not of course being candid in pretending that no one might read his diaries. He would not have carefully preserved them if he seriously believed they would be ignored. Certainly he was aware of a basic rule in diary keeping, and he was not often guilty of infringing it. Whenever he did so the retouching showed through and lameness was the inevitable consequence. He avowed that a good diary ought to be like correspondence with a clever person. And for many years he had that person in his sister Harriet. But in her widowhood the flow of their letters slackened and all but stopped; moreover enthusiasm for his journal was not otherwise enhanced. Without Harriet's interest in his daily rounds and thoughts the impulse for recording them correspondingly waned for a time. He even liked to fancy that William might after his death burn all that he had written; and in a fit of disgust actually destroyed three months of the journal. He was in a destructive mood, and also jettisoned an immense number of his parents' letters from 1784 to 1801, claiming that what were left would contribute enough to the social history of that epoch. Luckily the Duke's mood did not last long.

On 12 October Lord Carlisle died after prolonged agonies from that most aristocratic of complaints, gout. He was a good man who had played little part in public life; and a good husband of an arranged marriage in so far as he begot thirteen children which Hart thought excessive although he came to love most of them. As early as 1822 Hart told Georgiana that he hoped her next child would be her last and then she must 'retire from business' for child-bearing was 'so very dangerous a pastime'. Morpeth wrote his uncle touching letters about his father's three days of gradual sinking, surrounded by an affectionate family, at peace with God and secure in futurity. 'And here am I, vile slave of indulgence and worldly passions, broken, humbled, prostrate.'

One senses that there was by now something perfunctory in the Duke of Devonshire's protestations of his unworthiness in God's eyes like the repetitive tunes from a musical box denoting habit rather than conviction. He fairly poured them into the confidential pages of his resumed journal, as it were in loyalty to the dead Blanche who had in her lifetime so persistently evoked them with the aid of Dr Beamish. Indeed immediately after her death his religiosity had reached fever pitch. When a visiting clergyman preached at him from the pulpit of Chiswick church as the 'Mammon of Unrighteousness' he was plunged into such a turmoil of guilt and self-denunciation that he nearly lost his reason. The offensive accusation turned him temporarily against all social activities, to which as we have seen he returned in full measure in a sort of desperate bravado on the outbreak of the 1848 troubles on the Continent. If every civilized nation, he decided, was going to the dogs he might as well enjoy himself in a final fling and be damned to potato Beamish.

A far worse blow than the deaths of Benjamin Currey and Lord Carlisle was that of Mrs Arkwright. In April 1848 he called on her at

Sutton. Frail and wearing her blue spectacles she lamented that she was 61 and that her daughter, the beautiful, forthright and frigid Fanny was still unmarried. Towards the end of the year he heard bad tidings of her health, followed by a letter from her so ambiguously phrased that he failed to understand its meaning. On 2 March 1849 he wrote in the journal the words, *'In great grief with Mrs. Arkt.'* underlined. And on 12th,

> No better – and struck down today by news of Mrs. Arkwright's death. I had known how very ill, but settled that paralysis would be conquered; her letter understood now, and all that people say. Of all the strong attachments I have had in my life mine to her has been the purest the truest the most salutary. O how I loved her!

It was true. His love for her had been platonic but emotional, free from flirtation yet constant (notwithstanding the silly tiff over politics). There was little he kept from her. She knew about his liaisons, sympathized when they went wrong, even giving him a ring the day that Eliza first miscarried, wept with him when he mourned Blanche, and shared his enthusiasm for his houses (though herself devoid of taste having, he maintained, ruined Sutton Scarsdale), his collections (though her attitude to works of art was philistine) and of course his musical parties to which she often contributed with her singing (which he criticized – 'I cannot bear her high notes').

As usual when in deep sadness he sent for friends to comfort him. Good Mrs Lamb his half-sister was first on the scene as an old admirer of Mrs Arkt. And as usual he wisely sought distraction. He went to Ealing Park and made Mrs Lawrence, a plantswoman, show him her *Amherstia nobilis,* which the tiresome woman had admirably succeeded in making bloom. He simply had to congratulate her. The flower was of miraculous beauty, although the actual plant, which at first he thought was the wrong sort – it wasn't, it was the right sort, and really grand – she had forced up very quick. Kind Mrs Lawrence sent him a spike in bloom, and another to Windsor Castle. 'It is fine beyond my expectations, the crimson stalks! the gold labellum!' And then he went to Mr Byam Martin's to see a glorious camellia also finer far than his own. Probably as a result he got the two *Camellia reticulata* which still grow at Chatsworth.

The Duke had a lithograph made of a posthumous drawing of Mrs Arkwright's head by Sir George Hayter. It was adapted from an early portrait at Sutton Scarsdale. The round, youthful head, with straight hair parted in the middle, wears a bonnet and wide ribbons under the chin. The large eyes look upward. The slightly parted lips suggest that the subject was taken singing. It is a childlike, guileless likeness of a pretty, not strictly handsome woman, perhaps a bit too soulful. Under the drawing are written in the Duke's hand the fervent lines,

> So came thy ev'ry glance and tone
> When first on me they breathed and shone
> New, as if brought from other spheres,
> That welcome – as if loved for years.

The Duke had 120 copies taken and distributed to the deceased's many friends and admirers, whose letters of thanks he stuck into a special album dedicated to her memory.

In May of this year the Duke received a long and entertaining letter from William Makepeace Thackeray. He had met the famous novelist on the Lake of Geneva in the summer of 1839 at a party where the historian Sismondi bored him very much and which even the tentative advances of a certain Madame de Tracy did not enliven ('if the Geneva ladies were not renowned prudes I should think her fond'). He and Thackeray shared the friendship of Caroline Norton, seeing each other from time to time at her London house, without forming an intimacy. Like thousands of his countrymen the Duke was engrossed in the serialized instalments of *Vanity Fair*, then about to reach an end. He wrote to the author asking for a portrait of the heroine Mrs Rawdon Crawley, better known as Becky Sharp. Not only did Thackeray send him an enchanting drawing of Becky, 'whom I saw last week and whom I informed of your Grace's desire to have her portrait', but enclosed an account of the other principal characters, couched in the make-believe style of a current gossip writer. The drawing was of course done by Thackeray (most of the illustrations in *Vanity Fair* were his) purporting to be from a sketch, ' "made in happier days", to quote Becky's words with a sigh', by Sir Martin Archer Smee, PRA.

Mrs Rawdon Crawley is depicted lying in a nonchalant attitude of well-being, propped by cushions on a sofa. Her voluminous dress and shawl droop seductively to the floor. While she holds the open pages of a French novel (to judge by a copy of *Les Liaisons Dangereuses* thrown on the carpet) a searching eye is turned in the direction of the artist; and her tight little mouth reveals a whole packet of malice. 'Mrs. Crawley', he continues, now lives in a small but very pretty little house in Belgravia; and is conspicuous for her numerous charities wch always get into the newspapers, and her unaffected piety. Many of the most exalted and spotless of her own sex visit her and are of opinion that she is *a most injured woman.* There is *no sort of truth* in the stories regarding Mrs. Crawley & the late Lord Steyne.

Thackeray goes on to describe how

she has lost what little good looks she once possessed, & wears false hair and teeth (the latter give her rather a ghastly look when she smiles).

She lives on interest from the rupees which Jos Sedley left her. The fact that her infamously neglected son Sir Pitt Crawley does not see his mother 'is a cause of the greatest grief to that admirable lady'. The virtuous Amelia and honest Captain Dobbie live happily married in Hampshire. As for Amelia's son George Sedley-Osborne by her rotter husband, killed at Waterloo, he was seen 'in a most richly embroidered cambric pink silk shirt with diamond studs bowing to your Grace, at the last party at Devonshire House'. A postscript announces the utter ruin of the Bank of Calcutta in which all Mrs Crawley's money was deposited. 'Will Fate never cease to persecute that suffering lady?'

This was just the sort of satire to delight the Duke of Devonshire. Two months later the final instalments of the novel appeared, differing only in a few minor respects from the story outlined in Thackeray's letter.

Thackeray dined at Devonshire House in January 1850 and stayed the night of 26 September 1851 at Chatsworth, sleeping in the bedroom known as The Armoury which formerly contained muskets, broadswords, buff jerkins and penny trumpets. He was treated as an honoured guest and shown round the house by his host. His rivalry with Charles Dickens who had just preceded him on a visit was sometimes expressed in caustic innuendo. On his arrival at Chatsworth he had asked Freddy Leveson Gower, who was present, if Dickens had toadied the Duke much.

In spite of the Duke's raptures over the beauties of Lismore, the delightful company of the neighbours and the plans which he and Paxton had concocted for improvements to the castle during his visit in 1844, he did not return there until September 1849. Thereafter he went every year until his death, with the exception of 1852 when he had his first serious illness. Freddy who accompanied him declared in his *Recollections* that his uncle's primary object was to alleviate the extreme poverty of the Irish people, in so far as it lay within his power. During the intervening period the general condition of tradesmen as well as agricultural workers in Ireland, brought about by the potato blight and famine, and by high taxes and high rents demanded by absentee landlords, had certainly become deplorable. It is true that in his journal and letters the Duke makes no overt allusion to this state of affairs, of which his subsequent acts of relief prove that he was only too well aware. His journal is on the contrary a continuous catalogue of jollifications. Day after day he entertained friends from near and far to dinners, and night after night to balls which lasted till dawn. It was by no means the gentry only whom he invited. He gave balls for the tenantry and townspeople who flocked to the castle because their host treated them exactly as he did his own family, providing the same lavish food and drink, and dancing with their wives until the small hours. The members of his family who were staying, including William Burlington and his son young Cavendish, joined in the fun. Indeed the Duke protested that he loved Lismore largely because of the uninhibited, unsnobbish inhabitants whom he contrasted favourably with those of any English town of the same size. He told Freddy that

> A week at Lismore goes like an hour anywhere else. My neighbours throng to see me, and all are admitted. They have got a natural *bonhomie* and want of pretension that makes them very captivating, never wanting to appear what they are not ... They are always gay.

It was true. Moreover they returned his feelings for them with an affection that was, as far as he could judge, sincere. One tradesman went so far as to announce to the press,

> I would rather have a title of dignity conferred on me by that man, and be prouder of HIS touch on my shoulder than if the Imperial Eagle of immortal France was laid thereon, and there are thousands here who, if they were asked the question, would reciprocate my feeling.

The Irish may have a tendency to gush, but they are one and all susceptible to charm.

Each year the welcome he received on arrival became more and more spontaneous, more and more effusive, the words of the testimonials presented to him and the reports in the local newspapers more and more eulogistic, and the sobs on his departure that much louder. The reason was that besides bringing sunshine he dispensed a great deal of money to schools, churches, chapels and charities, Catholic as well as

Protestant. He would suffer no religious prejudice, if anything favouring the Catholics because they were oppressed. For work on a
vast scale at the castle during the 'fifties he employed Catholics and
Protestants alike, with the consequence that during these very lean
years the inhabitants of Lismore were less deprived than those of
neighbouring towns.

There were of course those who had grievances. The Association
of the Protestant Operatives of Youghal presented an address objecting
to the Duke's nomination of a Papist representative to some unspecified
office. It may have been a political nomination, in spite of the Duke's
endeavour since the passing of the Reform Act and the increasing
violence of political feeling in Ireland to avoid exercising more than
what he claimed vaguely as his 'legitimate interest' in parliamentary
candidatures. Before 1831 he had indulged, like all Irish landlords, in
widespread borough-mongering in Dungarvan and Youghal, quite
half of both towns being his property. Those days were now gone,
and he was the first to acknowledge the fact.

The address of the Protestant Operatives of Youghal was not
accepted by Francis Currey, the agent. Its rejection produced an out-
burst of indignation from the descendants of the bold adventurers of
Queen Elizabeth's reign who had made Youghal 'a bulwark against
rebels and rapparees'. They now made their vexation publicly known.

> His Grace had *virtually*, might we not say *ungraciously* and we suppose
> *advisedly* refused this Address because it told him plain truths in a plain
> way, but subsequently *a few* of his Grace's interested admirers concocted
> a testimonial of most aromatic frankincense ... flattering fawning and
> crouching (which was heeded). Alas, alas, Lismore Castle is not the only
> domicile where nowadays Sycophancy's painted face in purple and fine
> linen is met with kindly graciousness, while honest worth in 'hodden grey'
> is driven from a closed portal.

The implications of this effusion were clearly sectarian and explain
why Francis Currey ignored them.

During this visit a Cornish water-colourist, Samuel Cook, recommended by Lady Morley of Saltram, travelled to Lismore. He
executed a series of exterior and interior views of the castle and also
views up and down the Blackwater from the windows. His charges
were moderate – one to two guineas for each sketch, and five for the
finished thing. His patron getting to like Cook removed him from the
inn, lodged him in the castle and encouraged him to roam and draw

whatever he felt inclined. The result is a fascinating record of the castle before the Duke and Paxton embarked upon their very extensive alterations during the last half of the decade.

Before the Duke left Lismore at the beginning of November a letter came from Paxton announcing, 'The last leaf of Victoria is 4ft 8½ins in diameter. As it bears the Queen's name perhaps his Grace will want to send her the first flower.' A bud was already showing. The exciting news made him hurry to London where he took an express train up to Chatsworth.

Victoria Regia, the immense waterlily named after the Queen, was discovered in 1837 on the Berbice river in British Guiana by Sir Robert Schomburgk who sent seeds and drawings to England. At Kew Gardens the lily never flowered, just as the precious *Amherstia nobilis* had refused to flower at Chatsworth. Paxton acquired a plant from his friend Sir William Hooker, Kew's director, and spent three weeks preparing a special tank and glass house for its reception at Chatsworth. By September 140 large leaves and 112 flower heads had formed. Twice Victoria Regia outgrew her tank and twice Paxton had to build bigger ones. The final Lily House – in the Duke's words, 'the parent of the Great Exhibition' – which emerged was given supporting roof ribs copied by the ingenious Paxton from those of the plant's leaf. When the Duke reached Chatsworth on 17 November he found Dr Lindley and auditor William Currey with Paxton admiring the prized plant. He pronounced the lily stupendous. Chatsworth too was stupendous, 'but after Lismore seems to me a splendid desert, where for society I can only depend on people at a distance'. Nevertheless he spent a happy time sharing all sorts of confidences and concocting further fantastic schemes for Ireland with Paxton.

For the next few days, which were like summer, he could not keep away from Victoria Regia. On 20th he paid her no less than four visits, one with Lady Hunloke whom he had fetched from Wingerworth, and one with Mrs (Isabella) Thornhill who had driven over from Stanton. All the world was congregating at the tank's edge. On 22nd Sir William Hooker arrived to covet; and on the same day Annie Paxton, Joseph's little daughter of 7, was to her great delight made by the Duke and Lady Newburgh to stand on one of the leaves. The proud possessor of the lily was in the seventh heaven of happiness when 'My day was spoilt by a cruel, vile, anonymous letter'. The specific nature of this vile letter was not vouchsafed. The Duke was subjected to several such attacks, and if he never ignored he grew to shrug them off. 'The thing is not to fret or magnify evil,' he wrote philosophically.

In April of 1850 the Duke travelled down to Brighton. After church on 7th while walking along the cliff he met Louis-Philippe and Queen Amélie who talked and were friendly, but he, poor man, looked like death. Three days later having just returned to 1 Lewes Crescent from a long drive the Duke spied from a window the French King and Queen approaching the door on foot, accompanied by an ADC. The doorbell rang. In they walked and stayed an hour, examining everything. They raved over the view and the flowers in the gazebo. They studied the sketches of Lismore. 'When at length they departed,' he informed Georgiana, 'I was worked up into a great state of enthusiasm – muzzy, and Mr. Meynell at the door had tears in his eyes. Did you ever? And what an exciting life is led at Brighton.' In August the poor King died.

For his sixtieth birthday the Duke gave at Devonshire House one of the most splendid of the very many splendid balls which had been staged in this incomparable London palace. Eight hundred of the pick of English and cosmopolitan society were assembled. 'The grand saloon when crowded with company about midnight, presented a brilliant scene, of which none but those who had the good fortune to witness it could form the remotest conception,' wrote the press. Among those of good fortune who danced till dawn were the Duke and Duchess of Cambridge, the Infante Don Juan of Spain and His Serene Highness Prince Edward of Saxe-Weimar. The Duke opened the ball with, as might be expected, a young person, his great-niece Lucia Agar-Ellis.

In 1846–7 Devonshire House, repeatedly altered since being rebuilt by William Kent after a fire in George II's reign, was transformed into its ultimate splendour. The architect Decimus Burton and decorator John Gregory Crace were the artists chiefly responsible. Burton added a portico to the Piccadilly front, thus enabling guests to enter from ground level instead of struggling up an outdoor perron where in bad weather they might get soaked to the skin. From a new lower hall he contrived what was one of the most beautiful and graceful staircases of Queen Victoria's reign. It necessitated building on the garden front a bowed bay to contain it. Within a complete circle and under a domed skylight a flight of wide and shallow steps of white marble (specially brought from Carrara) rose to the state rooms on the first floor. The balustrade consisted of metal uprights forming scrolls and wreaths and alternately gilded. The breathtaking feature was the swirling handrail of glass; hence the name crystal staircase of this miraculously lovely creation.

Having mounted the crystal staircase guests entered a new ballroom fashioned out of two adjacent drawing-rooms, and the saloon. Both apartments were decorated by Crace. From photographs which survive the ballroom must have been rather overpowering with heavy compartmented ceilings and an ungainly remnant of the former partition wall left standing. Yet it displayed some of the finest paintings in the Devonshire collection. But the saloon must have been very magnificent, with its high barrel ceiling painted in the manner of Le Brun and blending architectural effects with groups of figures and flowers. Five great glass chandeliers hung from the flat of the ceiling. The walls were panelled with silk brocade and framed, as were vast looking-glasses, with highly ornamented and gilded wood carving. When we compare illustrations of this final achievement of palatial grandeur with William Hunt's water-colour of the Duke's earlier decoration of the saloon about 1822 we must admit that the change evinced little improvement in taste. Nevertheless the destruction of Devonshire House in 1924 will always be accounted one of the direst acts of architectural barbarism to disgrace London in our century.

From the crystal staircase to the Crystal Palace (always spelt by the Duke *Chrystal*) is a far cry, and there is little connection between them. If the first gave the Duke of Devonshire an ephemeral satisfaction the second was a source of enduring enthusiasm and vicarious pride. The first was certainly his project and probably his inspiration. The second was neither the one nor the other. Yet the creator of it was in nearly all senses his creation. Whereas Paxton subsequently acknowledged at a public dinner in his honour that the glass palace owed its erection to the Duke who had moulded him according to his tastes and wishes, so the Duke proclaimed to all and sundry that he was under an eternal obligation to his gardener who had achieved fame, fortune and honour, some of which had rubbed off on him! It was a charming and generous way of paying tribute.

The Duke followed every chapter of the romantic story (vividly told by Violet Markham): how Paxton by sheer genius roughed out his revolutionary design for a vast building to house the Prince Consort's proposed 1851 Trade Exhibition on a piece of blotting paper; how by tough persistence he induced the Prince, the Board of Trade and the Exhibition's Royal Commissioners to accept it, although the building committee had already decided upon a conventional and lumpish design in red brick from its own office. The Duke's delight could not have been more sincere had the Crystal Palace been solely his achievement. When at one moment it looked as if the whole scheme of the exhibition might break down because serious objections to the Hyde Park site were raised the Duke offered land at Chiswick for the purpose. Prince Albert was touched and grateful; but the House of Commons decided to stick to Hyde Park.

Among the Royal Commissioners Paxton had powerful friends to support him in Robert Stephenson, George's son, who happened to meet him on the train from Derby to London and, having been handed his finished plan, at once saw that it was a masterpiece of invention; and Lord Granville, the Commission's vice-president, who was equally enthusiastic. But the commissioner whose influence was the most telling of all was Sir Robert Peel. At the fateful meeting on 29 June – fateful both for Paxton and himself – when the scheme was discussed Peel gave it his unequivocal blessing. On riding home his horse stumbled in Hyde Park and threw him to the ground. After enduring tortures of pain he died on 2 July. Although Peel was out of office at the time his death was regarded as a national calamity for he was revered by Tories and Whigs alike. It drew from the Duke of Devonshire an appreciation of an eminently honourable, just and compassionate statesman who was possibly the only Tory minister he had ever admired without stint because of his genuinely liberal instincts and understanding. At all events the tragedy, following so closely upon Peel's authoritative persuasion, tipped the balance in Paxton's favour. The original blotting-paper plan of the Crystal Palace was adopted.

On 24 July the Duke and Paxton went up to Chatsworth together. Their reception was triumphant. 'It looked like the most brilliant fête.' Seven hundred 'pleasure hunters' (whom we would call sightseers) were about. 'I was cheered on arrival as if in Ireland,' the Duke wrote, as if indeed the real hero of the occasion was himself. Relaxed master and man at once went to exult over the new lily house and the improved pleasure grounds. 'Paxton the quite unaltered gardener,' the Duke exclaimed complacently.

In September 1850 came the autumn visit to Lismore which was now part of the pattern of the Duke's life. The years 1849 to 1858 marked the last and major phase of the Lismore Castle improvements, with a pause only in 1851–2. The improvements were carried out by Paxton and John Gregory Crace in amicable partnership. The one was responsible for the architecture, the other for the decoration. Paxton had sent from Chatsworth his head mason, John Brown, to take charge of his concerns in the role of clerk of works. Brown supervised the carriage by boat of dressed stone, quarried and even cut to measurement at Chatsworth, for windows and doorways of the castle. Crace, incorrigible fusspot about travel though he was, with a mortal terror of the Irish Sea, made several journeys to Lismore. Extraordinary was the speed with which the work ensued. On 30 March 1830 the Duke recorded a meeting held in London with Paxton, Crace and William Currey to settle the Lismore campaign. On 2 April Crace submitted to Paxton his proposals for a banqueting hall to be made out of the ruined chapel. Throughout the summer letters flew between Lismore and Chatsworth about the choice of wallpapers for the Duke's sitting-room and a suitable looking-glass for the drawing-room. On 15 July Crace wrote to the Duke that the castle was already transformed. By 14 September, the date of the Duke's arrival, the banqueting hall was ready.

The high open roof of the banqueting hall is supported by rather flimsy timbers painted in vivid red, blue and gold. The space between the velvet-patterned wallpaper and the roof is stencilled with armorial shields mantled with foliage. Two large Gothic windows at the longitudinal ends are filled with brilliant stained glass like theatrical jewellery, supplied by John Hardman of Birmingham. Hardman also forged the huge concave chandelier, a confection of spidery branches, and the Gothic wall brackets en suite, all of brass. The spectacular stone chimneypiece, a galaxy of carving like a 'tomb in a Gothic cathedral, came from the Great Exhibition and was inserted later, as were the Minton tiles of blue, red and yellow within the fireplace. Against the walls pew-like benches under coved canopies resembling choir stalls offer very unrelaxed sitting for guests 'when wearied in the mazy circles of the dance', as one newspaper suggested. In this colourful yet over-ecclesiastical and certainly high Victorian setting the Duke was to give at least two mammoth entertainments a year, one for the local gentry. the other for the tenants and tradesmen of Lismore and the neighbouring towns.

Unexpected disasters occurred in the early 1850s. The old north-east 'Bloody' tower fell down. A fire swept through the south-west wing, and the bridge across the Blackwater collapsed. These disasters instead of disheartening merely spurred the Duke into further activity. Practically the whole architecture of the castle, except the main rooms in the north range and the gatehouse, was remodelled to Paxton's designs with the aid of his son-in-law G. H. Stokes. What was ruinous was built up. Skyline and façades were much altered from what went before. Pointed gables were done away with and flat roofs with battlements took their place. No less than eight towers were renovated and embellished as befitted the mid-Victorian notion of what a medieval castle ought to look like, with crenellations, embrasures, bartizans and arrow slits. These appurtenances accrued throughout the decade.

On 10 December the Duke left Lismore for Cork where he listened to Mendelssohn's *Elija*. On 12th from Crewe he notified the staff at Devonshire House by telegraph of his impending arrival before midnight. Paxton was there to receive him, and they sat up for hours talking eagerly while the room grew colder and colder and the dawn edged a way through the cracks of the curtains.

Next day he was too tired to go to Hyde Park, but on 14th he drove, with Paxton, into the skeletal Crystal Palace. The 'Great Work [was] too beautiful, harmonious, mystic light'. He spent more than three hours with Paxton, Charles Fox the ingenious contractor for the palace, and his partner Charles Henderson, men for whom he had the greatest admiration and with whom he was proud to be seen. At first he expected to be 'snarled' by these experts for his ignorance of technology. Not a bit of it. They made him feel one of them, a conspirator, a creator. The glass palace was bringing him more happiness than anything he had been associated with since the days when he intrigued and joked with George IV. Once more he was truly in the swim.

Drawing by W. M. Thackeray of Becky Sharp in her declining years, sent to the Duke in 1848

9

Eclipse
1851–1858

───────◆───────

THE FIRST FOUR months of 1851 were spent in a crescendo of excitement over preparations for the opening of the Great Exhibition. The Duke remained in London with occasional dashes to Brighton and back. Scarcely a day went by that he did not visit, usually on foot when alone, the Crystal Palace in Hyde Park. The year opened warm like summer which was a great help to the builders. On New Year's Day the Duke noted, 'Paxton alone I wish to see, but besides his business, he is showing London to Miss Victoria and Master George', one of his daughters and the only son, who turned out a misfit and cause of great sadness and disappointment to his parents. Instead the Duke took one by one Harriet, his brother Black Rod, sister Lamb, Caroline Norton, the Normanbys, Lady Newburgh, Erskine, and anyone he could enlist to share his delight and enthusiasm. On 27 January he wrote that the translucent structure was approaching completion. 'Too beautiful and I like the colour employed.' On 29th, a red letter day, Paxton went with him. Another time he met Queen Marie Amélie under the open girders. You never knew whom you might stumble upon. The place had become a haunt of society folk. In a *Journal for Freddy*, which from the end of March until November entirely usurped the confidences of his own journal, the Duke related another encounter.

The Exhibition becomes too interesting. There is a colossal Amazon in bronze on horseback about to spear a lion that has fastened on her horse's neck, made at Berlin by one Kiss. I was gazing at it when a small woman accosted me. 'Ma'am?' said I – and *Ecco!* it was the Queen. She walks there most days among the workmen and exhibitors and is very popular. Albert looks stupefied.

The Prince too could think of nothing, nothing beyond the glass palace. And when the Duke dined at Buckingham Palace, the first time for ages, he could talk of nothing but Paxton.

On May Day the Great Exhibition was formally opened by the Queen with the Prince Consort at her side, amid a loud flourish of trumpets, salute of guns, roar of applause from hundreds of thousands of loyal throats assembled outside, and the strains of the Hallelujah Chorus to the booming of the organ installed by Mr Willis for the benefit of the privileged inside. A long procession marched into the palace headed by Paxton looking small and tubby, almost hand in hand with his partner, Charles Fox, followed by twenty-five Foreign Commissioners, twenty-four Royal Commissioners, the Diplomatic Corps, the Duke of Wellington Commander-in-Chief, aged 82, arm in arm with Lord Anglesey, aged 83, the Cabinet, the Archbishop of Canterbury and the Royal Household in Windsor uniform, some of them walking backwards. The rain which had been falling ceased as soon as the Queen approached and the first rays of the sun shone upon the colossal glass edifice. Prince Albert in Field Marshal's uniform read an address to the Queen who could barely contain her tears of joy in replying to it. The emotional and triumphant occasion has been recorded by countless eyewitnesses of the scene, including Her Majesty who finished her diary entry with: 'God bless my dearest Albert. God bless my dearest country, which has shown itself so great today.'

The Duke of Devonshire was prominently evident in the transept and like everyone else overwhelmed. 'I am hardly recovered from May day,' he wrote to Freddy when all was over.

> I was satisfied for Paxton, and so must he have been when at the mention of his name Victoria turned towards him and made a gesture of approbation. She did her part astonishingly well, with such composure and yet with joy in her face. She was wonderfully well got up, and contrived to be so dignified that it had the effect of beauty. The climate was perfect, there was no crowd, there was not a hitch except that you were not there.

His concern with the Great Exhibition did not hinder the Duke from forming a new friendship which meant a lot to him during the last few years of his life. In September 1845 he had attended a private performance at the retired actress Frances Kelly's theatre in Dean Street of Ben Jonson's *Every Man in His Humour*, in which Charles Dickens, John Leech the caricaturist, Henry Mayhew the humorous author, Mark Lemon the editor of *Punch* and Douglas Jerrold, play-wright and editor, took part. Amongst the invited guests were Alfred Tennyson and Jane Carlyle. The Duke was vastly amused by the performance. Yet he was blissfully unaware that Mrs Carlyle sitting opposite him was to observe snidely that His Grace's nose was 'looking towards Damascus', just as though revelations were in sight for the first time. As a matter of fact he had been a theatre addict all his life. That same year Dickens paid a flying visit to the Paxtons' house by the Barbrook in the Chatsworth walled garden. He had met Joseph presumably through his publishers, Bradbury and Evans, who were then launching a newspaper, the *Daily News*, of which Paxton was a principal backer and Dickens was to be the editor. It is unlikely that Dickens met the Duke on this occasion although he may have been introduced by Paxton at some later date.

As for Dickens he was so bitten by private theatricals and the applause of admirers that, however tenuous were his relations with the Duke, he boldly wrote to him on 4 March 1851 begging permission to stage a comedy by Bulwer-Lytton at Devonshire House in the presence of the Queen and Prince Consort in aid of his and Bulwer-Lytton's projected Guild of Literature and Art. The Guild's aim was to help needy men of letters and artists. Bulwer-Lytton even offered to erect and endow a building for the purpose on his estate in Hert-fordshire. Within two hours the Duke replied enthusiastically:

> My services, my house, and my subscription will be at your orders. And I beg you to let me see you before long, not merely to converse upon this subject, but because I have long had the greatest wish to improve our acquaintance, which has, as yet, been only one of crowded rooms.

Dickens was as delighted as he was surprised by the immediate response and wrote back a very flattering letter, in which he told the Duke there was 'no other on whose generous attachment to letters and art I so implicitly rely'. The two men then plunged into a correspondence about practical details. All the male actors were to be amateurs and the only two actresses professionals. Dickens disclosed that Bulwer-Lytton was taking infinite pains over the composition of the comedy, to be called *Not So Bad as We Seem*, and working himself into a great state of nerves. The Duke approached Buckingham Palace and obtained the monarch and her consort's august consent to grace the performance. By 24 April he was diffidently sending Dickens a few tentative corrections to Bulwer-Lytton's text.

The date of the first performance having been appointed by the Queen for 30 April Dickens's little daughter suddenly died. The Duke was all solicitude. The Queen consented to postpone the performance until 16 May. On that date *Not So Bad as We Seem*, dedicated to the Duke of Devonshire for his sympathy to literary men and artists in distress, was acted in the library of Devonshire House, the audience dominated by the royal couple sitting in the adjacent picture gallery. It was rapturously applauded. The cast included Dickens, Douglas Jerrold, John Forster, the novelist's future biographer, and Mark Lemon. A repeat performance took place, at the Duke's request, on 27th of the month, again before the Queen; but as it did not begin before nine o'clock Her Majesty got very restless by midnight. It then moved to the Hanover Square Rooms and went to Manchester and the provinces. It raised a respectable sum of money for the Guild which, in spite of the generous intentions and hard work of its sponsors, did not flourish. However it was a noble anticipation of subsequent charities held for theatrical causes. Bulwer-Lytton's comedy which Dickens was fain in later to years to dub *Even Worse than We Seem* died a natural death, and has never been revived.

Whatever its demerits the play cemented a firm friendship between novelist and Duke. On 1 June Dickens wrote to his new friend from a rented house in Broadstairs, a small picturesque Kentish resort where he took flying visits of refuge from the stage and pressing social activities:

I am in a favourite house of mine here, perched by itself on the top of a cliff, with the green corn growing all about it and the larks singing invisible all day long. The freshness of the sea and the association of the place (I finished *Copperfield* in the same airy nest) have set me to work with great vigor, and I can hardly believe that I am ever a Manager, and ever go about with a painted face in gaslight.

When I first had the happiness of seeing you in the room where we have since held so many a Council, you gratified me very much by your affectionate remembrance of *Copperfield*. I am having him put into a decent suit of morocco, and when he comes home in his new dress shall entreat you to give him a place on your shelves for my sake. You see how dangerous it is to give me encouragement!

When I saw you last I was quite full of the melancholy of having turned a leaf in my life. It was so sad to see the curtain dropped on what you made so bright and interesting and triumphant, that something of the shadow of the great curtain which falls on everything seemed for a little while to be upon my spirits. I have an indescribable dread of leave-takings; and the taking leave of such a gracious scene made me almost miserable – which I acknowledge here, because it was certainly and undoubtedly your fault.

With the utmost earnestness of my heart.

The letter may have a touch of melodrama – Dickens's whole life was melodramatic – but it also evinces sincerity. In the many missives he sent to the Duke in his meticulous handwriting over the signature with a flourish of underlining, which became his cypher, there is affability, prolixity, sometimes fulsomeness, but none of the toadiness of which Thackeray complained and with which poor Leigh Hunt was so lavish. There was always humour.

On 28 September Dickens again wrote thanking the Duke for his 'kindest of letters'. He was back in Broadstairs in the throes of a new book to be called *Bleak House*, and the arrangement of a newly rented dwelling, Fort House. He was walking by the sea every day:

endeavouring to think of both sets of distraction to some practical ends, but the prospect of renewing, even for a day, an intercourse which is perfectly delightful, which makes everything else fade out of my view ... Meanwhile I have thought and talked of you so often that I have insensibly seemed to be doing something (without exactly knowing what) to keep myself in your remembrance.

This I can simply affirm – that I continually come, in the spirit, into your room at Devonshire House, and add to that stock of noble and winning remembrances with which it will always be inseparably associated in my mind, and which is always enlarging.

From 3 to 5 October Dickens stayed at Chatsworth, being given the Centre Bedroom on the west front and sleeping in a bed 'like a brocaded and golden temple'. There was no question of Mrs Dickens going too, she remaining in Broadstairs with their quiverful of children. The visit which was not described from the Duke's point of view, his journal still being in abeyance, evoked a long Collins from the novelist dated 10th. He had taken with him a copy of his host's *Handbook*. Dickens was not gushing when he wrote:

As I travelled from Chesterfield in the railway carriage I read the little book I now return with a pleasure I can scarcely express to you. It was so like going over the house again with you, and hearing you talk about it, that it had a perfect charm for me: and besides this, I found it in myself so natural and unaffected, so gracefully sensible, and altogether so winning and so good, that I read it through, from the first page to the last, without once laying it aside.

I could mention some things in it which it would require a very nice art to do as well in fiction. The little suggestive indications of some of the old servants and old rooms – and the childish associations – are perfect little pieces of truth.

Very possibly some of 'the little suggestive indications' found an unconscious echo in the high-flown ruminations of Mrs Rouncewell, the venerable old housekeeper, upon the Deadlock ancestors at Chesney Wold.

They kept in touch. They dined together from time to time at Devonshire House, and once at Dickens's house in Tavistock Square for the Duke to meet the whole company of *Not So Bad*, who had become very attached and had asked to see him again. They exchanged gifts, the Duke sending loads of game to Mrs Dickens and the family as a sort of courtesy *douceur*, instead of meeting them. When the Duke, incapacitated by a stroke, was unable to write at length Dickens did not ignore him and dispatched occasional long letters when he found the leisure. He would tell him how, working solidly on *Bleak House* from 5 a.m. till midday he became practically insensible; and how he thought Mrs Stowe's *Uncle Tom's Cabin* an uncommonly fine book, even if Uncle Tom was a little too celestial – perhaps he was a little in the opposite direction. What was His Grace's view? He described the plays he had seen, and narrated stories to cheer his convalescence. On 5 July 1856 he sent him a long letter from a villa where he was staying near Boulogne. He was so pleased that the Duke liked Flora Finching in *Little Dorritt* who in days gone by was loved by Arthur Clenman but whom Clenman on meeting years later as a widow found a maddening figure of fun. Her beauty gone she was affected and kittenish, wishing to renew the old worn-out courtship. She talked torrents of verbiage in a malaprop way, never drawing breath and making little sense.

It came into my head one day [Dickens wrote] that we have all had our Floras (mine is living and extremely fat), and that it was a half serious half ridiculous truth which had never been told. It is a wonderful justification to find that everybody knows her. Indeed some people seem to think I have done them a personal injury, and that their individual Floras (God knows where they are, or who) are each and all little Dorritts!

November and December of 1851 and the New Year of 1852 were spent at Lismore. The chief event of this sojourn was the visit of Harriet Sutherland and her daughter Lady Constance Leveson-Gower The Duchess's presence caused an immense sensation. The whole population of Lismore turned out to gape at and cheer the Queen's Mistress of the Robes. For was it not rumoured that her visit would be followed the next year by that of the great Queen herself who had not yet deigned thus to honour her Irish kingdom? A ball was arranged for mother and daughter, and all the world admired them. Messrs Richardson & Son performed 'on their powerful and brilliant Rock, Bell & Steel Band', which today strikes an anachronistically modern note. A gallop, specially composed by Coote and accompanied by his son Robert at the violin, 'exquisitely grand and told with touching effect', was dedicated to Lady Constance.

But the Duke was not well. He was overcome by unaccountable, insupportable apathy and lassitude. He worried inordinately about the expense of keeping up Lismore, a thing those close to him had never remarked before. He was driven from room to room by nauseating smoke from the chimneys. He was anxiously waiting for Paxton, detained in London by disputes over the future of the Crystal Palace, to come over and resolve the smoke trouble. Instead Paxton wrote suggesting that they should heat the rooms in the castle by hot-water pipes.

Back in England the Duke passed a wretched winter and in March 1852 collapsed with a severe attack of influenza. He was moved to Brighton where he became seriously ill. Paxton wrote to Sarah that he would not leave him until he showed signs of improvement. 'He is so low and no one has been near him. Instead he looks a poor deserted neglected old man. It has almost made me ill to see him.' His face was haggard. Sir Joseph (for a knighthood had been awarded the Duke's head gardener after the closing of the Great Exhibition) begged his wife not to spread news of the illness about. On 22nd he told her that his patient coughed all night, that he, Paxton, was up with him all night, and the moment he left the room the Duke called him back. He was much frightened about him. Recovery was slow. On 11 April the Duke drove in his brougham from Devonshire House to Chiswick but did not get out. He feared he was being destroyed by a rapid consumption although the doctors swore themselves red in the face that he was not. He rejoiced that his solitude made it easier for him to bear the terrible expectoration and hoarseness he suffered.

Convalescence, when it came, was not made easier by domestic cares. Meynell, whose behaviour had been steadily declining with his health, exceeded all previous misdeeds and brought about a final fall from grace. He disappeared the whole of one day to a brothel, taking with him the Duke's little dog Vio. Sir Joseph with the police went in search of the miscreant in the red-light district of Soho. Meynell was found and Vio retrieved. The Duke was in a rage and under Paxton's persuasion immediately sacked Meynell. He was greatly upset by the incident. '3 years ago I thought him perfection & the model of service and trust & effort. All wrong!' Next day his anger turned as usual to sadness but not to a reversal of his decision.

> All is to be settled now about poor Meynell. He has slept for the last time in Devonshire House. His furniture will be kept for him, but his bed is pulled down & room dismantled. It seems to me incredible, but I try to look at it like Paxton, who says we ought to think that Meynell died two years ago, for then his change took place.

The inexorable Currey confirmed the dismissal in a formal letter to the valet. 'Do I live to see it?' the Duke wrote. 'He is to have 4 guineas a week, & in weekly payments, and to be admitted no more to D House. O poor fellow!' And that was the end of a service of more than a quarter of a century, marked by affection, amusement and much indulgence on the Duke's part, and devotion, presumption and total lack of subservience on the valet's. Meynell's misconduct had always been resented by the other servants and he was never liked by the Paxtons who referred to him as Beelzebub. As long ago as 1838 Paxton complained to Sarah that 'Meynell gets more than half seas over often, which annoys the Duke. I think that gentleman's sun will be set soon if he does not look sharply out.' But his master did not forget or neglect his old reprobate servant. He sent him an annual birthday present, defrayed the expenses of his wife's and his own illnesses, and even organized their funerals. Poor Meynell!

The Duke was not well enough to be present at Constance Leveson-Gower's wedding to Lord Lorne, son and heir of the Duke of Argyll and in due course to become a prominent Whig politician. Instead he watched the procession pass the Devonshire House gate. Dr Nussey was now a little worried. The Duke made alterations to his will, informing William Burlington that he was leaving Chiswick to his two sisters for their lifetimes. 'Dear William's manner was perfect about it.' To Chatsworth Bienaimé came and settled about the statues bought by the Duke when last in Italy. *Venus* and *Cicero* were to go down to the west garden. Unfortunately the Duke hit his toe against a ring in the shower bath which caused much pain and lameness and meant he had to be wheeled in a chair.

On 15 July the Duke 'sat today to Mr. Banquet for a lithograph, having been struck by one he did of Coote'. This was Charles Baugniet, a Flemish draughtsman who had appeared in London where he was taken up by the Prince Consort. Whether the idea of a family group was the Duke's or his relations' is not clear. He complained that he loathed sitting in a group of eight Cavendishes. But he took great trouble over the crayon portrait of himself and when the group was complete spent a deal of time distributing copies of the lithograph to relations and friends. He had Baugniet down to Chatsworth where he sat to him in his bedroom while Coote strummed away at the piano and Mlle Celestine Jacob, a most accomplished young Jewess, pedicured his bruised toe. He considered the first attempt at his portrait too disagreeable to be lithographed and persuaded Paxton with his immense politeness to condemn it in front of the artist, 'all the time obliging his victim (according to custom) without offending him.' Baugniet was thus persuaded to do better. When in early October the final group was completed the Duke was depicted seated in the centre with William, his sons, daughter, brother and his wife around him, and, prominently displayed in the background, a pedestalled urn with the simple message 'Blanche' carved upon its surface. The group was accounted by all those depicted a great success. About thirty copies of the lithograph were then distributed to a select few, of whom Harriet Sutherland wrote to her uncle, 'Yours [likeness] has your nobleness, your abandon, your acuteness, your kindness.'

The Duke was so pleased with the finished crayon of his own likeness which indeed made him look not merely patriarchal but handsome and benign that he had 500 prints taken of it separately. He compiled another list of people to whom they should be sent, together with a memorandum explaining how the lithograph came about. As he went on distributing the 500 to tenants, servants, gamekeepers, gardeners, mayors, to Dickens' band of amateur players, to the members of Coote's orchestra (few acquaintances were spared) they were soon exhausted; and he considered that a further 500 could easily find honoured recipients. The acknowledgements he received from his literary and artistic friends yielded such variety of opinion and such insight to their own characters that the Duke thought fit to record *in toto* or paraphrase each letter in a special album. Thus Dickens's thanks are preserved for the most wonderful portrait and the only perfect likeness of someone known to him which he had ever seen in his life.

> It is quite astonishing. After trying you with the greatest severity in every kind of aspect and position, I have suspended you at last in the hall: where a charming little gas lamp something higher than yourself shines on you after dark, and makes you radiant. If I were to tell you how much good it does me, to see you every time I go up or down stairs you would never believe me.

This letter is the nearest approach to that toadiness of which Thackeray accused him. As for Thackeray, he answered cannily in the third person which more or less precluded fulsomeness:

> Mr. William Makepeace Thackeray waited to acknowledge the picture till he could offer a copy of *Esmond* his new novel. Wishes the story had been more amusing, but the author not being in a lively mood the hero to be consistent must be glum. Salve & Vale.

Against a letter from Augustus Egg RA who wrote that the lithograph was one of the most beautiful drawings of the kind he had ever seen the Duke scribbled, 'which is great from an artist'. Letters from dear friends and relations were expectedly eulogistic. Elizabeth Lady Stuart de Rothsay had an agreeable surprise on coming into an empty house to see the familiar visage staring at her. The only *dérangement* she had yet derived from the gift was a threat from the Dowager Lady Morley to scratch her eyes out if she were not also sent a facsimile. At the end of the Baugniet album the Duke wrote a postscript.

> My task is done, up to the present day. On looking back at what occurred I feel astonished at my own cool impudence in dashing off all these bits of egotism to all the world àpropos to nothing without letters to explain or to request acceptance.

The Duke of Devonshire was by now extremely popular. He was recognized to be a great nobleman on the fringe of royalty, whose privilege and right it was to receive under his roof the illustrious of all nations. As one apart from the common herd he was expected to live grandly and entertain lavishly. He did not disappoint his admirers. For instance during one September week of 1852 in all 426 persons were fed at a Chatsworth house party. Of these 70 sat at the Duke's table, 105 at the steward's room table, and 251 in the servants' hall. The Duke's riches may have been coveted but they were not resented. He had become a national figure. Provided they live long enough national figures are forgiven their sins and taken to the public's big sentimental heart. The Duke had few sins that it was aware of and his weaknesses were venial. By now he was looking frail, and frailty is a considerable bonus to any good old man's popularity. While standing on Derby station platform in September of this year seeing off the Queen who had stayed a night at the Midland Hotel on her way from the Isle of Wight to Balmoral, the cheering for the Duke was so prolonged that he was embarrased, even displeased. He had to put a finger to his lips and indicate that his admirers had in the circumstances gone far enough.

In between the entertainments at Chatsworth of two Russian Grand Duchesses he made his great-nephew Cavendish accompany him on a long morning's visit to All Saint's Church in Derby to approve the repair and cleaning of the family monuments. The Duke was very attached to the 19-year-old youth who was to be his eventual heir. He allowed him free access to Devonshire House whenever he cared to call, and on Cav's coming of age was to give him an allowance of £2,000 a year. He did his best to induct him into the domestic responsibilities which would one day be his. But he was too lame and out of sorts – all aches and pains – to go to Lismore this year which almost broke his heart. Nor did he feel able to attend the Duke of Wellington's funeral in November. Instead he sat with friends on his wall overlooking Piccadilly to view the procession to St Paul's.

The year 1853 was quiet and uneventful. A group of Derbyshire gentlemen commissioned Landseer to paint him. This the artist agreed to do and then stalled. He protested that he was 'more of an animal and beast painter than a delineator of the human form divine'. Eventually the Duke had to remind him that he had waited nearly three years. 'I urge you to begin in earnest and to conduct yourself like a man of honour and honesty.' He could be stern. The irascible note did the trick. Landseer's shamefaced retort was 'Certainly', followed by action. If the picture by Landseer at Chatsworth of his subject in an opera box with opera glass in his hands and a programme, or scroll, on the ledge, was the result of his endeavour at this date, then the artist had absolved himself. It is a fine portrait of a wistful and earnest theatre-goer.

A short letter in a rather shaky hand, dated 7 January 1854 and addressed from Brighton, exhorts Cav to stay at Chatsworth for as long as he wishes. 'Brother of my heart, though it grieves me to be kept away I think your going gives me as much pleasure as being there myself.' He always derived vicarious enjoyment from the happiness of the young, especially when he had been the purveyor of it. And he assured his sister Georgiana that he was going to improve his hand-writing just as Lady Bessborough did hers in old age – a rather poignant resolution in view of the knock-out blow about to befall him.

On 15 February the Duke, extremely distressed by deteriorating relations between Great Britain and Russia, wrote to Paxton that he had an inane desire to go to St Petersburg and talk matters over with the Emperor Nicholas. In his reply of 18th Paxton, who dreaded what might happen to Britain's trade if war were to break out, encouraged this idea 'as the only chance that still remains for peace'. He went on:

> I firmly believe the Emperor would care more for what you would say and suggest, than he would from all the diplomatists that could be sent to him. I sincerely believe that he too at present never knows the true state of feeling in this country and in France, but particularly in this country on the Eastern question, and I moreover believe that if he does know it the very point of your Grace going over would give a new channel both to his thoughts and actions and would do more to stop impending events than anything that has at present been devised. But how this is to be done is another question, so as not to endanger your Grace's health, which in my mind is more important than even Peace or War.

The government ought to fit him up a special ship, a perfect suite with Dr Verity and Lord Cavendish in attendance.

For the lamentable Crimean War into which this country was dragged Palmerston was chiefly responsible through his engrained hatred of Russia and fear of her threat to Great Britain's supremacy in India. Control of the passage to India through Afghanistan was to be a recurrent objective of British interests and a recurrent cause of anxiety throughout the nineteenth century, and even into the twentieth. Britain's pressing concern at the time was a belief that the Russian Tsar, convinced of the Turkish empire's inevitable disintegration, intended to give the Ottomans a *coup de grâce* and then partition the Balkans into satellite kingdoms. This Nicholas declared over and over again he never would do or allow, so long as no other country attempted it. In 1853 General Menshikoff, the overbearing Russian ambassador to Constantinople, came to London where he asserted his country's right to protect Slav Orthodox subjects in the Turkish empire and maintain guardianship of the holy places in Jerusalem. On the refusal of these demands by the Sultan the Russians occupied Moldavia and Wallachia. On 5 October Turkey declared war on Russia. On 28 March 1854 Lord Aberdeen, leader of the Whig and Peelite coalition, although anxious to preserve peace, was forced by Palmerston and Lord John Russell to follow suit on Great Britain's behalf.

Before the actual declaration of war the Duke of Devonshire, then in Brighton, answered Paxton's letter. 'It is now too late. The English bulldog has been let loose, and it is not for me to stop him if I could.' Apart from his feeble health the Duke's patriotism vetoed any interference on his part, even were Aberdeen's government disposed to give him the facilities suggested by Paxton. Yet he was overcome by unhappiness, not only on Britain's account but on beloved Nicholas's. What would be the consequences to the Emperor of the insane folly of his precipitate action?

Paxton maintained links with the Crimea through a close friendship with John Macdonald of *The Times*. He urged through that organ that engineers be sent to the Crimea. He urged through Lord Panmure, who was to be Secretary for War, that a corps of navigators should be employed there. He recruited navvies, who had worked for him at Sydenham, in an Army Works Corps, and who when they got to Russia turned out to be undisciplined, drunken, afraid of danger and unpopular with the troops. The Duke wholeheartedly supported Paxton's war efforts before they proved abortive.

At Chatsworth on 3 June 1854 the Duke suffered a paralytic seizure of his right side. Physically he was much incapacitated. Yet neither his head nor his speech was affected. He wisely had himself taken immediately to London. On 5th Paxton wrote to his wife: 'Well, what a whirl I am in at this awful calamity.' He was almost prostrate with worry and distress and begged Sarah to come to Devonshire House at once. Troubles piled upon him. The Crystal Palace, transported to Sydenham, was to be opened by the Queen and Prince Albert on 10th of the month. His father Jonas was dying and clamoured to see him. His son George was misbehaving worse than ever. And the Duke could not bear him to be out of his sight.

The Duke's courage was astonishing. He wrote little notes with his left hand. Thus on 26th to Georgiana:

Taylor says my progress is as good as might possibly be expected. I write much better than this most days, but the wind and the glare are against me. Leg stronger; I walk upstairs to bed. I drive every day.

There are even four words painfully written by him in the Devonshire House visitors' book under the actual date of the stroke, 'D to London (Palsiest)'. But it seems unlikely that he went to the opening ceremony at Sydenham. He certainly marked the occasion by the presentation to Paxton of some massive silver plate, and to Sarah of a bracelet inscribed, 'beloved and worthy'. Worthy indeed she was. No wife of a successful self-made man can ever have made more sacrifices for her consort's advancement. During Sir Joseph's prolonged absences from Chatsworth on business and parliamentary duties she acted as his unofficial deputy. In November 1854 Paxton became MP for Coventry. When a deputation of that city's worthies invited him to represent them he kept them waiting, so the Duke wrote to Georgiana, 'for his answer till he had asked my leave. So much does he continue my very good little boy always.'

Now Rockhills, a solid Victorian villa on Sydenham Hill, became Paxton's principal home, although Barbrook, the square-towered house aggrandized by him at Chatsworth, was to remain in his gift, so to speak. Henceforth the Duke was a frequent guest at Rockhills. He would turn up at any time that suited him and remain often for weeks on end. Without being aware of it he virtually took over the place, what with his retinue of Doctor Condell, secretary Erskine, pianist Coote, valets and footmen innumerable, not to mention his immobility and feebleness which made heavy demands on his host's household. The Paxtons may have been honoured. They certainly never complained, although they must have found the visitations exacting, and when the Duke positively suggested that he might live at Rockhills permanently, even proposing certain alterations to the house, Paxton blenched. 'It will cost at least £100,' he wrote to his wife, 'and then he will change his mind.'

Sarah much resented the break with Chatsworth and never liked Sydenham, which she referred to as 'that haunt of vice'. This was going rather far, even allowing for her lower middle-class suspicions of the aristocratic way of life and her standards of what suited the Paxton social status. For five years after Joseph's knighthood this robust woman had refused to be presented at court. Finally she gave way only to the persuasions of Harriet Sutherland who had always been good to her and won her affection. She never cared for Joseph's business associates whom she suspected, sometimes with reason, of sharp practice, and blamed as the cause of his too frequent absences from her and the children. Nor did she feel at ease among the great society people who now ostentatiously opened their doors to them, although usually receiving Sir Joseph alone on the valid assumption that Lady Paxton preferred to remain at home. While not the least wishing herself to dine at Londonderry House or dance at Grosvenor House Sarah nevertheless grew to resent the imputations that he was wanted, and she was not. Although Paxton never lost his head or got above himself he undoubtedly trod dizzy heights. And why not? 'The Queen of the Netherlands and a party of about 25 or 30 lunch at Rockhills tomorrow,' he informed Sarah in July 1857. 'I had not told you that the place is in an uproar ... I was at Lady Holland's great party on Saturday, all the *ex*-Royal family [of France] were there and all the most fashionable people.' The distancing of his and his wife's sympathies in their old age was the Paxtons' tragedy. It was made the more poignant by the Duke being an unwitting contributory factor. Not only did he introduce his protégé into circles alien to Sarah but he made first claims upon Paxton's attentions. He had merely to raise a finger – a metaphorical gesture fully accepted by Lady Paxton – and off Sir Joseph went to wherever his master was, there to remain no matter how great might be her and the children's need of him.

It is a matter of conjecture how far the war with Russia contributed to the Duke of Devonshire's stroke. There is no question that it brought about the Emperor Nicholas's death in March 1855. This well-intentioned sovereign had learned from bitter experience that a high state of national morality could be supported only by despotic rule, and that despotic rule over an unwieldy continent of amoral peasants and nobles, with no intervening class of any consequence, must fail with the first relaxation of strength within or attack on the frontiers from without. When both these eventualities happened to Russia at once he died quite simply of a broken heart.

The Duke's conflict was purely personal, and no less stressful. It lay between his patriotism and a subjective sympathy. The solution of his friend's awful predicament, which must mean England's defeat, was a totally unacceptable prospect. His friend's stupendous fall was equally appalling. One or the other was inevitable, and was more than a stricken mind could lightly entertain. Since diplomatic relations between the belligerent countries were not severed the two friends managed to correspond for a time. On 26 July 1854 the Duke wrote to the

Emperor's secretary Count Perrotski that as long as he had a drop of blood left in his body – he explained how he had been *'subitement frappé par une maladie qui m'a privé de l'usage d'une moitié de ma personne'* – he would cherish his affection for the two beings (he included the Empress) who were part of his existence. On 23 August the Emperor wrote to the Duke appealing for help for Russian prisoners of war who were being treated in England worse than the English prisoners in Russia. *'Mon cher Duc,'* the letter began, *'vous êtes le seul ami qui me reste en Angleterre,'* and scribbled in his own hand at the bottom, *'Je suis pour la vie et similement votre vrai ami.'* In part answer to this appeal the Duke sent £250 for the Russian prisoners' relief, adding to his scribe's letter in very wobbly spelling and grammar, *'Adieu, Sire, vous qui m'êtes tourjours de la même indulgence, qui me comprenez, que Dieu vous bénisse sera tourjours la orière de votre affectioné et tout devoué Devonshire.'*

On 25 October the harbour of Balaclava in the Crimea was occupied by the British forces as the stronghold for future operations. The fight for it was signalled by the famous Charge of the Light Brigade, the noble six hundred who were cut to pieces. It was followed by the Battle of Inkerman in which the British lost 2,612 and the Russians 12,000 men. 'When will the lists come of the slaughtered? I am so miserable at the war and at all the horrors that are coming,' the Duke wrote to Harriet Granville. With one of the severest of winters on record the horrors came thick and fast. The pacific Lord Aberdeen, faced with reverses from the elements as well as Russian reinforcements, resigned, and Lord Palmerston took his place. In December the allied fleet in the Baltic was broken up.

At Kemp Town on 2 March 1855 the Duke was handed a telegram from his nephew Gink Granville, Lord President of the Council. It announced the death of the Emperor of Russia at one o'clock that morning. He had expired on a camp bed while talking to his grandson. The Duke left no record of how he received this grievous news, torn asunder as he was by his country's poor showing in the war and the loss of the person most dear to him in the world. His countrymen on the other hand were unanimous in their detestation of the Emperor as the devil incarnate. This opinion was evidently shared by God if we are to believe Harriet Granville's words: 'He hath put down the mighty from *his* seat.' In those British theatres where the news was announced the audiences rose in a body, and cheered lustily. With the tyrant's departure they saw hopes of peace. It came a year later with the Treaty of Paris, concluded by the allied Powers on 30 March 1856. Turkey's integrity in the Balkans was guaranteed and she was admitted to the Concert of Europe. This integrity was duly flouted in 1861 by the union of Moldavia and Wallachia within the newly formed and independent state of Romania. Thus, as happens at the end of nearly all bloody wars, no one was the victor and everyone was the loser.

In June the Duke, after enduring two years of his infirmity which he had supposed did not allow much prospect of their renewed intercourse, was cheered to see Charles Dickens's handwriting again. 'I know you will be glad to learn', he replied to the novelist, 'that since my severe seizure my mind has not been materially affected and I had the blessing of retaining memory wholly unimpaired. It would indeed have grieved me to lose the recollection of our season of 1851.' A correspondence which gave the stricken Duke much pleasure was resumed. On 14th Henry Greville met the Duke at the Granvilles' house where he was wheeled in after dinner, presumably because he was shy about handling a knife and fork in company. He dreaded another seizure which might affect his reason. 'Tell me sincere & true', he beseeched Harriet, 'when you perceive traces of mind failing, a thing which I do not yet – but daily expect'.

In July he was at Rockhills which for the rest of the year he made his base. All his letters written there paid tribute to Paxton's ministrations. Practically every night the ubiquitous Lady Hunloke – for whom the Duke had a house built at Sydenham – bringing her daughter Charlotte, dined. Other friends gallantly came down to Sydenham, or wherever he might be, for he still made flying visits of a day or two to Chatsworth, Kemp Town and even Bolton.

From Chatsworth he went on a pilgrimage to pay homage to the country's heroine, Florence Nightingale, back from the rigours and travail of the Crimea. She was then living with her parents, members of a Derbyshire family of gentry, at Lea Hurst, Dethick, a tiny village south-west of Matlock. The Duke described the expedition in a letter of 24 August to Harriet.

I rattled off with the four ponies through Matlock, along river, then up the hill to the abode of Florence Nightingale. A charming abode, lovely valley and mountain scenery. House not large but prettyly furnished, many servants at the door. My thought wandered as to which might be the butler, of four. I was shown into a drawing room, saw at a glance that it contained the parents, and Parthenope [the elder daughter who was shortly to become Lady Verney of Claydon] and alas Colonel Jebb and his precious Mealy. Much interesting talk with Mrs. N— and then in walked what is more like an angel than aught ever seen by me. Composed, unaffected, tall, blue eyed, without trace of fatigue, or of nervousness, natural, *entrainant in few words*, sensible, unpretending. I made them all go lunch, and then joined them, happy parents. Was not I think to be admitted ... It was I assure you most deeply interesting – to see that slight and gentle creature who has shewn such astonishing courage and judgement and firmness, with her tiny hands, which have so worked and endured and persevered it was beyond measure affecting. It is true that the sufferers said that the Scutari hospitals and others after had been like Hell *before she came*. I could not conceal my emotion and did not give way to it.

That was just as well because Florence, in spite of her ethereal appearance, was tough and not inclined to succumb to the sentimentality of any man. But the susceptible Duke was deeply smitten. He promptly invited her to Chatsworth. He also invited a number of admiring friends to meet her. It was not at all in her line to be gaped at by society ladies who would fire off silly questions at her. On 1 September the Duke wrote again to his sister.

The short and the long and the plain prose of the above is that the angelic one had given me hopes that she was coming here today, and instead sent me all the rest of the family. Oh small comfort were Lady Downe in Thornhill hand, Louise, G and Alice ...

He was much put out by what he took to be a snub. But to his delight he discovered that this was not her intention, and great was his joy to receive a letter from her, dated 10 September:

I have been so touched by the repeated instances of your Grace's kind thoughts for me that I will beg you to allow me, in these few words, to give expression to my feeling, since I was unable to join my father and mother in their gratifying visit to Chatsworth.

With this county, the home of my earliest affections, your name, never mentioned by any class but with respect and regard, has always been a principal association in my thoughts. I was early taught to think with affectionate admiration of your general and unwearied kindness & that steadfastness of purpose which enabled all to count with certainty upon your aid in every public struggle for truth and right. It has, consequently, been most gratifying and encouraging to me to find that the cause which I have endeavoured to serve has engaged so much of your sympathy ...

This was indeed a rewarding response for any man over 66 to receive from England's greatest and fairest daughter.

Another excitement that year was preparations for his nephew Lord

Granville's mission of goodwill in attending the coronation of poor Nicholas's successor, his son the Emperor Alexander II of Russia. Instead of nostalgically dwelling upon the similar occasion when thirty years before he in the glory of his youth and happiness so splendidly represented his sovereign at St Petersburg and Moscow, the Duke of Devonshire relished the prospect of his nephew's turn. Joyfully he lent the Devonshire jewels to Gink's wife Louisa. The mission was highly successful, for both Lord and Lady Granville were thoroughly cosmopolitan and spoke impeccable French.

During the last year of his life the Duke of Devonshire in spite of confinement to a wheelchair was just as restless as ever. Although he no longer travelled abroad he was constantly on railway and road between Chatsworth, Devonshire House, Rockhills, Chiswick, Hardwick and Brighton. Paxton was absolutely indispensable to him. This busy man did everything in his power to make his master's life easy. Whereas at Rockhills the Duke treated the household as though it were his own, at Chatsworth Sir Joseph and Lady Paxton acted as host and hostess, but always with the utmost tact and diffidence. Some vulgar fashionables resented what they mistook for overfamiliarity and Dr Condell's wife had the poor taste to make known her objection to sitting at the same table with a man who had once been an under-gardener.

In September Mrs Gaskell of *Cranford* fame went from Manchester with her daughter Meta on an expedition to Chatsworth. They stayed Friday night, 12th, at Rowsley, doubtless in The Peacock where they had a snug little sitting-room with fire and tea. Having applied beforehand for permission to view the great house they were issued with a green card which was to give them special treatment. House and grounds were open to the public every day of the year except Sunday from ten in the morning till five in the evening, and the waterworks were turned on for everyone, without exception. The number of visitors quoted by Paxton was about 60,000 annually. On Saturday morning Mrs Gaskell and Meta set off across the park in a little pony carriage. A nice-looking housekeeper took them round the rooms. To their surprise the Duke's valet sought them out with a message that his master, not yet up, expected them to luncheon at two o'clock and to stay the night. Consternation was caused by the fact that they had 'no clothes at all, in particular to start with – Meta's brown silk, & brown muslin; my grey carmelite, & black moiré, high, & next to no collars ...' which things were moreover at Rowsley. Nervously they asked if any visitors were staying. They were told that Mr George and Lady Louisa Cavendish, their daughters the two Miss Cavendishes, and Caroline Norton were guests. 'You may fancy how Meta and I looked at each other,' Mrs Gaskell wrote to her left-at-home daughter Marianne. Well, they bravely decided that it was a pity to miss so much for the sake of no gowns and sent word to their host, consenting. A maid was dispatched to Rowsley to fetch the unworthy clothing, and they were established in two grand rooms with private WC, the curtains of one bed being of thick white satin stamped with silken rosebuds which Meta proposed they should dress themselves up in. Presently the Duke came to them wheeled in his Bath chair. He was very deaf but Meta made him hear better than her mother. He took them into the sketch gallery (not shown to the public) until luncheon time. Round the dining-room table ladies only were present for the Duke retired to his private room to eat. Then Sir Joseph Paxton came in. 'He is quite the master of the place as it were.' He had been deputed to organize drives for the afternoon, with carriages and horses to ride. Meta, Mrs Norton, Sir Joseph and Mrs Gaskell (who was made to feel like Cinderella) were driven in a little low carriage drawn by pretty circus-like ponies. They went first to call on 'fat and pleasant' Lady Paxton at Barbrook in the grounds, and then drove through the kitchen gardens to a point where the Duke and Lady Louisa were awaiting them. They talked and admired everything. Then they moved off again, seeing views and improvements, and marvelling at the fountains and waterworks at play. In the miniature carriage they drove through the Great Conservatory, and so home to dress for dinner. Meta was done up in one of the good-natured Caroline Norton's dresses, Mrs Gaskell having to be content with her black silk.

In the library what seemed like half the clergy of Derbyshire and their wives were assembled, as well as the county MP and his wife. Both Sir Joseph and Lady Paxton and a daughter were present, 'he almost like the host'. After dinner all wandered through the statue gallery and orangery which were lighted up. Seven performers of the Duke's private band played selections of music for which printed programmes were handed out. Mrs Gaskell sat next to the Duke who, hearing better when music was played, talked throughout. Lady Louisa, whom the Duke described sometimes as a great swan-like love and sometimes as a perfect nonentity, complained that the county Member and his wife stayed too late. It was twelve o'clock before they got to bed, and they were to breakfast at a quarter past nine. 'And my dear, there is not a bell in the house because you are expected to have your own servants waiting in the ante-chamber.' Mrs Gaskell had forgotten to ask to be called but mercifully woke up in time.

In September the Duke decided to move to Hardwick where he had not stayed for a long while. He wanted to revive memories of his extreme youth when he had been so happy in this desolate and anti-quated place of sleeping beauty with his mother's undistracted atten-tion. In November he drove over to Chatsworth to receive the committee of the Manchester Art Treasures Exhibition. Staged in Manchester by Thomas Agnew, founder of the venerable firm of art dealers, the exhibition was the first attempt to show the public some of the treasures contained in English country houses. It naturally received the patronage of the owner of the greatest collection of paintings in the North Midlands, one of the great art connoisseurs of the age. A banquet and ball, graced by the Lord Mayor of Manchester, were given by the Duke to launch the exhibition. Before the end of the month the Duke insisted on returning to Hardwick in spite of Dr Condell's warning that the cold of that huge house might be very detrimental to his state of health and recommendation that he should go south. But he resisted, saying he was so happy among his friends at home. Paxton later observed how he had a desire to make himself out to be in better health than he was, whereas formerly it had always been the other way round. So William Condell and Paxton, who were close friends, agreed that henceforth one or other of them should never leave him.

On 14 January 1858 Paxton accompanied his master on his last expedition, to make a day call on the Duke of Newcastle and his beautiful daughter Susan at Clumber, thirteen miles away. 'The Duke has borne the journey very well,' Joseph wrote to Sarah, 'and is all on tip about the *Swan* dinner tomorrow.' The Duke, having been presented with a swan, decided to call a party of male friends to eat it. He asked Paxton to issue invitations to a dozen neighbours. Considering the short notice given it is surprising that all but one turned up. Paxton protested in vain over their sitting down thirteen to table. The Duke laughed and made light of it. But Paxton noticed that during dinner the Duke often looked across at him, and when the meal was over retired to his room.

The next morning, Saturday, Paxton before leaving for Bolton Abbey went early to talk with the Duke, who seemed rather low. The Duke spoke of his parents at Hardwick in the old days, then asked

Paxton to invite Peter Cunningham, the art critic, to come and re-hang the pictures in the long gallery. When Paxton said goodbye the Duke replied, 'Remember Thursday,' adding, 'Very probably you will find me gone when you return.' Paxton had often heard him say that and was not particularly struck by the remark. While he had his hand on the door the Duke called him back. 'Look at this,' he said, pointing to a copy of the *Charivari* in which the principal caricature represented two old gossips discussing superstition. One was made to say to the other, 'Well, thank God, I am not superstitious but I don't like thirteen to dinner.' Paxton laughed at the caricature and disappeared. 'This was my last interview with one', he wrote afterwards, 'who had unceasingly during a connection of 32 years been more than a father to me.' He left his master in the care of the doctor and Cottingham who had succeeded Paxton as agent.

On Sunday evening the Duke ate as usual in the dining-room on the mezzanine floor of the west front. Then as now it was hung with old family portraits blackened by smoke from the fireplace and oil lamps. Did he ruminate upon his father sitting in this room, 'as he supp'd at Brooks's, with his hat on, which his friends gave as the reason for his being so fond of Hardwick'; and remember with amusement how as a boy he turned the recess 'into a kind of menagerie' where behind a nailed up fishing-net rabbits, hedgehogs, squirrels, guinea-pigs and white mice were confined, 'and the smell was overpowering'? Before leaving the table he gave special instructions to Cottingham that his portrait by Archer Shee, then in the great gallery, should be moved next morning and be hung alongside his mother's in this room. The frugal meal over he was wheeled across the draughty gallery spanning the hall into the drawing-room, its chimneypiece decorated with a pair of heraldic stags in the round, their brown antlers rising above the cornice. Over oak panelling 'six peeces of tapestrie hanginges with personages and my Ladies Armes in them' remain today exactly as described in Bess of Hardwick's inventory of 1601. Suddenly the Duke asked Cottingham and Condell whether they had not seen two female figures pass and stop before the fireplace. No, they said, it was his fancy.

He had his chair wheeled close to the piano at which the faithful Coote was playing. Wrapped in a plaid shawl, for he was feeling the cold, he beat time with his foot to the accompaniment of Bellini's *Angel of Peace*. At half past ten, unable to get warm, he asked Charles Harris the footman to prepare his bed. When he got into it he complained of a slight pain in the head. Condell thought it merely muscular and gave him a sleeping draught. Returning an hour later he found his patient composed, sat with him for three hours until he fell asleep, and then was relieved by the usual night-attendant. At seven o'clock on the morning of Monday, 18 January, the Duke was found dead in his bed.

Paxton returned post-haste from Bolton to find Lord Burlington already at Hardwick. William, with true understanding and kind feeling, allowed him to make all arrangements for the funeral, and alone to accompany the Duke's body on the seventeen-mile journey to Chatsworth by night. There the coffin, swathed in red velvet and covered with a black pall emblazoned with the arms of Cavendish, Clifford and Boyle within an embroidered Garter chain, was placed in the centre of the chapel, the wall panels of which were draped with black cloth festooned with silver. Eight large flambeaux from massive silver candelabra cast flickering shadows upon Laguerre's dusky ceiling of the Ascension. Five days later the Bachelor Duke was buried amongst old friends in the churchyard of Edensor village.

Bibliography

BOOKS

Acland, Alice, *Caroline Norton,* 1948.

Airlie, Mabell, Countess of, *In Whig Society, 1775–1818,* 1921.

Anthony, John, *Joseph Paxton,* 1973.

Apponyi, Comte Rodolphe, *Journal du 1835–1843* (3ème édition), 1914.

Arbuthnot, Mrs, *Journals, 1820–1832,* ed. F. Bamford and the Duke of Wellington, 1950.

Askwith, Betty, *Piety & Wit: Biography of Harriet Countess Granville 1785–1862,* 1982.

Berry, Mary, *Extracts of Journals and Correspondence, 1783–1852,* ed. Lady Theresa Lewis, 1865.

Berry Papers, The, ed. Lewis Melville, 1914.

Bessborough, Earl of, *Georgiana: Extracts from Correspondence,* 1955.

—— *Lady Bessborough and Her Family Circle,* 1940.

Boyd, Mark, *Social Gleanings,* 1875.

Brock, Michael, *The Great Reform Act,* 1973.

Broughton, Lord, *Recollections of a Long Life,* 5 vols., 1911.

Brownlow, Emma Sophia, Countess of, *The Eve of Victorianism, 1802–1834,* 1940.

Burn, W. L., *The Age of Equipoise: A Study of the Mid-Victorian Generation,* 1968.

Bury, Lady Charlotte (Campbell), *Diary of a Lady-in-waiting,* ed. Francis Steuart, 2 vols. (first published 1838), 1908.

Byron, George Gordon, Lord – Letters and Journals, ed. Leslie Marchand, Vols. 1–4, 1973–5.

Calder-Marshall, Arthur, *The Two Duchesses,* 1978.

Cavendish, Lady Harriet: Hary-O, Letters, 1796–1809, ed. Sir George Leveson-Gower, 1940.

Cecil, Lord David, *The Young Melbourne,* 1939.

—— *Lord M,* 1954.

—— *Lord Melbourne,* 1965.

Chadwick, George F., *The Works of Sir Joseph Paxton,* 1961.

Charlotte, Princess, 1791–1811, ed. Professor Aspinall, 1949.

Clifford, Sir Augustus W., *A Sketch of the Life of the 6th Duke of Devonshire,* 1864.

Collier, J. Payne, *An Old Man's Diary, 1832–1833* (privately circulated), 1871.

Crainz, Franco, *The Birth of an Heir to the 5th Duke of Devonshire,* 1989.

Craven, Mrs Augustus, *The Life of Lady Georgiana Fullerton,* 1888.

Creevey, Thomas, *Papers,* Vol. 1, ed. Sir Herbert Maxwell, 1903.

Devonshire, 6th Duke of, *Handbook of Chatsworth and Hardwick,* 1844.

Devonshire, Deborah, Duchess of, *The House: A Portrait of Chatsworth,* 1982.

Devonshire, Georgiana, Duchess of, *The Sylph* (a novel), 1779.

Dino, Duchesse de, *Memoirs, 1831–1835,* ed. Princess Radziwill, 1909.

Eden, Hon. Emily, *Miss Eden's Letters,* ed. Violet Dickinson, 1919.

Evans, Eric J., *The Great Reform Act of 1832,* 1983.

Frampton, Mary, *Journal,* 1843.

Fulford, Roger, *Royal Dukes,* 1933.

—— *George IV,* 1935.

Fullerton, Lady Georgiana, *Grantley Manor,* 1847.

Gladwyn, Cynthia, *The Paris Embassy,* 1976.

Granville, Letters of Harriet, Countess, 1810–1845, ed. Hon. Frederick Leveson Gower, 2 vols., 1894.

Greville, Charles, *Memoirs,* ed. Henry Reeve, 8 vols., 1874–87.

Greville, Henry, *Leaves from the Diary of,* ed. Viscountess Enfield, 1884.

Gronow, Captain Rees Howell, *Reminiscences and Recollections,* Vol. 1, 1892.

Grosvenor, Caroline, and Beilby, Charles, Lord Stuart of Wortley, *The First Lady Wharncliffe and Her Family,* 2 vols., 1927.

Hawes, Frances, *Henry Brougham,* 1957.

Hinde, Wendy, *George Canning,* 1989.

Hobhouse, Christopher, *1851 and the Crystal Palace,* 1937.

Hodgson, James T., Revd, *Memoir of the Rev. Francis Hodgson,* 2 vols., 1878.

Holland, 3rd Lord, *Diary, 1831–1840,* ed. Abraham D. Kriegel, 1977.

Holland, Elizabeth Vassall, *Lady Holland to Her Son 1821–1845,* ed. Earl of Ilchester, 1946.

Howitt, William, *Rural Life of England,* 1840.

Hunt, J. H. Leigh, *Autobiography* (2nd edition), 1860.

Jenkins, Elizabeth, *Lady Caroline Lamb*, 1932.

Johnson, Edgar, *Charles Dickens: His Tragedy and Triumph*, 1977.

Knight, Cornelia, *Autobiography*, 2 vols., 1861.

Leconfield, Lady, and Gore, John, eds., *Three Howard Sisters, 1825–1845*, 1955.

Leveson Gower, Hon. Frederick, *Byegone Years: Recollections*, 1905.

Lieven, Dorothea, Princess, *Correspondence with Lord Grey*, ed. Guy Le Strange, 1890.

—— *Letters during Residence in London 1812–1834*, ed. L. G. Robinson, 1902.

—— *Unpublished Diary*, ed. W. V. Temperley, 1925.

—— *Private Letters to Prince Metternich 1820–1826*, ed. Peter Quennell, 1937.

Lincoln, W. Bruce, *Nicholas 1, Emperor and Autocrat of All the Russias*, 1978.

Linstrum, David, *Sir Jeffry Wyatville*, 1972.

Londonderry, Edith, Marchioness of, *Frances Anne: Life and Times of Frances Anne Marchioness of Londonderry*, 1958.

Lyttelton, Lady Sarah Spencer, *Correspondence*, ed. Mrs Hugh Wyndham, 1912.

Malmesbury, 1st Earl of, *Memoirs of an ex-Minister*, Vol. 1, 1884.

Markham, Violet, *Paxton and the Bachelor Duke*, 1935.

Masters, Brian, *Georgiana Duchess of Devonshire*, 1981.

Matthews, Henry, *The Diary of an Invalid*, 1820.

Moore, Thomas, *Memoirs, Journals and Correspondence*, ed. Lord John Russell, 1860.

Morris, Revd F. O., *Chatsworth* (Vol. 1, 'Picturesque Seats'), 1880.

Oldfield, Hon. Susan, *Some Records of Harriet Lady Granville*, 1901.

Pearson, John, *Stags and Serpents: The Story of the House of Cavendish and the Dukes of Devonshire*, 1983.

Pope-Hennessy, Dame Una, *A Czarina's Story* (written by Empress Alexandra Feodorovna, wife of Nicholas 1), 1947.

Pückler-Muskau, Prince Hermann von, *A Regency Visitor: The English Tour of described in his Letters 1826–1828*, ed. E. M. Butler from trans. by Sarah Austin, 1957.

Renier, G. J., *The Ill-Fated Princess: Life of Princess Charlotte, daughter of the Prince Regent*, 1932.

Robinson, Henry Crabb, *Books and Their Writers*, Vol. 2, 1859.

Robinson, John Martin, *Cardinal Consalvi*, 1987.

Russell, Lord John: Early Correspondence, ed. R. Russell, 1913.

Russell, Lord William and his Wife 1815–1846, ed. G. Blakiston, 1972.

Scott, Sir Walter, *Journals*, Vol. 11, 1890.

Somerset, Lady Anne, *William IV,* 1980.
Stendhal (M. H. Beyle), *Pages d'Italie en 1818,* 1824.
—— *Promenades dans Rome,* 1828–9.
Stockmar, Baron E. von, *Memoirs,* ed. F. Max Müller, 1872.
Stokes, Hugh, *The Devonshire House Circle,* 1917.
Stuart, Dorothy Margaret, *Dearest Bess,* 1955.
Surtees, Virginia, *A Second Self; Letters of Harriet Granville 1810–1845,* 1990.
Sykes, Christopher Simon, *Private Palaces: Life in the Great London Houses,* 1985.
Taine, Hippolyte, *Notes on England,* trans. and ed. W. F. Rae, 1872.
Thackeray, William Makepeace, *Vanity Fair,* 1847–8.
Thompson, Francis, *A History of Chatsworth,* 1949.
Thompson, F. M. L., *English Landed Society in the Nineteenth Century,* 1963.
Trollope, Anthony, *Lady Anna* (for a description of Bolton Abbey), 1873.
Waagen, Dr G. F., *Art and Artists in England,* 3 vols., 1838.
—— *The Treasures of Art in Great Britain,* 3 vols., 1854.
Wagener, Françoise, *Madame Récamier, 1777–1849,* 1986.
Wheatley, H. B., *Notes on the Life of John Payne Collier,* 1884.
Wilson, Harriette, *Memoirs of Herself and Others,* 1825.
Young, G. M., *Victorian England: Portrait of an Age,* 1960.
Ziegler, Philip, *King William IV,* 1971.

PAMPHLETS AND ARTICLES

Barker, Nicolas, 'The Chatsworth Library', *Christie's Review of the Season,* 1974, pp. 300–16.
Boase, George Clement, 'William 6th Duke of Devonshire', *Dictionary of National Biography,* Vol. III, *c.* 1885.
Cannadine, David, 'The Landowner as Millionaire: The Finances of the Dukes of Devonshire, *c.* 1800–*c.* 1926', *Agricultural History Review,* Vol. 25, Part II, 1977.
'The Czar's Visit to Chiswick', *Illustrated London News,* 15 June 1844.
Devonshire, Deborah, Duchess of, 'The Gardens at Chatsworth', *Country Life,* 5 September 1968.
Donner, Peter F. R., and Brooks, J. Marchant (photographer), 'Edensor', *Architectural Review,* Vol. 95, January–June 1944.
Girouard, Mark, 'Lismore Castle Co. Waterford', *Country Life,* 6 and 13 August 1964.
Hall, Michael, 'Village Eden (Edensor Village)', *Country Life,* 10 August 1989.
Kenworthy-Browne, John, 'Pauline and the Bachelor Duke', *Country Life,* 28 January 1971.
—— 'The Age of Marblemania', *Country Life,* 27 January 1972.

—— 'A Ducal Patron of Sculptors', *Apollo,* October 1972.

Lees-Milne, J., and Cornforth, J., 'Chatsworth Home of the Devonshires', *Country Life,* April–September 1968.

Proudfoot, Lindsay, 'The Management of a Great Estate: The Duke of Devonshire's Irish Property *c.* 1816 to 1891', *Irish Economic History,* Vol. xiii, 1986.

Spring, David, 'Ralph Sneyd', *John Ryland's Library Bulletin,* Vol. xxxviii, 1956.

—— 'Aristocracy, Social Structure and Religion in the Early Victorian Period', *Victorian Studies,* Vol. 6, March 1963.

Warner, Tim, 'The Railway that Never Was', *Derbyshire Life,* January 1989.

MANUSCRIPTS
(in addition to those at Chatsworth)

Charles, 2nd Earl Grey, Correspondence, 1830–1833, Grey of Howick MSS 6228, Dept. of Palaeography, Durham University.

Georgiana, Countess Carlisle, Correspondence, c. 1795–1857, Howard MSS 24681, Hon. Simon Howard, Castle Howard, Yorks.

Harriet, Countess Granville, Correspondence, 1825–1845, Leveson Gower MSS 8654, Public Record Office, Chancery Lane, London.

Mary Berry, Correspondence, 1802–1818, British Library Add MSS 37726, London.

Princess Dorothea de Lieven, Correspondence, 1813–1835, British Library Add MSS 47289–293, London.

Ralph Sneyd, Correspondence, 1824–1851, Sneyd MSS 1248, Keele University Library, Staffs.

Viscount Morpeth (7th Earl of Carlisle), Diary, 1843–1858, Howard MSS J19/8/1, Hon. Simon Howard, Castle Howard, Yorks.

Index

NOTE: For the sake of brevity the 6th Duke of Devonshire is referred to throughout the index as 'Hart', his familiar name.